Holy Matrimony:
The Image of God in the Family

Dr. Steven W. Waterhouse

Westcliff Press
P.O. Box 1521, Amarillo TX 79105
(806) 359-6362
www.webtheology.com
email: westcliff@amaonline.com

HOLY MATRIMONY:
THE IMAGE OF GOD IN THE FAMILY

Other Resources By Steven Waterhouse

Not By Bread Alone; An Outlined Guide to Bible Doctrine
(Hardback; also CD Read-only Version)

Strength For His People; A Ministry
For the Families of the Mentally Ill

Blessed Assurance; A Defense of the Doctrine of Eternal Security

What Must I Do To Be Saved?
The Bible's Definition of Saving Faith

Life's Tough Questions

Outside the Heavenly City: Abortion in Rome and the Early Church's Response

First Edition 2006

Copyright 2006 by Steven W. Waterhouse

Westcliff Press
P.O. Box 1521, Amarillo TX 79105
1-806-359-6362
www.webtheology.com
email: westcliff@amaonline.com

ISBN: 0970241895
Library of Congress Control Number 2006930667

Printed in the United States of America

ABOUT THE AUTHOR

Dr. Steven W. Waterhouse has served as the Pastor of Westcliff Bible Church in Amarillo, Texas, since 1985. He has degrees from Dallas Theological Seminary (D.Min.); Capital Bible Seminary, Lanham, MD (Th.M., Hebrew and Greek); Spring Arbor University, Michigan (B.A., Social Science) and Cornerstone University in Grand Rapids, MI.

Dr. Waterhouse and his wife, Marilyn, have three children, Carlton, Nathan, and Rachel.

Information about this book and others written by Dr. Waterhouse can be accessed at his web site at:
http://www.webtheology.com

Suggested Cataloging-In Data

Waterhouse, Steven W.
Holy Matrimony: The Image of God in the Family/Steven W. Waterhouse
    224 p. 24cm
      Includes biblical references, topical and biblical indexes.
      ISBN 0970241895
      1. Personal Counseling 2. Marriage Counseling 3. Marriage – religious
Aspects 4. Divorce – religious aspects 5. Family Counseling 6. Family – religious
aspects 7. Child Rearing – religious aspects.
      Suggested Library of Congress Number: BV4012.2
      Suggested Dewey Number: 253.5

PREFACE

God made countless angels. He created only two people and intended marriage and the family to take the human race forward. This complete contrast shows God deliberately ordained the family as a sacred institution with a unique purpose in His plans for the world.

Sometimes even Christians treat this topic with superficiality. Marriage is more than flowers, chocolates, and romance. God's purpose is much deeper. It involves the admiration and imitation of His own character within marriage and the family.

Marital and family problems are ultimately spiritual problems. Those who try to find happiness in marriage while excluding God from the relationship will experience futility. Those who understand and obey God's wisdom for the family will not only have fulfillment in their homes but also experience God Himself.

ACKNOWLEDGEMENTS

Westcliff Bible Church deserves gratitude for its support of Bible research. Among the many who worked on this project special thanks belong to my secretary, Mary Daily, to Matt Holley for the website design, and to those who edited the many drafts: Dr. Dan Bentley, Alan N. Good, Bonnie Huff, E. Jay O'Keefe, and Rachel Waterhouse.

DEDICATION

Marilyn, you are my blessing, and my reward
Proverbs 18:22, 19:14; Song of Solomon 8:6-7 (NIV)

ABBREVIATIONS
Old Testament

Genesis	Gen.	Ecclesiastes	Eccl.
Exodus	Ex.	Song of Solomon	Song
Leviticus	Lev.	Isaiah	Isa.
Numbers	Num.	Jeremiah	Jer.
Deuteronomy	Deut.	Lamentations	Lam.
Joshua	Josh.	Ezekiel	Ezek.
Judges	Judg.	Daniel	Dan.
Ruth	Ruth	Hosea	Hosea
1 Samuel	1 Sam.	Joel	Joel
2 Samuel	2 Sam.	Amos	Amos
1 Kings	1 Kings	Obadiah	Obad.
2 Kings	2 Kings	Jonah	Jonah
1 Chronicles	1 Chron.	Micah	Micah
2 Chronicles	2 Chron.	Nahum	Nahum
Ezra	Ezra	Habakkuk	Hab.
Nehemiah	Neh.	Zephaniah	Zeph.
Esther	Esth.	Haggai	Hag.
Job	Job	Zechariah	Zech.
Psalms	Psa.	Malachi	Mal.
Proverbs	Prov.		

New Testament

Matthew	Matt.	2 Thessalonians	2 Thess.
Mark	Mark	1 Timothy	1 Tim.
Luke	Luke	2 Timothy	2 Tim.
John	John	Titus	Titus
The Acts	Acts	Philemon	Philem.
Romans	Rom.	Hebrews	Heb.
1 Corinthians	1 Cor.	James	James
2 Corinthians	2 Cor.	1 Peter	1 Pet.
Galatians	Gal.	2 Peter	2 Pet.
Ephesians	Eph.	1 John	1 John
Philippians	Phil.	2 John	2 John
Colossians	Col.	3 John	3 John
1 Thessalonians	1 Thess.	Jude	Jude
		Revelation	Rev.

Miscellaneous Abbreviations

NASV	New American Standard Version		
KJV	Authorized King James Version		
NIV	New International Version		
ff.	Two or more verses following Scripture reference		
v.	Verse	vv.	Verses
Cf.	Compare (confer)	i.e.,	For example

Holy Matrimony: The Image of God in the Family

Dr. Steven W. Waterhouse

HOLY MATRIMONY:
THE IMAGE OF GOD IN THE FAMILY

Table of Contents

Chapter 1: Purposes For the Family   1

Chapter 2: Pattern For Marriage   11

Chapter 3: Procedures to Form a Marriage   17

Chapter 4: Preserving Marriage   23

Chapter 5: Prohibitions/Policies on Weddings   35

Chapter 6: Principles of Gender Equality   51

Chapter 7: Plans For a Husband   61

Chapter 8: Plans For a Wife   69

Chapter 9: Procreation (and Sexuality)   81

Chapter 10: Parental Philosophy   91

Chapter 11: Parental Practices   103

Chapter 12: Preventing Family Conflicts: Healthy Emotions   125

Chapter 13: Preventing Family Conflicts: Unhealthy Emotions   137

Chapter 14: Preventing Family Conflicts: Finances   167

Chapter 15: Preventing Family Conflicts: Communication   189

Conclusions   209

Index   213

Chapter One

Purposes for the Family

"What God has joined together . . ."

A destination begins with the first step. Therefore, the point of origin and direction greatly influences the outcome. No one ever won an Olympic medal by starting from the wrong line. Those on the wrong highway can hardly be expected to make the correct turns.

The outcome for a marriage can depend upon a couple's views of its origin. A traditional wedding ceremony will quote the Lord Jesus Christ's teaching, "… what therefore **God has joined together** …" (Matt. 19:6).

God did not just inaugurate the first family in Genesis or bless the institution of marriage in general. The holy and flawless God joins **every** couple since creation. Every marriage, every family, is holy.

Perhaps the quote "God has joined together" gives an example of familiarity causing thoughtlessness. God ordains and blesses every marriage.

The importance of this foundational conviction can be easily seen by contrast. Consider a common alternative view in the modern world: the family arose because primitive humans discovered units of people allowed greater ease of hunting and food gathering. Also, family units created superior defense and led to constantly available sex partners.

Views on the origin of marriage greatly influence a couple's direction and final result. Those with a humanist view can easily reason that marriage is now optional if not totally irrelevant. We no longer need family units to obtain food and defense. In our time sex partners seem quite available.

By considering an alternative (also false and painful) starting point, the importance of the origin becomes evident. By the authority of the Lord Jesus Christ every marriage has been formed and blessed by God. The conviction that the family is sacred makes a huge difference when marital stress comes. One can give up on a food gathering and a defensive unit, but never a work of God.

Mr. Right, Miss Right

By the authority of the Master, God forms and blesses every home. Does God control, even predestinate, the selection of every spouse? I personally believe He does.

Those who have defied God in their past may wonder if they missed out on God's best. To them I say with all pastoral care, "Don't worry about it." God's omniscience means that His "Plan B" can be so wonderful that those who obey Him starting now will never feel they have missed the best. For those married, their husband or wife is the right one.

The Bible gives evidence of God's supervision in the selection of a husband or wife. Adam used the phrase, "the woman whom you gave to be with me" (Gen. 3:12). From the Proverbs we know that God's involvement in selection of a spouse did not end with Adam. "A prudent wife is from the Lord" (Prov. 19:14).

The story in Genesis 24 supports the concept of a "Miss Right." Abraham sends his servant across the desert to find a wife for Isaac. The servant goes 800 miles to Mesopotamia, stops at a well, and prays for guidance. The kind and hard-working girl who offers to draw water for the camels will be the "one whom You have appointed for your servant Isaac" (Gen. 24:14). The belief that God has a plan in match-making arises from both Scripture and personal experience.

Why Marriage? Why the Family?

We seldom think about the miraculous (and weird) nature of the family. One day I took my sons camping in a Texas canyon. My purpose was to teach the facts of life. Carlton and Nathan started giggling and protesting, "that can't possibly be true!"

The Creator made the angels all at once. They have no marriage and never reproduce (Luke 20:35-36). God created myriads of countless angels. Given that believers in the Lord Jesus as Savior will rule the angels, reason concludes the number of angels surpasses the number of humans. The Bible compares the angelic host to the stars that cannot possibly be counted. By contrast, God created only two people and let the family take history from there. What an incredible difference! Obviously, God planned the difference, but why?

God's Purposes for Marriage - Companionship

"Then the Lord God said, 'It is not good for the man to be alone' " (Gen. 2:18). Companionship is a primary reason for marriage. Solomon said, "Two are better than one ... if either of them falls, the one will lift up his companion ..." (Eccles. 4:9-10). Then he adds, "how can one be warm alone?" (v. 11). The Bible calls a husband "companion" in Prov. 2:17 and a wife a "companion" in Mal. 2:14. In The Song of Solomon the bride and groom call each other "brother" and "sister" (4:9, 10, 12; 5:2). With great concern not to hurt the feelings of single people, the Scriptural point must be stressed that being single can be painfully lonely. God designed marriage for friendship.

Dating is not the subject of this book, but it relates to the point that marriage should arise from a deep friendship. As a pastor, I have been asked to discuss dating with our youth group. The Bible gives much instruction on how to treat other people. God's Word honestly says nothing specific about dating. General wisdom on relationships can be applied to dating (love one another, lie not one to another, be ye kind, and so forth).

The goal of Christian dating should be to make friends with the other person. Unbelievers tend to make the immediate goal of dating to get into bed. Christians may tend to make the immediate goal of dating to get to the wedding. One is morally better, but neither is sensible. Christians can unwisely begin dating at an extremely serious level. From the start the goal is marriage. If the relationship does not lead to marriage, they often break up with hostility, gossip, and avoid each other even at church.

3

Since Christians should already love each other with Christian love, the initial goal of dating should be to make a better friend, not to rush to marriage or certainly not sex. If the relationship ends in friendship alone, the result is totally satisfactory. If marriage results, it should arise from friendship. Make many friends of the opposite sex. I married my best friend in life. We have known each other since infancy. Marry your best friend.

God's Purposes for Marriage - Procreation

The command to be "fruitful and multiply" occurs in the Bible's first chapter and has never been withdrawn. While the Church is not under the Law of Moses (unless a command has been repeated in the New Testament), the command to have children is pre-Mosaic. This means married Christians who are unable to conceive should entrust themselves to God, but those who can produce children should have children. A long list of Bible verses teach that children are one of the great blessings and rewards in life. One of God's purposes in marriage is raising children. Chapters 9, 10, and 11 give detailed consideration.

As for you, be fruitful and multiply; populate the earth abundantly and multiply in it [Gen. 9:7].

Behold, children are a gift of the LORD, the fruit of the womb is a reward [Psa. 127:3].

God's Purposes for Marriage - Sexual Satisfaction

God created us male and female. The sexual design of the human race displays God's intelligence and God's intent to bless us with joy.

His commandments on sex are intended to protect us from danger, not to destroy "fun" in life. The purpose of a fence around a playground is not to destroy fun but to protect children from potential harm. Totally unrestricted sex can be no safer than unrestricted traffic. A popular counselor uses the phrase "covenantal sex" on her radio program and tells her married listeners to enjoy fully "covenantal sex." This is a helpful phrase. Within the emotional (and medical) safety of a lifelong covenant, sexual union becomes a wonderful blessing. God's will and His command is that married people enjoy each other. "Marriage is to be held in honor among all, and the marriage bed is to be undefiled … "(Heb. 13:4). Celibacy **before** marriage is a command. Celibacy **in** marriage is a sin (1 Cor. 7:2-5). The rather obvious fact is that married Christians make love thousands and thousands of times over the course of a marriage as God intended.

God's Purposes for Marriage - Spiritual Growth and Service

One pastoral and counseling illustration concerns a triangle. God is at the peak. Husband and wife are on the sides with arrows going up. The point is that the closer a husband and wife draw to God, the closer they draw to each other.

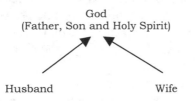

God
(Father, Son and Holy Spirit)

Husband   Wife

The illustration may be odd, but the conclusion is biblical. 1 Pet. 3:7 teaches that husband and wife are "fellow heir(s) of the grace of life." Ephesians 5 gives the picture of marriage as that of Christ and the church. The world is supposed to observe Christian marriages and see an example of Christ's unconditional love and the Church's dedication to Christ.

When God created Eve to be a helper, this did not primarily refer to making fruit salad (Gen. 2:18). God designed wives to build up their husbands spiritually. Likewise, other Scriptures teach that a husband's task involves leading his wife and children spiritually (1 Cor. 14:35; Eph. 6:4). God created the family for spiritual growth and witness to the world. We will shortly explore the deeper aspects.

God's Purposes for Marriage - Security, Protection

In Ruth 3:1 a mother-in-law, Naomi, asks her widowed daughter-in-law, Ruth, " … shall I not seek security for you …?" By "security" Naomi literally means the financial and protective security found in marriage. Before we jump to the conclusion that modern women do not need a hero to protect them or that financial security need not involve marriage, step back and look at real life.

Strong marriages reduce poverty regardless of whether the husband or wife makes the income. Experiences in pastoral care quickly teach that there is a huge difference in a crisis between those supported by strong families and the unfortunate person who lacks the security of a home. Some crises are financial. Many troubles have nothing to do with money. However, in either kind of affliction, it's hard to beat the support of a strong family rallying to its afflicted member. Even in modern times the family unit provides the best security, whether financial or emotional, and we should not be totally confident that the need for protection from physical danger was only a problem for Bible days. A family will still protect its own whether facing hurricanes, crime, or sickness. Soldiers will still fight and die with the motivation of protecting their family back home. Companionship, procreation, sexual enjoyment, spiritual growth/service and security in life are all part of God's purpose in joining a couple together. These truths are explicitly taught in the Bible. God also intends marriage to be a major part of His plan to make us more like Himself.

Spiritual Predictors of Marital Success

Pre-marriage counseling is a blessing. The eager bride and groom come to the church to learn what the Bible teaches about the family. We study finances, the tongue (communication), sex and parenting, decision-making and emotions. Every subject is vital, but none of these alone will create a strong relationship if we try to solve potential family conflict but ignore God Himself. We cannot fully solve marital problems by only studying potential marital problems. Furthermore, there is some value in flowers, boxes of chocolates, cards, eating out, and marriage enrichment seminars. These can improve an already healthy marriage, but they will not resurrect a dead marriage. They can become examples of the Lord's proverb, "these things you should have done without leaving the others undone " (Matt. 23:23, KJV, the author's paraphrase). Many practices will improve a marriage, but they alone will not overcome a rejection or neglect of basic spiritual truths.

A marriage will have success or failure, joy or misery, marital heaven or hell, based upon the answer to two questions. First, is there a sense of obligation to **respect the authority of the Bible**? Is there a conviction that God ordains marriage and that His authority rules? He is the ultimate marriage and family expert. In a marital conflict, if both believe they must obey God's Word, then every problem can eventually be resolved. If husband or wife (or both!) feel free to disregard God's wisdom on the home, then the marriage will at best continue to be unpleasant.

Secondly, is there an **admiration of and desire to imitate the character of the Lord Jesus Christ**? (Or all Persons of the Godhead; Father, Son and Holy Spirit.) What we worship we become. A little boy who idolizes a football star wants to play football. A little girl who "worships" a ballerina wants to dance. Christians who genuinely worship God will want to become like Him. Those of us who are married will strengthen our marriages by the admiration and imitation of Christ or weaken them by disinterest in becoming like Him. The Lord Jesus Christ forgives, loves unconditionally, and gives grace (kindness even when we do not deserve it). His traits lived through a husband and wife determine the strength and quality of a marriage.

Concluding that **admiration and imitation of Christ** is a predictor of a successful marriage is not identical to assuming the imitation of God is the underlying purpose for God designing the human race in families. However, it's close. The most basic purpose in marriage and the family may not even be companionship, children, sexual enjoyment, spiritual growth or security. By creating the human race in families, God intends that people, not angels, have a deeper experience of His own nature.

Life in General

What is the meaning of life? Humans were created to worship and enjoy fellowship with God (Rev. 4:11). Those who refuse to do so will never find contentment. God allowed suffering and evil into this world in order for His otherwise hypothetical virtues to be experienced.

By being exposed to evil we learn forgiveness. By observing suffering we learn long-suffering. By encountering the unworthy we can display God's grace. By loving unconditionally we imitate the glorious nature of God.[1] Life in general is about exalting God, especially knowing God and becoming like God in character. God's main purpose for marriage and family must relate to this (see Phil. 1:21; 3:8).

Marriage and the Family in Particular

Only a tiny step exists between viewing God as the role model for marriage and then inferring the main purpose of the family is the experience of imitating God's character in a deeper way. Both the Old and New Testaments not only portray God as the Creator of life, but God also presents Himself as the model for marriage. In the Old Testament the LORD is the husband to Israel (Isa. 54:5; Jer. 31:32; Hos. 2:19). In the New Testament, Christ is not only the model for husbands (Eph. 5:25) but also for wives (1 Cor. 11:3).[2] It may be an inference, but the Bible's own illustration of God as the role model in marriage is sufficient to prove God ordained the family in order to deepen the human experience of God's own character. Angels will never know God as fully as humans because they have no family experience.

God is the Creator. By God's plan humans become "creators" by reproduction. God loved and endured the pain of sacrificing His Son. All humans who have lost a family member to death can relate to God the Father. As part of life in general, marriage and the family enables us to live out forgiveness, longsuffering, graciousness, and unconditional love. As the Persons within the Godhead are One, and

---

[1] See Steven Waterhouse, *Life's Tough Questions* (Amarillo, Texas: Westcliff Press, 2005) pp. 1-15 for further comments on suffering deepening ones experience of God's virtues. Marriage and the family seems to be another part of the same process.

[2] The Lord Jesus Christ is the role model for both husbands and wives. In His relationship to the church He is the Master who serves. He gives sacrificial love and uses authority in our best interests. Thus, He serves as a model for husbands. (Eph. 5:23ff). Less emphasized in articles and sermons is the Lord Jesus' role model for wives. His relationship within the Trinity is one who is co-equal in Person and worth but willingly submits to the Father in terms of position and work. Paul makes this parallel in 1 Cor. 11:3.

every believer is one with Christ, marriage teaches union, oneness, and intimacy as a parallel to a believer's spiritual union with God and the unity among the Persons of the Trinity. Finally, God's purpose for marriage must have something to do with His own nature of being committed and loyal to a covenant.

God Keeps His Vows

Questionnaires for admission to my doctorate program included two basic questions:

♦ In one sentence, what is the message of the Old Testament?

♦ In one sentence, what is the message of the New Testament?

The New Testament is elementary. The message of the New Testament is in John 3:16. *For God loved the world, that He gave His only begotten Son, that whoever believes in Him shall not perish, but have eternal life.*

It is far more difficult to summarize the entire Old Testament in a single sentence. "New Testament" means "New Covenant" and "Old Testament" means "Old Covenant". In one sentence, the Old Testament teaches that God is loyal to His covenants. The Old Testament constantly repeats that God is abounding in "lovingkindness" (see Ex. 34:6, Psa. 103:8). Every verse in Psalm 136 uses the same word to repeat 26 times that "His lovingkindness is everlasting." The Old Testament is full of various covenants God has made. One could even view John 3:16 as part of God's offering and keeping a promise. The Hebrew word *chesed* translated as "lovingkindness" or "loyal-love" stresses God is faithful to His relationships. God keeps His promises and commitments to His people. He has loyal-love and faithfulness to us. It is no coincidence that the LORD of the Old Testament is Israel's husband or that a covenant (vow) initiates a marriage.

The Admiration and Imitation of God in Loyalty to a Covenant

God keeps His promises. God is loyal to His covenant and faithful in His relationship to believers. Marriage begins in a covenant (Prov. 2:17; Mal. 2:14). **A major part of God's plan in ordaining**

marriage is that we could experience and share His own attribute of loyal-love in keeping a covenant. This main purpose for marriage also forms the secret to a lasting and strong marriage. We must never worship a husband or wife or the institution of marriage as an end in itself. God is the object of admiration and worship. What we worship we become. **God's purpose for marriage is to make us more like Himself, especially in the matter of loyalty to a vow and a relationship.** When both husband and wife seize this purpose, they also ensure a strong and lasting marriage. [3]

---

[3] Few characteristics are more unlike God than treachery to a covenant. The Bible does not give flattering terms to those who intentionally break vows, especially a marriage covenant. See Deut. 23:21-23; Eccles. 5:4-5, and especially Mal. 2:14-16. God warns His people to guard their spirit against treachery and calls those who make casual vows "fools".

Chapter Two

Pattern for Marriage

"Male and Female... two shall become one ... let no man separate..."

... Have you not read that He who created them from the beginning made them male and female, and said, "for this reason a man shall leave his father and mother and be joined to his wife, and the two shall become one flesh"? So they are no longer two, but one flesh. What therefore God has joined together, let no man separate [Matt. 19:4-6, cf. Mark 10:6-9].

The Lord Jesus Christ in this passage endorses the pattern for marriage given by God to Moses (Gen. 2:24). God's ideal includes monogamy, heterosexuality and permanence. "Two shall become one" gives an uncomplicated pattern. Since marriage teaches us about God, unity and oneness mirrors the spiritual oneness of the believer with God and perhaps the Persons of the Trinity with each other. Polygamy hinders this spiritual oneness in marriage and fosters dispute rather than intimacy and oneness. Homosexuality moves even further from God's pattern. In case we do not get the message, the above text actually gives a triple reference to heterosexuality (male/female, father/mother, man/wife). Neither aspect to God's pattern for marriage gives the fair reader trouble with interpretation. Other Scriptures show that God tolerated polygamy in the Old Testament as a less than ideal concession. By comparison, homosexual "marriage" would be so far removed from the pattern as to be unthinkable.

The Old Testament and Polygamy

The Lord's teaching ratifies God's pattern for marriage given through Moses. Though polygamy fails God's ideal, He did not punish those with multiple wives. Instead, He regulated the practice (Deut. 21:15-17) and allowed misery by experience to teach the hard lessons of polygamy. Old Testament examples of polygamy do not show a pattern of intimacy and oneness, rather constant squabbles and often spiritual harm. Abraham with Sarah and Hagar, Jacob with Rachel and Leah, Elkanah with Hannah and Penuel; all give stories of polygamous pain.[1] Most believers mature with age. Solomon regressed spiritually. "… his wives turned his heart away" (1 Kings 11:3).

The New Testament forbids church leadership to polygamists (included within the teaching of 1 Tim. 3:2; Titus 1:6). In areas of the world where those with Muslim backgrounds come to faith in Christ, it is often necessary to restrict polygamous men from leadership. The Bible presents monogamy as God's pattern with polygamy ruining the ideal. Polygamy can be safely classified as a failure. It was endured (not approved) by God to teach a lesson. By the time of their exile, Jewish custom had returned to God's ideal of monogamy. By contrast, God has never tolerated homosexual acts. The "homosexual marriage" debate would never have occurred at any point in Bible history.

Homosexuality and Marriage

Biblical material on the subject yields the unmistakable conclusion that God disapproves of homosexuality, and any so-called marriage defies His pattern for marriage.[2] The Bible does drop the death penalty as God's revelation moves from Old Testament to New Testament, from strict Law to Grace. Also, Paul gives the hopeful example that some of the Corinthians had been cleansed from a homosexual past by faith in Christ (1 Cor. 6:9-11).

God's Word gives sufficient evidence that God would never approve homosexuality as a marriage pattern. A pastor (or church) adhering to Christ's authority should decline to participate in any homosexual wedding ceremonies regardless of the prevailing civil law. To be balanced on the subject we must continue with some material that technically goes beyond the scope of a book on the Christian home.

Ministry to Homosexuals

---

[1] See Genesis 16 and 21, Genesis 29-30, and 1 Samuel 1 for the stories of conflict in these homes. Solomon did not enjoy his polygamy as evidenced by statements about contentious women (Prov. 19:13, 21:9, 19, 25:24, 27:15) and not finding one woman in a thousand to be acceptable (Eccles. 7:28).

[2] Gen. 19:4-5; Lev. 18:22,29, 20:13; Deut. 23:17; Judges 19:22; Rom. 1:26-28; 1 Cor. 6:9-11; 1 Tim. 1:9-10.

Rejection of homosexual marriage does not mean hatred of homosexual persons. A man with AIDS came to my office one afternoon. The counseling session ended with a tour of the church. When we reached the pulpit, he hugged me. The Lord's example was to be a friend to sinners but an opponent to those leading others into sin. He extended grace to those in sin but would severely rebuke those who deceive and lead others astray. His ministry model shows the way. Some homosexuals possess a militant attitude. They will debate, influence, and recruit. In order to protect others from their influence, Christians should regularly defend morality both by teaching and by refusing church membership to homosexuals.

However, the Lord's example and the tone of the New Testament encourage grace as a first course of action. While homosexuals may not join our church or serve in any ministry, especially youth work, those who inquire are always given a welcome and blessing to attend. If they offer no debate or disrespect, and do not attempt to influence others, they may be in the process of seeking and finding truth. Christians should not tolerate any militant attitude, but many homosexuals are in deep pain. Love means we would never use derogatory terms. I personally avoid the word "gay." Many are not in the least happy people. Some were lured and molested at a young age. For others, homosexuality has brought them to an empty dead end. With exception for those of a militant nature, ministry to those bearing a broken condition should not include harsh rebuke. The Lord's righteous indignation would have involved tough talk to arrogant people trying to harm others but grace extended to the broken.

One man told me he had been molested as a child. He kept reliving the memories in his mind. He wished his head would explode like a watermelon to stop the memories of homosexual molestation. A few days later I visited him in the local suicide prevention unit. He asked if I would smuggle something out for him. After I declined to handle any illegal substance, he showed me the razor blades hidden inside a CD case. I took the hidden razor back to the church with an appreciation that people, including homosexuals, need God's love and grace reflected in His people. Ministry should begin with grace. If one later finds blasphemy against God or dangerous influence to others, then one can choose tough-talk (2 Tim. 2:24-26).

On one occasion, a mother asked me to contact her homosexual son in a distant city. He accepted my visit. The next thing I knew I was sitting in a homosexual restaurant. Beginning with grace, I tried to express two main ideas: one, that God's prohibition of homosexuality expresses His love and concern for our welfare and, two, many sins, including homosexuality, are attempts to find a good thing but in an evil and, therefore, harmful way.

I said to him, "I believe that homosexuality is evil, but I traveled here because our church cares about you and does not want to see you hurt. What you want is good, but you are going about it in a destructive way. Your goals (intimacy and love) are good, but this is the way to harm and misery. God prohibits this not to hinder your joy in life but to protect you from self-inflicted harm. If you will trust in Christ, God will meet your needs in a way that blesses and improves you. Be honest, you are not happy are you?" He replied, "This is a very miserable life." I parted with expressions of grace and a plea to stop trying to meet legitimate needs in a harmful way. A few weeks later his mother told me he had rejected homosexuality.

Let us first offer grace to the broken and then use righteous indignation and rebuke for those who prove to be militant. However, in no case would God ever include homosexuality within His pattern for marriage.

Till Death Us Do Part

By the Lord's authority marriage involves a man and woman, two becoming one. The final element to the simple pattern given in Matthew 19 is permanence. The traditional phrase "till death us do part" may not be a biblical quote, but the traditional English wedding liturgy gives biblical truth.

The Lord's actual phrase "let no man separate" (Matt. 19:6; Mark 10:9) might be so familiar as to have lost meaning. Here is a suggested paraphrase, "when a man and woman are married all others are forbidden to break up that union." God will not approve of anyone trying to split the marriage by stealing another's husband or wife. While the Lord's warning applies more directly to any outsider as a potential adulterer trying to split a married couple, it also tells the extended family (such as in-laws) and even the government to regard marriage as a permanent union.

The Bible teaches that marriage is a life-long but earthly relationship. Stating the principle negatively, death ends marriage. Most Bible texts on this subject are addressed to widows. Therefore, they state the truth negatively. Paul says in Romans 7:2 "for the married woman is bound by law to her husband while he is living, but if her husband dies, she is released from the law concerning the husband." 1 Corinthians 7:39 teaches marriage is indeed binding for life, but Christian widows are free to remarry. In 1 Tim. 5:14, Paul encourages younger widows to remarry. Though the main topic was life after death, Jesus mentioned that marriage is not a heavenly institution (Matt. 22:30; Mark 12:25; Luke 20:35).

Engaged couples, newlyweds, and even couples married for a long time often dislike the thought that marriage is not forever. It helps to realize that God's purpose for marriage prepares believers for heaven through experience of His attributes. Furthermore, husband and wives will love each other more in the beyond than we can in our fallen state in this world. Marriages end with this life, but love will be deeper, purer, and without end.

Bible texts giving freedom for remarriage to widows must necessarily stress the word "part" in "till death us do part." However, those contemplating marriage and those in a marriage may profitably stress the words "so long as you both shall live." From the prospective of those entering a marriage, God's pattern is permanency. A married couple's conviction should be that of a life-long commitment. A couple on their wedding day may suppress thoughts of death and view marriage as permanent through all of life. Neither bride nor groom may separate to join another. No outsider has any right to try to split the union. Of course, the life-long permanency of marriage brings to mind the topic of divorce. That subject needs a separate chapter, but it is good that we cannot proceed directly to biblical studies on divorce. We must first study the procedure for initiating a marriage. God joins a couple together, but how?

The need for further studies on the institution of marriage is providential. God hates divorce (Mal. 2:16). Divorced people hate divorce. This unpleasant topic must be covered, but let us suppress that for a moment to emphasize divorce is not part of God's pattern for marriage.

Bible texts giving instruction to widows or the freedom to remarry give important information but would make poor choices for wall plaques for newlyweds. More appropriate would be "Let no one separate." By Christ's authority, the pattern for marriage is man and woman (heterosexuality), two become one (monogamous) and permanence (let no one separate).

Chapter Three

Procedures to Form a Marriage

"I now pronounce you husband and wife."

Perhaps other ministers feel discomfort with the phrase "by the authority invested in me...." The word "me" seems a bit presumptuous. It is God's authority that joins every husband and wife in marriage, "what, therefore God has joined together ... " (Matt. 19:6). How? What procedure or magic words form a legitimate union in God's sight?

A graduate student challenged the New Testament professor about the need for a wedding license; "Show me in the Bible where God commands to get a marriage license. Why do we need a worthless piece of paper? Many who have licenses get divorced. So those living together have just as valid a relationship as those without any paper!" How should we respond?

Submission to the Government

The Bible allows civil disobedience if a government commands an action contrary to God's higher law. The midwives refused to throw the Hebrew babies into the Nile (Ex. 1:17). Daniel continued to pray when it was illegal (Dan. 6:10), and his three friends refused to worship a statue (Dan. 3:18). When the authorities ruled that the message of Christ's death for our sins and His resurrection was illegal, the apostles responded, "We must obey God rather than men" (Acts 5:29). The technical term for this is "hierarchical" ethics. All of God's moral commands are absolute. In a perfect world, we can and must comply with all commands (the opposite of situation ethics). However, misuse of human authority can force a believer to choose to suspend the lesser human command in order to fulfill the higher command of God. Yet, Christians have no authorization from God to disobey a government whenever we feel like doing so. There must be a higher moral principle at stake before God permits civil disobedience (such as Pharaoh ordering the midwives to throw male babies into the Nile).

Marriage licenses present no such moral dilemma. Thus, believers must submit to such regulations. We must obtain a state wedding license, so long as it conforms to God's pattern for marriage (Chapter 2): male/female, two become one, lasting until death.

I once lived in a district where the congressman proposed revision to marriage laws. He wanted to issue a three-year wedding license similar to a driver's license. At the end of the term, the marriage would expire unless the couple renewed their license.

Unfortunately, some nations and states issue marriage licenses for homosexuals, and some nations allow polygamy. Licenses according to these arrangements should be rejected as not conforming to God's pattern. God joins a couple but not in these ways.

Christians should respect civil authority (Rom. 13:1-4). This involves obedience in obtaining a wedding license as long as it conforms to God's marriage pattern. Regardless of any odd type of wedding regulations that may arise, it is impossible to imagine conditions where the traditional (i.e. biblical) pattern would not be among the options for civil marriage contracts. Therefore, yes, we must obtain a piece of paper.

Still, in all fairness, Isaac and Rebekah had no wedding license. Abraham sent his servant across the desert. Rebekah agreed to leave Mesopotamia (Iraq) and go to Israel to become Isaac's wife. He took her into the tent and "… she became his wife, and he loved her …" (Gen. 24:67). Some details of this wedding may be missing to keep the narrative short (such as vows and a ceremony), but Isaac and Rebekah did not go to any courthouse to buy a license.

Evidently, in a hypothetical situation where no government exists, a couple could be wed without a certificate. In our politically organized world, a Christian should respect civil authority and obtain a marriage license. Nevertheless, Isaac and Rebekah illustrate that God, not the state, is the ultimate authority for marriage. The critical wording in a marriage ceremony is not, "by the authority invested in me by the state of …." The basis for a valid wedding is reflected in the defining phrase, "I pronounce you man and wife *in the name* (**i.e., the authority**) *of the Father, and the Son and the Holy Spirit.*"

Christians should comply with the government and obtain a license. However, God forms the union of man and wife. What procedure does God recognize as creating a legitimate marriage?

Cohabitation without Any Wedding

Concluding that a legitimate marriage does not primarily arise from government authority does not equal approval of living together without a wedding. One of the great stories in the life of Christ is the woman at the well in John 4. In order to prove His identity to her, he revealed that He possessed all knowledge of every detail in her sinful past. Jesus said, "Go call your husband ..." (John 4:16). She replied, "I have no husband." Jesus agreed and then shocked her with His omniscience. She had been married and divorced five times prior to her present cohabitation with a man without the benefit of marriage. The Lord agreed that she was indeed presently unmarried. "You have well said, 'I have no husband'... and the one whom you now have *is not your husband*" (John 4:17-18). She was living and sleeping with a man, but the Lord refused to define this relationship as a marriage.

In fact, just living together is actually the antithesis of true marriage. Given that **the primary purpose of marriage is the admiration and imitation of God**, a relationship with less than total dedication in a covenant of love can hardly qualify as a marriage. God possesses unending loyal-love to those in a covenant with Him (by faith in His Son). A fundamental purpose for marriage is sharing God's experience of loyal covenantal love. This is hardly possible when two people reject any covenant to each other.

The Marriage Covenant

God joins a couple, not so much the state, the denomination, the local church, or the minister. Though the Bible does not contain required wording for a wedding ceremony, God's Word teaches the need for a marriage covenant. Proverbs 2:17 calls a wife's wedding vows, "the covenant of her God." Mal. 2:14 teaches that God witnesses the promises made by a man and woman. Malachi also warns a husband to guard his spirit and not deal treacherously against his "wife by covenant."

19

God joins together every husband and wife by witnessing their covenant (modern language, wedding vows). The Bible gives truths to be applied to diverse cultures over generations. God has given freedom for the precise wording of wedding vows. In fact a couple can compose individualized vows. The only restrictions would be that the wording conforms to God's pattern for marriage. Vows must include the promise of a man and a woman to live together in a permanent union (heterosexual, monogamous, lifelong, permanent duration). God witnesses and approves such vows. The **covenant** is the basis of God joining a couple together.

Couples who live together without any marriage covenant rationalize sin and delude themselves. They think they can test each other to see if the relationship works. Thus, by definition cohabitation involves less than a total commitment. It stresses hesitance and reluctance to join together with sacrificial love. Cohabitation by definition involves a mental reservation against giving self totally to another. Plan "B" is to ditch the other party if times get rough.

In fairness one could make casual or treacherous vows.[1] Yet, serious marriage vows with honorable intentions have nothing in common with the trial or probationary nature of mere cohabitation.

A man and a woman vow before God, family, and friends their intent to a commitment for life. They love each other based on what they know, but will from this point on continue to love despite any unknown trait or characteristic that arises after the marriage. Real love commits totally without reservation, come what may about flaws in the spouse discovered after the wedding. Cohabitation rationalizes an easy escape. Vows made by God's pattern for marriage burn those proverbial bridges. The two mindsets are actually direct opposites.[2]

---

[1] See footnote 3 in Chapter 1 for verses about foolish casual vows. No one making vows on a wedding day should take the words as a joke or entertain thoughts of an easy divorce as a way of escape.

[2] One might apply Jesus' words that any one who starts to plow should begin with a dedication to a successful finish. Those who never really care about the task in the first place are unfit for God's service (Luke 9:62). Salvation comes by grace through faith alone, but God's full will for us involves complete

God joins together a couple by witnessing their vows which pledge themselves to each other according to His holy pattern for marriage. Tentative relationships with partial dedication do not meet God's definition of marriage. If there has been no covenant, it is not a marriage.

Just as the Scripture does not command certain words for a vow, it does not require a set of customs for a ceremony. However, God approves and blesses a diversity of customs so long as the cultural marriage pattern conforms to His biblical pattern for marriage. The Lord Jesus participated in the wedding at Cana (John 2:1-11), and His Second Coming is compared to a wedding celebration. The universal Church (defined as all who trust in Christ as Savior) is now like an engaged bride with the wedding coming upon the Lord's return (Rev. 19:7, 21:9).

God blesses and must personally rejoice at the diversity of wedding customs among the many tribes and nations in the human race. The actual details of procedure matter little except God wants to witness vows that pledge a man and a woman to permanent loyal love. When words fail to convey the beauty of the heavenly city, God selects His choice for the most beautiful image on earth, "a bride adorned for her husband" (Rev. 21:2).

---

dedication. This includes marriage vows made with sincerity with no reservation to complete loyal-love.

Chapter Four

Preserving Marriage: Divorce

"Is it lawful... to divorce ... for any reason at all?"

The Lord's teaching on divorce comes in a direct answer to the above question. His enemies planned their trap with a remarkably modern cast. "Is it lawful for a man to divorce his wife for any reason at all?" (Matt. 19:3). In Jesus' time the proponents of Rabbi Hillel believed in a long list of grounds for divorce, including burning supper. The followers of Rabbi Shammai limited divorce to various sexual offenses. [1]

If anything, the Lord Jesus Christ's teaching is more conservative than the conservatives of His day. The disciples responded to His rigid views by saying that if marriage is that binding it would be better to be single (Matt. 19:10). The Lord's comeback may be paraphrased, "Permanent marriage or permanent celibacy ... Take it or leave it." The Lord simply had no sympathy for the "divorce for any reason" point of view.

Two passages in Matthew (Matt. 5:32 and 19:9) qualify the overall prohibition against divorce by giving adultery as a very important exception clause. However, the parallel teachings in Mark 10:2-12 and Luke 16:18 omit the exception clause. It helps to remember that the Lord's instructions on divorce arise in a direct answer to the question "Can we get a divorce for any reason?" The answer is a loud and clear "NO." In modern writing style, adultery would perhaps be placed in parentheses or probably in a footnote. Granted it is a vital footnote, but the Lord's emphasis gives this direct answer to the hostile question: "No, you may not divorce for just any reason!" Because of the flow of the argument in its original setting, Mark and Luke do not even include the "footnote." The Lord continues

---

[1] Most commentaries will mention the rabbinic background to the Pharisees' challenge to Jesus on His divorce views, for example Louis A. Barbieri, Jr., "Matthew" in *The Bible Knowledge Commentary*, edited by John F. Walvoord and Roy B. Zuck (Wheaton, IL: Victor Books, 1983), p.63.

beyond the blunt answer to the question, giving the Pharisees more than they ever wanted to hear.

A Second Honeymoon as Adultery

Jesus taught if a man or woman divorces and marries another (with adultery excepted), even in a perfectly legal second marriage, the second honeymoon is itself an act of adultery. The Lord did not care if the state recognized the divorce or the remarriage as legal or even if the new couple abstained from sexual relations until remarriage.[2] That point set the disciples off and causes modern Christians to get up and walk out on a sermon. Read it without emotion with the intent of interpreting and following the authority of the Lord Jesus Christ.

> And He said to them, "Whoever divorces his wife and marries another woman commits adultery against her; and if she herself divorces her husband and marries another man, she is committing adultery [Mark 10:11-12].

> Everyone who divorces his wife and marries another commits adultery, and he who marries one who is divorced from a husband commits adultery [Luke 16:18].

The Apostle Paul gives further instructions for those who get a legal divorce (without grounds of adultery). They are supposed to remain single or reconcile (see 1 Cor. 7:10-11). The Bible's viewpoint on divorce when neither party is guilty of adultery is that grounds for divorce do not exist in God's sight. This places a Christian couple in a "stand-off" relationship. So long as neither have sexual relations with another (including a remarriage), there is hope for the original couple. Only adultery by sexual union to an outside party or even by a remarriage seals the demise of the original marriage in God's sight. Given contemporary disrespect for biblical authority and even to red-letter portions of Scripture (the words of Christ), it is usually just a

---

[2] Of course, this raises the issue of the Christian response to the many remarriages that occur after divorce lacking biblical grounds. Should there be a second divorce to the improper remarriage and a return to the original spouse? This topic will be covered later by footnote four.

matter of time before a man or a woman pairs up with another after divorce. Therefore, God's grounds for divorce (immorality) often take place soon after a purely legal divorce that originally lacked any biblical basis for the dissolution of the marriage. However, (adultery excepted), the Lord Himself did not grant any other grounds for divorce. [3]

In His conclusion, the Lord was probably enforcing the true interpretation of the Law of Moses. He began by asking them if they had ever bothered to read the Old Testament carefully. The Law of Moses does not appear to give any grounds for divorce that God approves. The Law only regulated sinful divorces that inevitably occurred under the Law and now under the Church. [4] Old Testament

---

[3] Adultery is the only biblical grounds for divorce. Adultery can, however, take place long after a court action led to a divorce on other grounds. Either one party commits immorality or remarriage (which Christ regarded as adultery). Thus, after the time of the original legal divorce, the first spouse to join to another gives the remaining spouse grounds for the demise of the original marriage.

[4] Deut. 24:1-4 does not give God's approval for divorce. It controls practices that displease God. If a divorce takes place, then it must be in writing, and no man may change his mind and take his wife back after she marries another. She may not return either after a second divorce or as a widow. God hated divorce (Mal. 2:16). Adultery under the Law required stoning. Since people would divorce anyway, Deuteronomy 24 merely controls an action that people do because of "hardness of heart" (Matt. 19:8).

God did not permit wives bouncing around back and forth. By principle, Deut. 24:1-4 answers the question as to how to handle divorces and remarriages that occur without any adultery in the previous marriage. Remarriages that take place when there was no adultery by either party in the original marriage are biblically wrong. However, a second divorce to return to the previous marriage is now out of God's will. God prohibits any "marital" rebounding in a mistaken effort to fix a broken past. Even when remarriage is an act of adultery, the marriage covenant is binding. No pastor should advise trying to "turn back the clock" by shuffling husbands and wives back to past spouses.

In Chapter 5 we will see that God prohibits the marriage of a believer to an unbeliever. However, when the prohibited marriage takes place, the vows are holy and binding. Once contracted even a marriage that should not have taken

allowances for divorce should not be confused with Old Testament approval for divorce. Under the Law, adultery was a capital offense (Lev. 20:10; Deut. 22:22). The New Testament drops the death penalty.[5] Grace permits divorce for adultery instead, but the evil of the "divorce-for-any-reason" philosophy of life remains constant whether Old or New Covenant.

Objections: Bible Times and Now

The Bible teaches marriage is for life. God says, "I hate divorce" (Mal. 2:16). No one likes to use the ugly word sin, but objective Bible interpretation forces the conclusion that every divorce involves someone's sin. Of course, "we all stumble in many ways," (James 3:2), but as to the actual guilt for a divorce it is possible for one party to be innocent. Yet, it is not possible for both to be innocent. Every divorce involves someone's violation of a sacred and permanent covenant (the opposite of God's nature to be loyal to a covenant). Maybe the husband sins. Maybe the wife sins. Maybe both sin. Only a false prophet tells people what they want to hear (Isa. 30:10-11; Jer. 5:31; Micah 2:6,11). The Lord Jesus Christ reveals God's truth. His views on marriage and divorce give the only ways that do work. They are not rooted in strictness for strictness' sake, but to protect us from sin. Far from being mean, the Lord's marriage and divorce policy assumes marriage is far too holy to destroy for problems that have a hope for solution simply by obedience to God. Even the disciples disagreed with the Lord's no-divorce policy. They regarded His views as impractical and instantly questioned Him (Matt. 19:10; Mark 10:10). They felt the divorce-for-any-reason view gives a practical solution to immediate need. Why should anyone yield to the Lord's authority and

---

place is still permanent (1 Cor. 7:12-14). Bible truths about the marriage of a believer to an unbeliever show that marriages, even those begun in defiance of God's commands, become sacred once such vows are made. God does want us to try to fix all the pain but to regard the present marriage as sacred.

[5] By God's example in divorcing Israel for spiritual adultery (Isa. 50:1; Jer. 3:8; Hosea 2:2), He may have given indirect permission for the Jews to drop stoning for adultery and substitute divorce even within the period of the Old Testament prophets.

change character habits? Why should couples reconcile their problems when divorce is an "easy" option?

We might consider whether divorce for any reason improves life. The Lord Jesus Christ compared His commandments to a yoke used to harness oxen for heavy labor. He also adds that His ways are "easy" and His burdens "light." As hard as Christ's teachings can be, rejection of them brings a much harder journey. Life cannot be made totally carefree and easy. The Lord's wisdom gives an easier option for life's problems than the world's foolishness (Prov. 16:2).

Holiness and Hope

Christianity provides hope in a world of humanly impossible problems. All other world views are ultimately dead-ends. Sometimes those who reject God's wisdom end up foolishly concluding death is the best answer (Prov. 14:12). By a figurative parallel, marital death seems a quick and painless solution to marriages with trouble.

Just as faith in Christ as Savior offers hope to an individual whose problems cannot be solved without the Lord, God's wisdom has a solution to every marital conflict. Let us repeat the two factors that predict a strong marriage: **the admiration and imitation of the Lord Jesus Christ and submission to the Bible's authority**. The most seemingly hopeless individuals can find salvation by faith (e.g. Saul of Tarsus, i.e. the Apostle Paul). The most seemingly hopeless marriage can be saved if both husband and wife will yield to God's wisdom for life and for the family. No one should think the Lord's views on divorce are unworkable. They certainly are not cruel. They may be an insult to human pride and autonomy. Sometimes we would rather do things our way than admit to flaws, learn, and change. The disciples may have regarded the Lord's teaching as restricting mankind to hopeless marriages. The Lord's policy in reality restricts us to God's authority as the hope for all marriage. The underlying reasons for narrow divorce grounds are the **holiness** of marriage and the **hope** that God can solve any marital difficulty. Rather than seeing Christ's teaching as unworkable and hopeless, they spring from the presumption that marriage is far too sacred to break easily and that God can give hope for every marriage. How absurd to conclude Christ's ideas are unworkable. He gives the only truth that could possibly work. Marital problems are spiritual problems. God can solve them. The Lord's rejection of easy divorce stems from the sacred and holy nature of marriage. Marriage is too holy to destroy for problems that have a remedy if only stubborn people will submit to God.

What Is a Man (or Woman) To Do?

While the Bible only allows divorce on grounds of adultery, in the real world other serious problems can arise. We might argue that the worse case scenario is domestic violence. Anyone can quickly compose a long list of other horrible possibilities that threaten a marriage, but domestic violence can well serve as a test case that might destroy a marriage. A pattern for dealing with this serious issue could be applied to other troubles.

Questions about domestic violence usually present the most serious challenge to the view that Scripture gives no grounds for divorce beyond adultery. "You mean I (or my daughter or sister) must put up with that? This cannot possibly be true. I will never accept such teaching." The Lord's restrictive views as to grounds for divorce do not mean the government, or the church, or a family, or a spouse should tolerate abuse. Peter assumes that a wife should live "without being frightened by any fear"(1 Pet. 3:6). Peter assumes even an unsaved husband would act this way. Given that a woman's security is one of the most basic purposes of marriage (Ruth 3:1), domestic violence constitutes a serious violation of a covenant patterned after God's loyal-love. It hardly qualifies as "nourishing" and "cherishing" a wife as is Christ's model for a husband (Eph. 5:29).

No one should tolerate domestic violence. This does not, however, change the fact that adultery alone gives grounds for divorce. A separation may be needed. An attorney may be needed for potential financial and child custody protection. However, even a separation for any other reason short of adultery need not be the same as immediate action for divorce.[6]

---

[6] In situations where domestic violence is charged, some caution is in order unless a pastor actually witnesses the abuse. It is not helpful if the charge is untrue or exaggerated, and the report back home is "the pastor told me to leave you." Separation is appropriate for a wife who feels danger, but that decision

With marital problems not involving adultery, the Bible recognizes that separation (even legal divorce) occurs. The commandments in such circumstances are to "… remain unmarried, or else be reconciled" (1 Cor. 7:11).

Immediate divorce may not be in order but tough-love, tough-talk, legal advice, and separation may be very much in order. Still, initially the option of reconciliation must be part of a Christian's thinking. Also, a separation with a view to working on problems does not give the moral freedom to either party (yes, even the victim) to start a new romantic relationship. "Let no one separate" warns third parties not to break up a marriage, including those vulnerable because of serious difficulty. Short of adultery, the marriage covenant remains binding in God's sight. Thus, separation (negatively for protection, but optimistically to work out serious problems) may be necessary, but it is not a green light to fornication for either the husband or the wife (which would be adultery and would give grounds for ending the marriage). Human sin often demands a tough and skeptical response. Serious marital troubles may need time to resolve, including time with a biblically informed pastor or counselor. Furthermore, there is an emotional side to forgiveness (dropping resentment) that is always in order, but one of the shades of meaning to forgiveness involves accountability. The Hebrew and Greek words refer to canceling a debt or removing a crushing load. One should always forgive a spouse in the sense of dropping hatred and vengeance. One should not always remove moral accountability. In cases of domestic violence, it would be necessary to insist upon a probationary relationship, even a second courtship, in order to reestablish trust and security. However, without adultery, the Bible's commands restrict our actions to remaining morally faithful and hoping for and working toward an eventual reconciliation. If both have convictions about the admiration and imitation of Christ, and both agree they must obey the Bible, even serious marital problems have solutions.

If All Else Fails, Then What?

must be hers, not a counselor's. Also, if she feels protection is needed, law enforcement should be consulted as the problem is beyond the scope of ministry.

Despite honorable intentions to reconcile and against strong objections to divorce, sometimes a good person is served with divorce papers. Neither party has committed adultery but legally the marriage ends. Does this morally bind a Christian to a single status for life? How should the newly divorced Christian who is seeking God's plan respond following divorce despite the best efforts and against his or her will? The pattern for separated but not divorced couples holds true for those in divorce situations on grounds other than adultery. Christians legally divorced for any other grounds have a duty to work toward reconciliation.

It is foolish to deny the gravity of such situations. The psychological problem of acceptance (not denial) must begin. However, one may still possess a willingness to reconcile and refuse to enter into a relationship with a view to remarriage (and certainly not promiscuity).

God can do the humanly impossible (Matt. 19:26; Luke 1:37, 18:27). I know of several couples who remarried each other after an earlier divorce from each other.

Realistically, it is improbable that a couple can save a marriage after divorce court. Those who have been divorced on grounds other than adultery should pray and hope for the best but prepare emotionally for the worst.

In such a spiritual test, the overall goal remains honoring God even if a marriage simply cannot be preserved. A Christian who remains faithful to marriage vows despite legal divorce and despite the dismal prospects for recovery proves sincerity in allegiance to God. By choosing to remain single and reserving the slim possibility for reconciliation, a Christian proves to the former husband or wife, to the extended family, to the church and to God that he or she did not desire the divorce. Even afterward, he or she still desired to obey, please and serve God.

Fidelity to marriage vows even after a legal divorce shows the entrusting of one's future to God and honor to God's Word. Does this mean a life of being single?

Separation, or divorce on grounds other than adultery, creates a moral stand off. The parties are still supposed to reconcile and remain single (including not rationalizing other relationships whether sinful sexual acts or even with a view to remarriage). Even after a perfectly legal divorce, the first party who engages in any sexual union (even after a perfectly legal remarriage) is committing an act of adultery according to the Lord Jesus Christ. Though it be after the time of a legal divorce, any sexual union now gives moral grounds for a divorce. After this occurs, the original spouse may consider himself or herself free of their original marriage covenant. Prior to such adultery, one who is divorced on other grounds should submit to God by waiting in purity and offering reconciliation. Once adultery occurs, the remaining original spouse will have demonstrated obedience to God to the end.

Sometimes divorced people ask, "How long does God want me to wait?" "How will I know my marriage is totally beyond any hope of recovery?" The answer is when your spouse joins to another either by illicit sexual union or even by a remarriage. Even when a divorce originally occurs without a Scriptural basis, adultery after the fact means the marriage can now be considered beyond hope. Such adultery gives a basis for its final demise.

The divorced person who remains has demonstrated integrity and a desire to please God during the interim. He or she has now experienced a legitimate basis for divorce. Given our sinful world this is often just a matter of time. This involves freedom to begin new relationships and a freedom to remarry.

Adultery: The Lord's Important Footnote

Solomon claims "there is nothing new under the sun" (Eccles. 1:9). Contemporary views of marriage reflect the casual divorce-for-any-reason of Jesus' own time. However, older readers likely will remember days when most Christians held to a no-divorce policy for any reason including adultery. At times in Christian history even those who divorced on grounds of adultery and eventually remarried were still stigmatized. If this material were being written decades ago there may have been a need to emphasize the Lord's secondary point that divorce based on adultery forms an exception to His primary teaching against divorce. Matthew 5:32 and 19:9 give the exception clause.[7]

Some have viewed the exception clause to pertain to Jewish couples in an engagement period. Joseph and Mary were engaged but not yet married. In their culture, a divorce was required to break even a betrothal. Before angelic revelation that Mary was a virgin, Joseph had considered a divorce to break off his engagement to Mary (Matt. 1:19). This is an accurate understanding of the historical account regarding Joseph and Mary.

However, the Lord's teachings on marriage and divorce occur in the context of Adam and Eve (Matt. 19:4), and definitely refer to a man and wife (v. 5) not just an engaged couple. Even Joseph himself became an example of the principle that unfaithfulness can be a moral basis for the ending of a relationship. Not only do the exception clauses in Matthew present adultery as grounds for divorce, the Old Testament figuratively pictures God as divorcing Israel for her spiritual adultery (see Isa. 50:1; Jer. 3:8; and Hosea 2:2). Though such texts are poetic word pictures, is it conceivable that God would even figuratively portray Himself in an action that is sinful?

Adultery need not result in divorce in all cases. The entire book of Hosea tells a story of loving an unfaithful spouse. The grieved party has control over the decision. If he or she can forgive the treachery, then grace is a loving and noble action. However, God does not require that one remain in a marriage after adultery (even one occurrence). In addition, continuance in a marriage along with ongoing adultery hardly contributes to the sanctity of marriage.

Adultery breaks the covenant of marriage. If there is repentance and a complete forsaking of immorality, reconciliation is a possibility when the grieved spouse so chooses. However, the reason adultery permits divorce, **the sacredness of marriage**, is the reason one should not extend marriage to another who refuses repentance and continues in adultery. Though Paul's phrase refers to a different

---

[7] Homosexual adultery is adultery.

situation, it applies to divorce for adultery. "… the brother or the sister is not under bondage in such cases …" (1 Cor. 7:15).[1]

God originated marriage and the family for a blessed purpose. His pattern is without complexity (man/woman, two become one, separated only by death). The procedure for a legal wedding involves a covenant (vows) made by this pattern. Obedience to God gives hope for solving any marital troubles. The main peril to a marriage is adultery. In all this, we must still study the Bible for its teaching on eligibility for marriage. Sometimes a marriage fails because the wedding should have never happened.

---

[1] 1 Cor. 7:15 does not give additional grounds for divorce but does give grounds for remarriage when an unbeliever divorces a believer for religious incompatibility. Paul had just taught that a believer should not divorce an unbeliever if the non-Christian is content to remain married. Thus, the situation is not grounds for divorce. If, however, the unbeliever refuses to continue in marriage to a believer, the Christian is free. There needs to be caution here against rationalizing that an ex-spouse be suddenly transformed from being a Christian to the heathen category. Mixed marriage occurs when a believer disobeys God and marries an unbeliever. The situation Paul had in view occurs when one person converts through faith in Christ but his or her spouse declines to trust in Christ as Savior. The marriage is still permanent unless the unbeliever abandons the believer because of objections to Christianity.

Chapter Five

Prohibitions/Policies on Weddings

" . . . Speak now or forever hold your peace!"

This offer serves to give public awareness that not all marriages are morally proper. Obviously, screening for eligibility for marriage must take place long before the wedding date. "If anyone knows just cause why these two should not be lawfully wedded," is probably best deleted from a public ceremony. Some couples should be discouraged from marriage or even refused approval for a church wedding date.

By observation I believe some clergy have adopted an "anything goes" policy in order to keep everyone happy. Sometimes standards are not enforced or overlooked for purposes of favoritism or church politics. God's commandments are not a burden (see 1 John 5:3). Modern language would paraphrase that His commandments are not a "pain" or a "hassle." God's prohibitions keep us from making extremely painful mistakes.

Mixed Marriages (Believer to Unbeliever)

Since spiritual growth and Christian service are core purposes for the family, a marriage of one who has faith in Christ to one who rejects (or simply does not care about) faith in Christ will be off target from the start. The admiration and imitation of God produces character traits essential for strong families (forgiveness, grace, unconditional love, faithfulness to a covenant relationship). Those who have not experienced the Savior's forgiveness, grace, and love, simply have a sub-standard experience in life to make the best husband or wife. Unbelievers are poor prospects for a strong and happy home.

The Old Testament on Marriage to an Unbeliever

God repeatedly prohibited marriage of Jew and Gentile under the Law of Moses. The reason has nothing to do with ethnicity. The great love story in the book of Ruth involves the marriage of Ruth (a

Gentile) to Boaz (a Jew) with the couple becoming ancestors of both David and Jesus. Old Testament commandments prohibiting mixed marriages clearly show that the concern is not ethnic but religious. Marriages to unbelievers threatened spiritual purity and unity. "Can two walk together except they be agreed?"(Amos 3:3 KJV).[1]

> ... and cause your sons also to play the harlot with their gods (i.e., spiritual prostitution) [Ex. 34:16].

> ... they will turn your sons away from following Me to serve other gods ... [Deut. 7:4].

> Did not Solomon king of Israel sin regarding these things? Yet among the many nations there was no king like him, and he was loved by his God, and God made him king over all Israel; nevertheless the foreign women caused even him to sin [Neh. 13:26].

Historical examples of mixed marriages give a pattern of disastrous outcomes. Esau's marriages to a pair of Hittite women "brought grief to Isaac and Rebekah" (Gen. 26:35). Poor Rebekah later said she was "... tired of living" because of Esau's foolish marriages. She suggested that Isaac send Jacob back to the old country (Mesopotamia, the place of Abraham and Rebekah's own origin) so he could find a wife in God's will. If Jacob made the same mistake as twin brother Esau by marriage to a pagan, Rebekah felt it would ruin her life. "If Jacob takes a wife ... like these ... what good will my life be to me?" (Gen. 27:46).[2]

Samson also ruined his life by not submitting to God's will in marriage. He had rather pagan standards for selecting a wife. His demand to his father to arrange his first marriage reflects a total lack of

---

[1] See also Josh. 23:12-13; Ezra 9:1-7, 12; Neh. 10:30, 13:23-25 on mixed marriages. The Old Testament also gives a long list of pairs that would be regarded as incestuous (Leviticus 18).

[2] By contrast to Esau, Rebekah herself is an example of seeking God's will in the choice for a spouse. She was Miss Right for Isaac (Gen. 24:40, 44).

36

concern and respect for God's authority. He insisted on marriage to a Philistine on the exalted basis of "Get her for me, for she looks good to me" (Judges 14:3). By definition, every good prospective marriage also involves sexual attraction. Samson could have married a beautiful believing woman. He simply did not care. His story continues with a visit to a Philistine prostitute (Judges 16:1). Finally, " … he loved a woman … whose name was Delilah" (Judges 16:4). The rest of the story confirms the foolishness of marriage to unbelievers.

Perhaps Solomon wins the prize for disregard for God's loving commandments. He was not the last to reject God's beneficial control over life. Solomon also presents an exception to the general rule that age brings maturity and wisdom. He coveted wisdom in youth (1 Kings 3:5-15). He got more reckless and foolish with age. His foolish marriages to many unbelieving women (mostly for political alliances rather than love) stained his otherwise good reputation (for example, 1 Kings 3:1).

1 Kings 11:1-3 makes the point that Solomon "held fast to these [unbelieving pagan wives] in love" (11:2). "When Solomon was old, his wives turned his heart away" from God (11:4). After concluding that Solomon's heart was no longer fully devoted to the Lord and that Solomon did evil by not following God fully (11:3,6), the account continues with God's anger at Solomon and God's decision to split up Solomon's kingdom in coming time. He entered into numerous (see Deut. 17:17) and prohibited marriages to unbelievers. His point was to strengthen his empire. Yet, this disobedience literally destroyed the material and political aspects of his life's dream (but in God's mercy not his intellectual and literary work). Also, the world's richest man had a miserable personal and family life.

Solomon's proverbs comparing a contentious wife to the annoyance of dripping rain arise from his polygamous marriages to unbelieving and fussy princesses (Prov. 19:13, 27:15). Evidently, marriage to an unbeliever is like the proverbial Chinese water torture. Solomon would have traded his cedar and golden palace for a humble home with godliness. A corner upper room or even the desert would have been happier (Prov. 21:9,19). He would have preferred vegetable soup with a happy marriage to royal banquets with his many pagan wives, but it was too late for Solomon (Prov. 15:17).

It was probably with a tinge of regret that Solomon concluded "a prudent wife is from the Lord" (Prov. 19:14). He had inherited property and riches from his father, David, but a wise wife or husband comes from obeying God's will. The verse that immediately precedes Solomon's admission to himself (and advice for us) tells of the opposite experience, "And the contentions of a wife are a constant dripping" (Prov. 19:13). Solomon was wise, but his advice on the matter of selecting a marriage partner was learned the hard way.

We may reverse the non-biblical proverb in the matter of a believer's marriage to an unbeliever. It should not be "live and learn" as if one must make foolish mistakes prior to learning wisdom. We should learn first by God's commands and tragic biblical examples. Then we can live better without making the same disobedient and reckless mistakes.

The New Testament on Marriage to an Unbeliever

Several New Testament phrases may be applied to the situation of a spiritually mixed marriage. The wise man builds his house on the rock. In its context, the definition of a solid foundation is obedience to the authority of Christ (Matt. 7:24). Abraham Lincoln applied the Lord's words about a house divided being weak to the nation (Matt. 12:25). The human household that is divided in beliefs also faces the probability of collapse.

Paul prohibits an unequal yoke (harness for pairing oxen or horses) of believer to unbeliever (2 Cor. 6:14). In the context, Paul prohibits a merger of Christianity with paganism. He permitted the Corinthians to have unsaved friends but not to join with them in pagan rituals and temple worship. While his point is not limited to marriage, this has been a common application of the text with good reason. If Paul forbade joint pagan temple worship in general, he would not have approved of participation in pagan rituals for one's own wedding service! The New Testament contains more than general warnings that may be applied to mixed marriages. Several verses specifically limit the choice of a husband or a wife to only believers. They come in contexts of remarriage for widows. Thus, the exact phraseology in this verse is not as memorable as the more familiar phrase, "Do not be unequally yoked" to unbelievers (2 Cor. 6:14). This quote makes for great preaching and gives a true application. However, several less familiar phrases specifically teach about marriage and definitely restrict a believer's marriage only to another Christian.

1 Cor. 7:39 grants Christian widows the freedom to marry again. However, it restricts marriage to believers, "... only in the Lord." In response to criticism, Paul defends his apostolic authority in 1 Corinthians 9. He reminded his readers that he actually had more rights than he chose to use. Among them, he could have chosen marriage. A single state permitted easier travel and less danger to a family. Like Peter (Cephas), Paul had the freedom to marry. Yet, Paul qualifies freedom to marry by saying any potential spouse must be a "believing wife" (1 Cor. 9:5). The Greek word is "sister."

Unbelievers lack the spiritual foundation and development to be good choices for a Christian to marry. They do not have interest in **the admiration and imitation of Christ** and will pull against rather than with a Christian spouse in the most important direction in life. The purpose for God's commandment against marriage to an unbeliever is His love and concern for our welfare.[3] God tries to protect us from our own stubborn mistakes and self-induced pain.

Of course, some Christians refuse God's warning and marry against His will. There are real consequences when a believer marries an unbeliever, and I decline to conduct such weddings, believing I would be assisting in disobedience to God's will recorded in Scripture. All those I have personally declined to marry have suffered divorce

---

[3] Pre-marital interviews and decisions about conducting weddings are not occasions for denominational squabbles. The core of the Christian faith includes: The Trinity (One God in three Persons, Father, Son and Holy Spirit), the virgin birth and deity of Christ who is fully God and fully human, His resurrection and Second Coming. All, in any denomination, who place faith in Christ and His death on the cross for our sins are genuine Christians bound for heaven. All, in any denomination who do not have faith in Christ as Savior are not Christians despite any church membership or ritual. They are in danger of eternal punishment because God is holy. He cannot overlook sin. Either one accepts Christ's substitute punishment in our place or enters into God's holy judgment without any covering for sin.

within a few years.[4] They found ministers who were not averse to performing mixed marriages; after a short time they became unhappy and the relationship finally ended with both parties suffering damaged emotions and lives. The absolute fact is that the Bible prohibits mixed marriages for our own welfare.

The Sanctity of Even Disobedient Marriages

Marriages not made in heaven, in terms of submission to God's commandments, are still sanctified (i.e. holy).[5] Those who defy God's restrictions for marriage to an unbeliever are personally unholy in behavior. However, the marriage covenant (vows) and the institution of marriage always remain holy even when the persons are not.

Peter and Paul both instruct that marriages of Christians to unbelievers remain binding once they have occurred. They assume a home that started with both husband and wife being unsaved. Later one professes faith in Christ while the other declines faith. In an ancient setting, they may even include marriages by slaves or arranged marriages by unsaved parents with little personal choice in the matter. Indirectly, the teaching still gives principles for a believer who deliberately enters into a marriage covenant with an unbeliever.

In the same way, you wives, be submissive to your own husbands so that even if any of them are disobedient to the word,

---

[4] One older couple began their marriage with the wife a believer and the husband an unbeliever. His military service, including serious wounds on D-Day, led to faith in Christ. He gave me the metal cross he crafted from a downed British airplane propeller as part of his rehabilitation.

In a big world there are obviously other examples of mixed marriages ending well, but there are far more examples of marital disaster. Times when a mixed marriage ends well are situations of God's grace and mercy in rescuing a couple despite themselves.

[5] Assuming the biblical pattern given in Chapter 1 (heterosexual, monogamous and binding for life)

they may be won without a word by the behavior of their wives [1 Pet. 3:1].

... If any brother has a wife who is an unbeliever, and she consents to live with him, he must not divorce her. And a woman who has an unbelieving husband, and he consents to live with her, she must not send her husband away. For the unbelieving husband is sanctified through his wife and the unbelieving wife is sanctified through her believing husband; for otherwise your children are unclean, but now they are holy [1 Cor. 7:12b-14].

Wedding vows that are made in disobedience to God's will are still binding and sacred. Children born in such homes are legitimate and holy.[6] Marriages are holy even if sinfully contracted in the first place.

Since marriages of a believer to an unbeliever often bring turmoil in the extended family, this is a good point to mention some practical advice. A proposed mixed marriage is both sin and a big mistake. Yet, once contracted, the wedding is binding. Relatives are placed in an awkward situation. It is wrong to give approval to such a proposed marriage. It is also wrong to undermine the same marriage after it takes place.

Application of these two principles is obviously difficult and may vary on a case-by-case basis. The best a family can do is remind of God's Word, instruct, warn, and oppose. In the end, it may be best to concede to attendance at the wedding as a witness to the vows. After the covenant has been sealed, the family should reverse direction and do all things possible to preserve the new family (including a courteous witness of faith in the Lord Jesus Christ). Biblical instruction on how to view the marriage of a believer to an unbeliever also helps with the next category of proposed marriages. What does the Bible say about marriages following a divorce or even those relationships begun in adultery?

Remarriage Following Divorce

---

[6] One true and helpful quote is, "There is not such thing as an illegitimate child, only illegitimate parents."

The first topic that a pastor should discuss with a couple requesting a wedding is their spiritual condition. Assuming both profess faith in Christ as Savior, a logical next issue is whether either has been divorced in the past.

Remarriage after a divorce is not a one-size-fits-all situation. Sometimes the Bible prohibits a remarriage. Sometimes Scripture permits a remarriage. There are four main situations following a legal divorce granted by the courts. They include: a couple who has just broken a previous home by their adultery with each other; a legal divorce but not based on biblical grounds (i.e., neither spouse has been adulterous in the past or present); a past divorce because of adultery with the innocent ex-spouse now wishing to remarry; and divorce that had not originally involved adultery but one of the original pair has since either remarried or has had a sexual relationship (i.e., adultery after the fact of a divorce).

Prohibited Marriages Following a Divorce

First, couples who have destroyed a previous home by their adultery with each other should not expect a church to bless a wedding to each other.[7] Obviously, a long list of verses condemning adultery could be quoted. [8]

A second situation following divorce involves a direct biblical prohibition of remarriage. 1 Cor. 7:11 gives guidance concerning a separation or a legal divorce when no adultery has occurred.[9] Paul

---

[7] Even if a marriage does arise from an adulterous start, the vows once sinfully contracted are binding. Often these marriages also fail. Life is short but long enough to make a mess from disobedience. Also, life is short but long enough to change for the better. Based upon God's mercy and evident repentance, I would consider performing a marriage for one who had destroyed a home in the distant past through adultery. However, the relationship must be to a new person who had nothing to do with the break up of a previous marriage. Churches should not bless unions of those in the process of wrecking a home. Indulgence is a false definition of love.

[8] See Chapter 9, pp. 82-83.
[9] See pp. 24-25, 29-31.

commands "but if she does leave, she must remain unmarried or else be reconciled...." When no adultery has ever occurred by either party to an original marriage, God's view is that all other marital problems have solutions. The couple should remain single or reconcile. Neither the man nor the woman in this situation should feel free to pair up with anyone else.

A court granting divorce for a marriage in which there has never been adultery does not give moral freedom for one to seek another partner for remarriage. This conclusion comes to a shock to many, but the Bible teaches it. The decision is whether to ignore or enforce 1 Cor. 7:11.

Permissible Marriages Following a Divorce

A third situation following divorce concerns the victim whose spouse has committed adultery. Adultery is a valid biblical ground for divorce.[10] The faithful spouse who has been betrayed by adultery is free to remarry.

A fourth situation follows a legal divorce that did not originally involve adultery. Neither the husband nor wife in this situation should feel free to pair up with anyone else. Because the state has granted a divorce decree, most people in society (or even the church) would not regard subsequent sexual relationships, especially a remarriage, as an act of adultery directed against the ex-spouse. After all, the court gave a divorce. However, by the Lord's definition, the first person who breaks the "stand-off", i.e., the command to "remain single or reconcile" is committing adultery (see Matt. 19:9; Mark 10:11-12; Luke 16:18; 1 Cor. 7:11). Even though it might occur long after a previous divorce granted by the courts, such adultery gives grounds for the demise of the original marriage. The remaining partner who had demonstrated a willingness to live celibately in hope of reconciliation should now be considered free of a spouse who commits adultery by pairing with another. Beyond this point, the remaining person could be ethically remarried.[11]

---

[10] See pp. 31-33.
[11] See pp. 24-25, 29-31.

To review, a church should not approve a wedding for an adulterous couple that has broken a home. It should also counsel those divorced on grounds other than adultery not to feel freedom to find other spouses.

Those divorced on the basis of adultery do have a moral right to remarriage. One may be the victim of adultery by immorality during the period of marriage. If not, one may still become the victim of adultery when the former spouse later disobeys Paul's command to remain single (remain single and also pure) or reconcile.

At this point all situations in which the New Testament specifically prohibits a marriage have been covered.[12] All possible problems for the wisdom of a proposed marriage have not. Perhaps the most difficult question involves pregnancy. Must a pregnant woman always become a bride?

Pregnancy and the Wisdom of Marriage

Common wisdom is that pregnancy requires a "shotgun" wedding. Is this response a biblical command or a cultural practice?

Ex. 22:16 requires a wedding after sexual relations among single people, with or without pregnancy. However, the Church is not under the Law but Grace (John 1:17; Rom. 7:4; 10:4; Gal. 3:24-25). All of God's Word is eternal (Matt. 5:17-18). Since God never changes His attributes (Mal. 3:6; James 1:17), one may study the theology of God's nature from either Old or New Testaments. Still, unless a truth is carried over into the New Testament, that truth may not be considered automatically binding on the Church. We must obey nine of the Ten Commandments as they are repeated in the New Testament. Saturday (Sabbath) worship is not required by the New Testament. A church could worship on Saturday, but most follow the New Testament

---

[12] Leviticus 18:6-18 lists relationships defined as incestuous. This may be profitably studied but hopefully a rare issue in those coming to a pastor seeking to arrange a wedding service.

example of Sunday worship in memory of the resurrection day. [13] The change from Law to Grace also involves the abrogation of blood sacrifice and the purely optional nature of Old Testament holidays (Jewish believers may practice them as a choice but not a requirement).

Ex. 22:16 may be used as one support for the opinion that a pregnancy demands a wedding. It does not, however, carry the binding authority as would a New Testament text addressed to the Church. It does give the principle that we are responsible for our moral behavior.

I believe the marriage of a believer to an unbeliever should not occur even if a potential bride is pregnant. Another consideration would be whether the couple had been in a courtship and/or engaged status; or whether they are really virtual strangers. Also, a pastor should watch for repentance and submission to Scripture, not an independent and defiant attitude.

If the couple had previously planned marriage or at least had been close to each other, Ex. 22:16 gives positive reinforcement for getting married. Still, this is a matter of wisdom not New Testament authority, (except on the restriction against mixed marriages and that abortion is a sin).

Cohabitation and A Church's Wedding Calendar

Those who are living together outside a covenant of marriage should either marry or move apart. If these wish to marry, counsel should be given with both issues (marriage, separation) at the same time. Such couples requesting a wedding are taking steps in a positive direction. Assuming biblical eligibility for marriage, the wedding should be encouraged and approved.

However, scheduling a wedding months in advance raises questions regarding honor to God and the example to others in the

---

[13] See Steven Waterhouse, *Not by Bread Alone*: *An Outlined Guide to Bible Doctrine*, (Amarillo Texas: Westcliff Press, 2003) pp. 309-11 for ideas on the use of the Law under grace.

community and church family. If a couple really wants God's blessing on their marriage, they should live in a way that God can favor.

Would continuing to live together for the next few months demonstrate repentance and a sincere desire to please God? Isn't it hypocritical to arrange a service with a view to asking God's blessing while engaging in a sin that God cannot bless? What are the lessons by such a wedding policy for the rest of the church, especially the next generation?

I agree to schedule future weddings for those who have been living together. However, the couple must agree to separate until the ceremony.[14] To date I have been able to persuade such couples that separation is really a condition for God's approval, as well as an example for the youth.[15]

Parental Consent

Even adult children should honor father and mother. Loving support from an extended family is best for newlyweds. Still, the basic text on God's pattern for marriage presents any new marriage as an act of leaving father and mother (Gen. 2:24, quoted by the Lord in Matt. 19:4-5 and Mark 10:6-8). Parental disapproval of a wedding may reflect concern over legitimate biblical objections to a child's proposed marriage. If so, the couple and minister should pay attention. The objections might also be matters of control or irrational fears.

In Bible times it was usually safe to assume older meant wiser. Today this may not be true at all. A couple and minister might consider a delay in wedding plans in cases where unity can eventually be

---

[14] One might yield on this demand to separate if a couple already has children in their home.

[15] One couple had already bought a marriage license and decided to repeat their vows before sunset. They called local family and friends to the church. This is also an acceptable option for a wedding of those who have been living together.

reached. The value of unity in the extended family exceeds the inconvenience of some delay. Yet, adult children have a need to break free from overly fussy, worried, or domineering parents. The mother of the bride who objected to my participation in the wedding because God would reject a wedding in any church outside her denomination comes to mind.

Marriages between Those of Different Races

The account of the Tower of Babel (Genesis 11) shows that God desired diversity among the nations. Global unity would produce a world united in wickedness. This otherwise true idea has been misapplied to interracial marriages.

A true parallel would be language study. God wanted the world divided by languages. This hardly means that learning a different language is a sin. The number of those who do so still does not pose any threat to language diversity on a world scale. Only for purposes of communication, do these paragraphs even contain the word "race." The Bible teaches diversity but classifies humanity as one race (Gen. 9:1,7; Acts 17:26; Gal. 3:28; Col. 3:11).

Moses' life illustrates that an interracial marriage can definitely create social problems but is not a moral problem to God. Brother Aaron and sister Miriam objected to Moses' wedding to an Ethiopian (Num. 12:1). This is the same passage that praises Moses for humility (12:3). God wanted to know why they were not afraid to criticize Moses (12:6-9). Next in anger God punished Miriam with leprosy that could only be cured by her brother's appeal to God (12:9-16). Evidently, God did not agree with criticism directed at Moses regarding his marriage.

Marriages between Unbelievers

God regards the institution of marriage as holy regardless of the spiritual status of the couple involved. Marriage vows are holy even when the bride and groom are not.[16]

Marriage is to be held in honor *among all* ... [Heb. 13:4].

Non-Christian couples who remain indifferent to faith in Christ have poor prospects for a strong and happy marriage. Yet, marriage is definitely the moral option as opposed to cohabitation or other sexual immorality.

If no other factors would cause ineligibility for a wedding, churches who agree to marry unbelieving couples may in good conscience schedule their services. They may also in good conscience decline for personal convictions or practical limitation of time or strength.

Those who deny Christ as Savior are in a condition that prohibits God's full blessing. A Christian wedding service appealing to God's authority and for His blessing has a measure of hypocrisy when bride and groom do not trust or obey Christ. One could conclude that a secular wedding is the consistent choice for secular people. Also, churches with beautiful buildings can be over burdened by those who only admire art and architecture with no thought that the place has been built to reflect God's beauty. I have discovered that unsaved couples can be willing to run volunteer church staff ragged on weekends conducting rehearsals, weddings, and receptions while they have no interest in God or His church. A church can find itself used as the second choice to Las Vegas merely because it will work for less. There can be no moral objections to a pastor not consenting to such requests. Yet, a church may also reason in favor of conducting weddings for unbelievers.

I knew a pastor in a resort area who willingly booked many weddings among non-Christian couples. Though it has become just a

---

[16] Positional holiness before God as Judge comes from faith in Christ as Savior. Practical holiness before God as Father comes after faith through confession of sin, repentance, and obedience in holy living.

cultural habit in a post-Christian society, he reasoned that the desire for a Christian wedding might produce more good than bad (even if a little hypocritical on the couple's part). Every wedding guest received a clear and repeated invitation to trust in Christ as Savior and submit to the Bible's authority over the home.

Each request must be considered on a case-by-case basis. The screening interview alone presents an opportunity to expose a couple to Christian kindness and the gospel. The couple who wanted to have dogs for groomsmen and bridesmaids in the church did, however, step beyond my limits of patience as do those who inconvenience a church's volunteer staff by expecting long hours and perfection from unpaid volunteers. Sensitivity to overworked lay staff has led me to reduce the number of weddings for non-church members. This is, however, a practical not a moral matter.

Summary

The Bible itself prohibits some marriages. Other times the concern over a proposed wedding might be more an issue of wisdom, not ethics. Assuming a man and woman make a covenant together according to God's pattern for a wedding, they are joined by God in a sacred institution. Only adultery or separation by death breaks the covenant between husband and wife.

A good marriage takes much more than even the most sincere vows. Next we turn to the Bible's command for a partnership in marriage. What does the Bible teach about a husband's role in marriage? What does the Bible teach about a wife's role in marriage? What does the Bible teach on the subject of the equality of the sexes?

Chapter Six

Principles of Gender Equality

An imbalanced washing machine shakes, thuds and rattles in an annoying way. Lack of balance relative to gender studies in churches sometimes wobbles the machine to the left by denying a wife should submit to her husband. Sometimes by clumsy communication the church machine wobbles to the right. One might hear a poor sermon where a husband's authority comes across like a chest-beating gorilla or a overbearing thug with a foot on a wife's neck. Usually, the problem on the right is just poor communication style. If, however, a speaker or author should actually assert that men and women are not equal, this is biblically false doctrine.

The Bible contains balance. Christians must learn to communicate the value given to women in Scripture. At the same time, we must use prudent words in balancing the truth that a wife should submit to her own husband. With efforts towards balance, God is honored and more in society would listen.

God's Word teaches that male and female are equal. The matter of a wife's submission to her own husband is a related but still different topic than gender equality. By voluntarily entering into a marriage covenant with me, Mrs. Waterhouse took the risk to trust my leadership. However, this has absolutely nothing to do with men in general. She has no obligation to the authority of the man next door or male readers of this book. Furthermore, while subordinate to me in the position and work of the family, she possesses equal value to me in person and worth.

The Bible does teach a wife should yield to her own husband. This point is actually irrelevant to the topic of gender equality. Obviously and categorically the Bible does not teach that all women are subordinate to all men.

A single woman has no obligation for any special respect to any man. She has not chosen to enter any marriage covenant. If she does find a man she loves and trusts, submission to him alone arises by choice. Even then she remains equal in value in terms of person and worth.

The Image of God

The creation account teaches that both male and female possess the image of God. "God created man [humans] in His own image, in the image of God He created him; male and female He created *them*" (Gen. 1:27). Genesis 5:1-2 defines "man" as both "male" and "female." Both possess the likeness of God.

A full study of the image of God would lead us away from specific consideration of gender equality. Some aspects of the image of God were lost by sin. This part of God's image is being renewed in Christ (Eph. 4:23-24; Col. 3:10). Humans, like God, were originally holy. We lost this in the fall. Other parts of the image of God in humans were retained despite the entrance of sin into the human race. God is spiritual and eternal. Though sinful, all humans remain eternal souls. This aspect of God's image remains so that life, believer or unbeliever, is sacred. All humans have infinite worth retaining aspects of God's image. Because God's image endures even in unsaved humanity, cursing and murder are evil (Gen. 9:6; James 3:9).

The image of God in both male and female means that women have equal and infinite value. Men and women are equally sinful and depraved.[1] Christ died on the cross and offers salvation by faith equally. In eternity men and women who trust in the Lord Jesus Christ will both enjoy the heavenly city.

God as Mother

Those who translate the Scripture into modern languages have a sacred obligation not to tamper with gender relative to God. *He* is God. The Persons within the Trinity are *Father* and *Son* and Holy

---

[1] In a theological sense, depravity does not mean every one is as wicked as possible. It means we are all equally hopeless in terms of solving our own sin problem. No one, male or female, has any hope of salvation without faith in the Lord Jesus Christ.

Spirit. The Lord's Prayer must remain, "Our *Father* who art in heaven ..." Still, God possesses feminine traits. This comes as no surprise since both male and female constitute man made in God's image.

One of the great attributes of God is "*compassion.*" Along with God's nature of being loyal to a covenant relationship, the same passages emphasize His "compassion." "The LORD, the LORD God, *compassionate* and gracious, slow to anger, and abounding in loving-kindness (i.e. loyal-love to covenant relationships) and truth" (Ex. 34:6, see also Psa. 103:8). While males can and should have compassion, primarily this is a feminine trait. The Hebrew word for "compassion" relates to the Hebrew word for "womb." This fascinating word used of God's attributes stresses the female and the maternal. The image of God within the human race includes traits that emphasize women's nature as in a mother's compassionate love.

God the *Son* "nourishes" and "cherishes" the church (Eph. 5:29). The Greek word for "cherish" was chosen by the ancient rabbis to translate a reference to a mother bird covering her eggs or covering the little birds with her feathers (Deut. 22:6 LXX [2]).

The Apostle Paul compared himself to a mother "But we proved to be gentle among you, as a nursing mother tenderly cares for her own children." (1 Thess. 2:7). The Greek word chosen here relates to feminine traits (1 Kings 1:2,4 LXX; Job 39:14 LXX).

References in the above paragraphs teach that Christian men, as husbands or church leaders, are supposed to have some feminine characteristics. The Bible teaches that both woman originated from man (Adam's rib) and that every man originates from woman (1 Cor. 11:12).[3] Evidently, in the Judeo-Christian world-view, even the ideal

---

[2] Because Greek became a universal language in the centuries before Christ, Jewish scholars in Alexandria translated the Old Testament from Hebrew into Greek. This translation is called the Septuagint. Because it is said 70 rabbis worked on the project, the abbreviation for the translation is LXX. This translation helped dispersed Jews for whom Hebrew became a secondary language. Today, it helps Bible scholars with word definitions.

[3] The genders are interdependent, males and females need each other.

for manhood involved an appreciation and inclusion of feminine traits. Men remain men but renewal from the fall into the image of God involves some feminine traits because they are also part of God's nature. [4]

The Lord Jesus Christ and Women

The world seems oblivious to the debt it owes Christianity relative to the status of women. The Old Testament made the point. Male and female are both in the image of God (Gen. 1:27, 5:1-2). A good wife has infinite worth (Prov. 18:22, 19:14, 31:10-31). Deborah was a political, even a military leader (Judges 4-5). Huldah was a prophetess respected and needed by both king and high priest (2 Kings 22:8-20). The books of Ruth and Esther gave God's view on the value of women. Judaism honors its matriarchs: Sarah, Rebekah, Leah, and Rachel. Compared to the surrounding pagan world the Hebrew Scripture elevated women. Still, not everyone applied such truth.

The disciples were shocked that the Lord would converse with the woman at the well (John 4:27). To deal with a Samaritan (heretic, half-breed in their thinking) was bad enough, but Jesus talked with a woman and probably even drank from the same vessel. This was

---

[4] Some non-Christian cultures have long regarded Judeo-Christian models as "weak." A contemporary perspective might be that church participation is for women, children, and weak men. Pagans with a barbarian mindset have long detested humility as a virtue and tenderness as weak. The ideal can become a violent and murderous rampage with little mercy. Jews and Christians can make first rate warriors, but the Bible commands a reflection of God's nature in the ideal of a father as "Abba, daddy." Humility that reminds us we desperately need God actually creates greater courage and strength in life, including battle. God's "compassion" and His tenderness "to nurture" and "cherish" is perhaps reflected more in women. However, men who imitate God also display these virtues. Men should not become feminine but do need to become civilized gentlemen. Any "new age" return to pagan ways will not be good for men, women, or children. Men who reflect God's image more fully also develop God's tender side. Those who hope for Christianity to decline will not find any blessing if a generation of men arises with the manners and actions of Vikings, Huns, or Mongols.

improper manners and quite disgusting.[5] Ancient rabbinic quotes reflect attitudes towards women at the time of Christ.

> Jose ben Johann said, "… talk not much with womankind." They said this of a man's own wife: how much more of a fellow's wife! Hence the Sages have said, "He that talks much with womankind brings evil upon himself and neglects the study of the Law and at last will inherit Gehenna." 6

> A man shall not talk with a woman in the street, not even with his own wife … [7]

> Rabbi Jose the Galilean was traveling on the road. He met Brurih (the wife of Rabbi Meier) and asked her, "Which way must we take to the city of Lud?" She answered "Thou Galilean fool! Did not our sages say, that thou should not converse much with a woman? Thou shouldn't have asked, "Which way to Lud?"8

---

[5] One Sunday, the author gave a sermon in a rural African church. The rumors were that one particular woman had been stigmatized because she was unable to have children. Yet, this same woman was caring for six orphans whose parents had died from AIDS. John 4 was a perfect choice for a text. Not only did the message apply to tribal hatred (modern "Jew-Samaritan" feelings) and evangelize, but the text asserts Jesus' concern for women in contrast to many in His own culture.

[6] See Leon Morris, *Studies on the Fourth Gospel* (Grand Rapids: Wm. B. Eerdmans, 1969), p. 219, fn 8. See also Marcus Dods, *The Gospel of John* in *The Expositor's Greek Testament*, reprint ed. (Grand Rapids: Wm. B. Eerdmans Publishing Co., 1976) 1:729. Dods translates "womankind" as "the woman" and says this is a prohibition against talking much even with ones own wife!

[7] Ibid.

[8] Homer A. Kent, Jr., *Light in the Darkness: Studies in the Gospel of John* (Grand Rapids: Baker Book House, 1974) p.79.

Blessed Art Thou, O Lord Our God, King of the Universe, who hast not made me a woman.[9]

Knowledge of such odd customs is vital to a true picture of the Lord's behavior by contrast. The Lord balanced His teaching ministry displaying equal interest in women. "For whoever does the will of My Father who is in heaven, he is My brother and sister and mother" (Matt. 12:50). The Lord balanced the story of a lost sheep with a woman sweeping the house for a lost coin (Luke 15:4-10). Both men in the field and women grinding at the mill must be ready for His Second Coming (Matt. 24:40-41). In the meantime, the kingdom of heaven is both like a man sowing seed (Matt. 13:24-30) or fishing (13:47-50) but also a woman hiding leaven in flour (13:33). The Lord's attention to and interest in women reflects an astounding difference to the culture of His time. The gospel authors who selected such comments and stories for inclusion indirectly show their value of women. Dr. Luke probably attended many women and children either in childbirth or sickness. Bible scholars have long noted Luke's interest in women and children in the accounts of both Luke and Acts. [10]

Modern feminists who disrespect Christianity actually undermine the world-view that has elevated women. Efforts to weaken Christianity cannot possibly improve future treatment of and views toward women. In all fairness, some Christians have been poor models or have communicated the Bible's views on women with bad attitudes and poor words. Women of the world are in debt to the Lord Jesus

---

[9] Charles C. Ryrie, *The Role of Women in the Church* (Chicago: Moody Press, 1978), p.8.

[10] Luke mentions 13 women not mentioned in the other gospels. In the book of Acts he records the raising of Tabatha (Dorcus) with the story of Cornelius (Acts 9-10). Rhoda forgot to open the door with Peter outside of Mary's house (Acts 12:12-17). Lydia was the first convert in Europe (Acts 16:14ff.). Since Priscilla's name comes first, she is likely the one who privately and respectfully informed Apollos there were some problems with his sermon (Acts 18:24-26).

Christ, Dr. Luke, and Matthew, Mark and John.[11] Oddly, given the abuse he receives, the Apostle Paul gives the clearest statement on gender equality.

Paul on Women

The Apostle Paul wrote most (but not all) texts that command a wife to submit to her **own** husband (e.g. Eph. 5:22). The Greek word "own" is *"idios"* from which we also derive "idiosyncrasy." A wife has an obligation to submit to her "own" husband as a unique relationship exclusive to her husband. However, Paul also gave a clear statement on overall gender equality in Galatians 3:28. " . . . there is neither male nor female, for you are all one in Christ Jesus."

Viewed as an entire classification, men and women are equal. They share equally in spiritual need due to sin. They share equally in the offer to trust in Christ for salvation. After faith in Christ, they share equally in union with Christ and will share an eternal destiny.

Women in Society

Scripture addresses the role of women in the home and church leadership. Within these spheres the Bible subordinates wives to husbands and women to male authority within church government.[12] Yet, the Bible gives no prohibitions on the role of women in politics, education , or business.

When we fail to enforce the Bible, we err by liberalism. When we go beyond the Bible, we err by legalism. Assuming a woman is single or married with her husband's support (and without maternal responsibilities), it is not a sin for her to have positions in society. Neither is it a sin for a man to be employed with a female supervisor or a male student to take a course from a female teacher. The election of a

---

[11] Spiritual blindness prevents many from giving any credit for societal blessings arising from Christian influence in world history. Some, however, can be convinced that Christianity has elevated women.

[12] For our purposes we need not delve into the role of women in church. See Steven Waterhouse *Not By Bread Alone*, pp 339-340.

woman to political office or serving in the Cabinet is not a moral issue just on the basis of her gender alone. It would be a different situation only if she has children to attend or her husband disagrees.[13]

The Importance of Gender Equality

The Bible's position on gender equality is actually a different topic than gender roles within marriage or church life. Balance on the topic casts a spotlight on the important contribution Christianity has made to the status and treatment of women.

Also, it is vital that married men understand the value of women. While a wife should submit to her own husband in position and work within the family, she remains of equal and infinite worth in

---

[13] Radical feminists can mistakenly target Christians as an object of wrath. Despite their stated purpose, to elevate women, their efforts may result in worse treatment for women. Women have tended to produce a civilizing influence in all societies by insisting upon manners and moral standards. Women with the contradictory attitude of sexual liberation mixed with a "who-needs-a-man" attitude help encourage the type of men who use and mistreat women. It becomes a self-defeating cycle. One cannot expect to reduce sexual harassment by ridiculing the standards of gentlemen. It will not help the status of women to attack the type of man who wants to take care of a wife.

On this topic, I found myself on a flight sitting next to a New York State official in the National Organization for Women. At first the conversation was awkward. I learned her attitude toward men had developed from mistreatment by men lacking any Christian integrity. Her bad attitude about all men was a reaction to experiences with men very much different from the men in our church. Furthermore, a preacher in her past told her that her child who had died was in eternal hell because it was not baptized. We had a long talk about the Bible on gender, on roles of husband and wife, and on infants who die before the age of accountability (see p. 99, Fn 6).

She gave me her card with a laugh and said she had sworn to never give her phone number to a man again. She also gave me $100.00 and asked me to mail her a box of Christian books. A balanced approach to the Bible's teaching on women that is carefully communicated can change some people's hearts.

her person. The role of helper means the poor guy needs help! The role of leader in a home is not that of a tyrant, for the Bible commands husbands to love as Christ loves, to understand their wives, and to communicate. The Bible's role for any leader is that of a master who is a servant. Christians in any leadership role in life are supposed to make decisions without selfishness and in the best interest of those under their authority. Careful communication of biblical ideas about gender equality and a true balance of male authority in the home allows for less confusion in society and stronger marriages.

Chapter Seven

Plans for a Husband
The Imitation of Christ in His Relationship to the Church

What does the "love" mean in the statement, "I love chocolate!"? In high school days, I went to a rock concert purely by accident. Our senior class went to an amusement park and discovered our trip had led us to an event involving the band at the top of the charts. After the first song the "star" invited women backstage afterwards to have some "love." Even the unsaved girls from our rural high school said they were frightened and left.

In the sentence, "I love chocolate" the definition of love is "consumption." When I consume chocolate it gratifies me. Everyone talks of the need for love, but not everyone has the same definition in mind. In the worst cases, "I love you" means "I will use and consume you for myself."

The primary Biblical command for husbands is " ... love your wives just as Christ also loved the church ..." (Eph. 5:25, see also Col. 3:19). God the Son is the ideal model for husbands. Good husbands imitate Christ in His relationship to the Church. His example of love could not be more different than consuming another for selfish purposes.

Four Words for Love:

The Greek language has four main words for love. *Eros* refers to sexual love. While the New Testament does not use this word, the Bible certainly blesses sexual love within the marriage covenant (Chapter 9).

A second Greek word refers to parental instinct, the normal love of a family bond such as maternal love. Paul used a negation of this word (*astorgos*) to say that many people in Roman Empire times had lost normal family affection (Rom. 1:31, "unloving", see also KJV). He also predicted in the last times humanity will lose normal family love (2 Tim. 3:3, "unloving", see also KJV). Yes, parents can be cold to their own children and siblings can hate each other. However, God's Word classifies this as abnormal psychology. Normally, people love their children, their parents and their siblings.

The next two words for love are *philos* and *agape*. Both of these concern love between couples.

Tender and Emotional Love:

Many who reject Christ would misdefine love as consumption. Yet, it is possible for even unbelievers to rise higher in their concept of love. Often when people use the word "love" they mean a good feeling. They have affection for another person based on tender and warm feelings. In a romantic sense their hearts throb in each other's presence. In a friendship they enjoy each other's company.

The Greek word for love based on feeling is "*philos.*" The New Testament contains about 94 uses among an amazing 26 different forms. They come down into English in such words as "Philadelphia" (brotherly love), "philosophy" (love of wisdom), "philanthropy" (love of humanity). The *philos* word family stresses emotions. Related words may be translated "friends" or "kiss."

Emotional love should not be regarded as unholy. The Father loves the Son with deep emotions (John 5:20). God the Son loved Lazarus evidenced by His crying at his friend's death (John 11:3, 36). The Lord asked if Peter loved Him with this kind of love (John 21:17).[1] Paul expects Christians to love the Lord Jesus with emotional love (1 Cor. 16:22).[2] Marriages should have the *philos* type of love. Couples

---

[1] The Lord asked Peter twice if he had a committed sacrificial love (*agape* in John 21:15-16). Then in John 21:17 the Lord asked if Peter even had affection (*philos*) towards Him.

[2] Does God love some people more than others? Does God love everyone equally? I think the answer is "Yes" and "No." In terms of *agape* love (sacrificial love), God loves everyone to the deepest degree. In terms of *philos* love (emotional love), He loves believers more than unbelievers. Furthermore, God has a deeper emotional attraction to certain believers over others because of their response to His love. Daniel was greatly beloved (Dan. 9:23, 10:11). Among the many disciples the Lord was closest to twelve and maybe even

need to feel good about each other. We should be married to our best friend. However, what holds the relationship at times when feelings either do not exist at all or have even become resentment and hostility? Lyrics to some old love songs speak of "loosing that lovin' feeling" or "trying to get the feeling again." If a marriage possesses only *eros* or *philos*, it will become vulnerable in periods of hard feelings, depressed feelings, or the absence of feelings.

Emotional love (*philos*) is neither unholy nor undesirable, but alone it is an insufficient foundation for a secure relationship. Those who think only in terms of a "50-50" relationship have a deficient concept of love. The deepest kind of love endures even when the feelings are gone, and the other person does not seem to be giving in return.

Sacrificial Love:

Husbands and wives should have good feelings towards each other. However, a lifetime of never ending good feelings is not realistic. Two people with sin natures will disappoint each other, usually sooner rather than later.

The actual Greek word used in the verse commanding husbands to love their wives is *always agape* (Eph. 5:25, 28, 33; Col. 3:19). The New Testament contains approximately 140 uses of the verb, 116 uses of the noun, and 62 uses of the adjective "beloved." 1 Corinthians 13:4-7 gives a classic description of *agape* love, and John 15:13 teaches the Lord Jesus Christ displayed the greatest love. All of

---

three: Peter, James, and John. The Lord Jesus loved John with emotional love (John 20:2).

God loves every believer with infinite *agape* love. However, even the same individual is closer to God at some times in life than others. We each please God more at some times in life than at other times. God's *agape* love never ends, but His feelings about us vary. We can grieve God (Eph. 4:30). We can please or displease Him (John 12:42-43).

the types of love are desirable. *Agape* love is the greatest and most necessary for life and marriage. [3]

Did it feel good for the Lord Jesus Christ to die for our sins? At the time were we returning love or keeping our responsibilities to Him? [4] Was His attitude one of using or consuming us for selfish ends?

Christ's example of love is to give oneself to do what is best for another regardless of how it feels or whether they reciprocate anything in return. Christ's love is giving, not taking.

Theologians often describe personhood as consisting of mind, emotions and will. The *philos* type of love stresses emotions. *Agape* type love stresses the will. With our wills we chose, we decide, we act, we commit. The Lord Jesus Christ chose to love us when it definitely did not feel good and when we gave nothing in return. [5]

Ideally, a marriage will often have both *agape* and *philos* love. However, only *agape* is a solid foundation. During periods of no feelings or even bad feelings *agape* love provides the commitment to fulfill one's promises. *Agape* love remains constant even if the cost is high and the feeling of perceived return from the other person is low.

---

[3] In many ways *agape* is superior to *philos*. The greatest virtue is love (1 Corinthians 13). The greatest commands are love (Matt. 22:36-40). Love fulfills the entire Law of Moses (Rom. 13:10; Gal. 5:14). Scripture definitely encourages the good feeling type of love (*philos*), but it regards *agape* love as greater. Such sacrificial love is unlike human nature, i.e. supernatural.

[4] *Agape* love continues without reciprocity. God loved us at a time that we hated Him. " ... *not that we loved God,* but that He loved us and sent His Son to be a propitiation for our sins (1 John 4:10). "We love, because *He first* loved us" (1 John 4:19). God loved at a time when we were enemies (Rom. 5:8; Eph. 2:1-9).

[5] The pain of the cross obviously did not feel good. Unlike *philos* love, *agape* love is not at all dependent upon feeling good. It rather is a sacrificial gift of oneself to do what is in the benefit of another even when the love is not returned (e.g. John 3:16, 13:1, 15:13; Gal. 2:20; 1 John 3:16; Rev. 1:5).

Agape love comes from the Holy Spirit, " ... the love of God has been poured out within our hearts through the Holy Spirit ... " (Rom. 5:5). "The fruit of the Spirit is love ..." Gal. 5:22.[6] An unsaved husband may have better character than to define love as selfish consumption. He may have good feelings towards his wife. However, the expectation that the feeling of "wedded bliss" can be constant is false. Non-Christian homes do not have the strong foundation of *agape* love because they misdefine love as primarily only a feeling, lacking experience with Christ's love through salvation and a motivation to imitate Christ's virtue. Sadly, many believers also lack the spiritual maturity and mindset to make the imitation of Christ's love central to life.

A husband who loves his wife as Christ loves the church will sacrifice his life (including one day at a time), will honor his vows, will chose to do what is best for his wife (and children) even when it hurts and nothing seems to come in return. That is love. Christ "gave Himself up" for the Church. He wants to "sanctify her" (i.e. cause holiness and spiritual growth). The Lord "nourishes" and "cherishes" the church (Eph. 5:25-29).

God's plan is the imitation of these traits by a husband towards a wife. Assuming obedience to "love as Christ loves the church," the biblical position of male authority in the home takes care of itself.

How to Treat a Wife

The Bible teaches male authority in the home, but the specific relationship envisioned hardly parallels an ignorant brute that likes to bark orders. Not only is the imitation of Christ's love commanded of husbands, several specific teachings clarify gender roles in the home. If obeyed, decision-making need not lead to friction but to appreciation for each other.

The Apostle Peter tells husbands to "live with your wives in an understanding way" and to "grant her honor ..." (1 Peter 3:7).

---

[6] Other verses stress that *agape* comes from God. It is nothing short of miraculous to love so unselfishly (see 1 Thess. 4:9; 1 John 4:7,9,12,19).

Numerous Scripture texts teach communication skills. God did not give such wisdom so that we could practice it on strangers and friends, but ignore it within the family. Husbands who obey the command to live with a wife in an understanding way will discuss all important issues. To understand means to take views, goals, interests, and opinions into consideration. Husbands who make decisions without understanding and honoring a wife are not only foolish but also disobedient to Scripture.

Important decisions should always be made together. By understanding and honoring each other, a husband and wife come to agreement on most issues. Independent decision-making by a husband can result in needless friction whereas talking before the decision would have produced the same result with unity. In the minority of times of disagreement one option is to wait. The Bible refers to the wisdom of waiting on God's timing (Psa. 27:14; 40:1; 130:5). In some cases, deadlines or other circumstances force a decision even when a couple does not fully agree. If a husband has tried to obey 1 Pet. 3:7 in understanding and honoring his wife, she should be able to trust him and leave the matter in his hands. God gives him the authority to make the final decision. She should yield without nagging (Prov. 19:13; 21:9, 19; 27:15) or causing grief (Heb. 13:17 by application).

In any Christian position of leadership, the master is always a servant. The Lord Jesus Christ is the Master who came to serve - not to be served (Matt. 20:28). Husbands have the authority in the home with the understanding they will imitate Christ. Assuming a wife is strong in her relationship with God, she will understand her husband's intent to do what he thinks is in her best interest (and/or the children's best interest) even on those occasions she might not fully agree.[7] It is possible to doubt the wisdom of a course of action but fully trust the motivation. If a husband loves his wife, a spiritual wife will return that love. So says Ephesians 5:28, "He who loves his own wife loves himself ...."

Views and Value

---

[7] One can appreciate another's intent without thinking the results will be superior.

The old saying goes, "You don't know what you have until it's gone." Hopefully, this would not be true of marriage. A husband's relationship toward his wife begins in his relationship to Christ. Of course, his attitude toward her personally also greatly influences the relationship. Solomon told husbands to view a good wife as a great reward from God. She is more valuable than any material possession.

He who finds a wife finds a good thing and obtains favor from the Lord [Prov. 18:22].

House and wealth are an inheritance from fathers, but a prudent wife is from the LORD [Prov. 19:14].

An excellent wife, who can find? For her worth is far above jewels [Prov. 31:10].

Men are supposed to view their wives as a great reward from God. Yet, Paul warns against the opposite attitude of resentment. "Husbands, love your wives and do not be embittered against them." (Col. 3:19) Any type of leadership can abuse authority when it is used not to benefit but to harm. How would we evaluate a parent who uses authority to harm children out of a motivation of bitterness and resentment? Likewise, Paul's command in Col. 3:19 assumes it is possible for even a Christian husband to make family decisions with an attitude of bitterness. A man might make decisions that purposely make life hard for the family just because he can do so. Knowing this, Paul absolutely forbids it. The antithesis of Christ's love would be to use authority in grumpy cruelty. Real love by contrast involves giving, nourishing, and cherishing (Eph. 5:25-33). Love does not keep a list of past wrongs (1 Cor. 13:5) and covers a multitude of sins (1 Pet. 4:8; Prov. 19:11).

Christ's example of forgiveness and unconditional love means that husbands will view and treat wives as valuable. The Bible definitely gives husbands primary authority in the home. Biblical teaching also restricts this type of authority to be exercised not in a grudging way but with the attitude that a wife is God's greatest reward.

Married Men as Family Leaders

The role of a husband as the provider may not be cast aside as limited to one culture or bygone days. It began in the original home (Gen. 3:17-19). Paul assumes men will want to provide for their wives, children and other extended family in need. If a Christian "does not provide for his own ..." he "is worse than an unbeliever" (1 Tim. 5:8). A truly amazing number of Bible references command hard work and prohibit laziness, sometimes with sarcastic humor (e.g. Prov. 26:13-16).[8]

Leadership for husbands includes but is not limited to material provision. God assumes the head of a household will know Bible doctrine and ethical truths. Most texts giving a husband responsibility to know Scripture occur in contexts of fathers teaching children and will be studied in Chapter 11 (e.g. Prov.1:8; 3:1-2; Eph. 6:4). Paul assumed that a husband would have searched the Scripture to the degree that he can answer his wife's questions (1 Cor. 14:35). Not every family man needs to be a theologian, but all are supposed to be thinking about God's Word continually (Joshua 1:8; Psa. 1:2; Acts 17:11). Personal obedience in Bible study and attendance at a church that teaches the Bible gives a man knowledge to become a spiritual leader at home. God's will for every husband is spiritual maturity and spiritual leadership in his household. A wife who obeys God will not just tolerate her husband trying to lead. She will **help** him.

---

[8] See chapter 14 on finances and work ethics.

Chapter Eight

Plans for a Wife
The Imitation of Christ in His Relationship to His Father

Informed Christians all know the command for husbands to love as Christ loved the church (Eph. 5:25ff.) The Lord Jesus Christ is the model for husbands in His relationship to the Church.

Fewer books and sermons include the truth that Christ is also the role model for wives. 1 Cor. 11:3 teaches, "… the man is the head of a woman, and God is the head of Christ." The article "the" in front of man means that the reference is not to men and women in general but to a husband and his own wife in particular. The comparison of a wife is to God the Son in relationship to God the Father. God the Son is co-equal to His Father in Person and worth. Yet, in the work of the Trinity the Son voluntarily chose to submit Himself to the Father. He remained equal in Person and worth but chose to submit in the position and work of the Godhead. [1]

A Christian wife's role is to imitate the Lord Jesus Christ in His relationship to His Father. Females are equal in person and worth to males. When a woman enters a marriage covenant, she is choosing to submit herself in position and work of a family while remaining completely equal in person and worth to her husband.

Male leadership in the home does not mean tyranny and cruelty. As Chapters 6 and 7 explain, the Bible commands husbands

---

[1] Would Christ in His relationship to His Father be a more important role than Christ in His relationship to the church? Of course, such matters are not contests. This is a question without an answer. Still, the role of Christ in His relationship to the Godhead would not be any less important than His relationship to the church. If a choice must be made, His example as God's Son would be the higher role. Therefore, a wife's role is not any less important than a husband's role in the process of the admiration and imitation of Christ.

to understand and honor wives (1 Pet. 3:7).[2] Numerous texts on the "tongue" must still be obeyed within a family and not just society in general (see Chapter 15 on family communication). Also, in the Bible the leader is always a servant. Husbands are supposed to love sacrificially and should be trusted in making unselfish decisions in the best interest of wives and children. With communication a couple agrees on most decisions. If a deadline forces a decision before consensus, the Bible gives authority to a husband with the understanding he will imitate Christ in sacrificial love. A wife is supposed to imitate Christ as He carried out the will of His Father (John 6:38; Matt. 26:39).

A Husband Needs Help

God's original design for marriage placed a wife as a "helper" for her husband. Gen. 2:18 states, "I will make a *helper suitable* for him." Then God created Eve (the name comes from the Hebrew word for *life*). Adam immediately recognized oneness but difference at the same time. "This is now bone of my bones, and flesh of my flesh; she shall be called Woman, because she was taken out of Man" (Gen. 2:23). The New Testament reinforces the idea of helper. "... for indeed man was not created for the woman's sake, but woman for the man's sake" (1 Cor. 11:9). [3]

Define Helper!

The Hebrew word for *help* relates to that great biblical name "Ezra." In the creation account, none of the animals provided suitable companionship for man. Animals can indeed be very nice, but none of us can imagine a satisfactory world of only animals for intimate friends. They have God's breath of life but are not made in His image. Adam quickly tired of trying to communicate with animals. They don't

---

[2] Chapter 6 argues for the equality of the sexes. Chapter 7 balances male authority in the home with Bible commands on communication and with commands to understand, honor, and love a wife.

[3] 1 Tim. 2:13 also supports the idea that the order of creation has a bearing on the wife being under her husband's authority (see 1 Tim. 2:11-15). However, the context deals with the role of women in the church.

say much of interest or much of anything new. After repeating that creation has been good, God concluded, "It is **not** good for the man to be alone ..." (Gen. 2:18).

The first woman would be from the man with all other men in the history of the world coming from woman. She would be part of him but different. The phrase "help suitable for him" means "helper opposite him." The animals are on a much lower plane. The woman would be on the same level. Still, she is opposite to him and fulfills his deficiencies and needs. When the man and woman stood face to face, they were on an equal level but opposite each other. [4] They were both one and different at the same time. Each had traits the other lacked and needed. [5] As a man is often lonely without a wife (Gen. 2:18), Gen. 3:16 seems to teach most women also feel a need for a husband, "... your desire will be for your husband."

A wife is on the same level as her husband but different. God wants her to help her husband become a man of God by spiritual growth and to become a servant of God by Christian service. She remains an individual, but a wife with a totally independent spirit that puts one's "own thing" first in life fails according to God's plan. Wives who are spiritual will want to help their husbands to spiritual achievements.[6] Yes, **God wants husbands to lead**.

---

[4] Must a couple have many identical interests, or do opposites attract? Compatibility on core spiritual values is absolutely essential. However, given that both admire and want to imitate the Lord Jesus Christ and given both feel obligated to the authority of Scripture, other secondary differences should not be major problems. In fact, they may enrich life. If a common and deep commitment to God exists, a couple need not be identical in many other respects. Each may provide something the other lacks and there can be discovery, growth, and new appreciation for secondary matters in life.

[5] "If God had meant woman to rule over man, He would have taken her out of Adam's head. Had He designed her to be his slave, He would have taken her out of his feet. But God took woman out of man's side, for He made her to be a helpmeet and an equal to him." Richard Strauss attributed this quote to Saint Augustine in Richard L. Strauss, *Marriage is for Love* (Wheaton, IL: Tyndale House, 1988), p.18.

[6] By declaring Himself to be our great helper, God reveals the value of a wife mirroring His own character by helping her husband. Among the numerous

Just as the Bible clearly teaches the equality of men and women, it clearly teaches wives should yield to husbands. The subject must be balanced, and some details may be debated; but a fair reading of Scripture supports the main conclusion:

… he will rule over you [Gen. 3:16].

… the man is the head of a woman…[1 Cor. 11:3].

The women … are to subject themselves, just as the Law [The Law of Moses] also says [1 Cor. 14:34].

Wives, be subject to your own husbands, as to the Lord [Eph. 5:22].

But as the church is subject to Christ, so also the wives ought to be to their husbands in everything [Eph. 5:24].

… the wife must see to it that she respects her husband [Eph. 5:33].

Wives, be subject to your own husbands, as is fitting in the Lord [Col. 3:18].

… being subject to their own husbands, so that the word of God will not be dishonored [Titus 2:5].

… you wives, be submissive to your own husbands … [1 Pet. 3:1].

… being submissive to their own husbands … [1 Pet. 3:5].[7]

---

references are the following: Gen. 49:25; Ex. 18:4; 1 Sam. 7:12; 2 Chron. 14:11; Psa. 30:10, 33:20, 54:4, 70:5, 121:1-2; Isa. 41:10, 13, 44:2, 50:7; Hos. 13:9; Rom. 8:26; Heb. 13:6.

[7] Many of these verses have the Greek word "*idios.*" English derives "idiosyncrasy" from this word. A wife is to be in subjection to her *own* husband, but not to every other male. The relationship is a matter of marriage, not gender relationships as a whole.

Paul qualified his command in Eph. 5:22 with the phrase "as to the Lord." Submission to a husband is obedience to the Lord. Other phrases include "in everything" and "with reverence" (related to the word for fear).[8] Peter gives the example of Sarah who called Abraham "lord" (1 Pet. 3:6).

The Greek word translated "subjection" or "submission" occurs approximately 40 times as a verb and 4 times as a noun. New Testament texts which use this word of other relationships include children submitting to parents (Luke 2:51; 1 Tim. 3:4), slaves submitting to masters (Titus 2:9; 1 Pet. 2:18), believers submitting to the government (Rom. 13:1,5; Titus 3:1; 1 Pet. 2:13), angels submitting to Christ (1 Pet. 3:22), demons submitting to the apostles (Luke 10:17,20). All things, including death, will submit to Christ in the end (1 Cor. 15:27ff.).

---

[8] These verses assume the husband is not asking a wife to violate a higher command from God. Scriptures contain many examples of civil disobedience (Ex. 1:17; 1 Sam. 14:45, 22:17; Dan. 3:18, 6:10; Matt. 2:8, 12, 16; Acts 4:19, 5:29). A government authority tells a believer to sin. In such cases, Daniel suspended obedience to a human law against praying in order to keep the higher law to God (Dan. 6:10). The apostles suspended obedience to the Jewish government in order to keep God's higher law to proclaim the Gospel (Acts 5:27-29). A magazine article reported a story of an unsaved husband telling his Christian wife to commit adultery in order to secure a business contract. This situation obviously involves a higher law of God. She must refuse. In some situations the command to respect a husband is the higher law. In my judgment, for example, a wife should not give money to the church if her husband forbids it.

Usually a husband's authority will not clash with biblical commands. On one occasion a Christian wife wanted to divorce her unsaved husband because of "child abuse." On further probing, she defined the abuse as the husband bringing the children candy. In this case the wife had a totally unreasonable attitude and a perfectionist expectation of motherhood. She felt she must be "supermom" and protect her children from sugar whatever the cost. She apparently believed that the children would be better off without candy than without a father. The situation would be different if the husband had asked her to commit actual sin against a moral command in the Bible. Obviously, the Bible does not prohibit a father from bringing home sweets after work. In such matters, a wife should submit.

Whether we observe the details of Bible texts that command a wife to submit to her husband, or do a word study of the Greek word in other contexts, the result is a strong assertion of male leadership. When a woman chooses to marry, she becomes a helper to her husband.

In Chapters 6 and 7 we argued for gender equality and for defining a husband's authority as the authority of one who "understands," "honors" and uses authority to serve. A husband should decide matters according to his wife's best interests. When he loves as Christ loved the church, when he uses leadership to serve her, following his lead will not be too burdensome. When both husband and wife obey the Bible and imitate Christ, a wife may find fulfillment in her role of helping him. [9]

Love Your Husbands

---

[9] Bible-based arguments against a husband's authority in a family are not very convincing. One cannot argue that there was a change from Law to grace (from the Mosaic system to the Church). Almost all the commands to a wife to submit to her husband occur in New Testament Scriptures (see page 72).

Some try to argue that the curse in Genesis Chapter 3 caused a wife's subordinate role and that the curse has been lifted in Christ. The curse indeed made gender roles in marriage far more difficult as both Adam and Eve became selfish with sin natures. Therefore, God had to command male leadership in Gen. 3:16, " ... he will rule over you." However, the order of creation, not the curse from sin, was the origin of male headship. "For indeed man was not created for the woman's sake, but woman for the man's sake" (1 Cor. 11:9; see also, Gen. 2:18 and 1 Tim. 2:12-13 on the order of creation making a wife a helper.).

Gender roles in marriage were made harder by sin but were in place prior to the fall as part of God's design for the home. Still, for the sake of argument assume the entrance of sin is the origin of male headship. This would hardly give grounds to conclude wives no longer need to submit to husbands. The Lord Jesus Christ will remove the curse of sin. However, in the present, thorns still grow, snakes still crawl, childbirth still hurts, men still have to work, and we still have funerals. All the various lines of argument commonly used to overturn traditional marriage fail to overturn the clear and repeated statements that God tells wives to submit to their own husbands.

Titus 2:4-5 is a key text on biblical studies about women. Mature Christian women are commanded to "... encourage the young women to love their husbands ..." (Titus 2:4). One interesting distinction is that when the Bible commands a husband to love his wife, it always uses the Greek word *agape* for love. In Titus 2:4 God commands a wife to love her husband with a *philos* type of love. Is there a reason for choosing different words for love?

It may be the case that Paul chooses different words for love purely for stylistic reasons. However, "husbands, love your wives," is *agape* love in Eph. 5: 25 and Col. 3:19. Wives love your husband is *philos* in Titus 2:4. The husband initiates. The wife responds. If and when a husband loves his wife with sacrificial and unselfish love, she will (assuming her dedication to God) return that love. The sun shines. The moon reflects. The speculative nature of my astronomical illustration is improved by biblical authority within the statement, "He who loves his own wife loves himself ..." (Eph. 5:28). If the conditions are true that a man loves his wife as Christ loves the church, she will reflect that love to him in return. Also, she will not have a hard time submitting to the leadership of a husband who "honors" her (see 1 Pet. 3:7) and makes all his decisions in her best interest.

The principle of not making a theological point on a single verse is valid. On the other hand, we only have Titus 2:4. Wives should love their husbands with a tender *philos* type of love. May I suggest that men are generally "rougher" than women. I think it is normal in most marriages for a wife to attempt to sensitize, maybe even civilize her husband. If she loves in a thoughtful, kind and warm sense, over time he may soften up. This process seems to take place in many marriages and may be the basis for the use of the word *philos* in the command for wives to love their husbands.

Perhaps God intends a process of wives tenderizing their husbands over time with constant *philos* type of love. This process may be normal in the course of a relationship. However, the Bible warns against wives becoming irritating nags (Prov. 19:13, 21:9, 27:15). Also, wives must never expect men to stop being men. There is room for individual variation in different marriages.[10] However, a man need not enjoy poetry, crafts, candles, gardening, or sewing to be a highly successful and faithful husband. Christian husbands should become gentlemen. Christian husbands should not become effeminate. Wives have a ministry from God to tenderize their husbands with a *philos* type of love. However, even a tenderized steak still remains a steak, not a marshmallow.

Domestic Duties

The world does not give trophies for homemaking or Nobel prizes for raising the best children. God does. Believers are saved through faith alone by God's grace. However, in the matter of degrees of reward in glory "the last shall be first and the first last" (Matt. 20:16). Faithful wives, mothers, and grandmothers will be highly blessed by God at the Judgment Seat of Christ. In some cases, Christian leaders with recognized names will obtain less praise and lower positions in the kingdom of God.

Christian homes should not use the phrase "just a housewife." It takes the wisdom of Solomon and the patience of Job to raise a family. Proverbs 31 praises a wife who gives primary attention to domestic pursuits.

> She rises also while it is still night and gives food to her household and portions to her maidens .... She looks well to the ways of her household and does not eat the bread of idleness. Her children rise up and bless her; her husband also, and he praises her ... [Prov. 31:15, 27-28].

Every Christian couple must wrestle with Paul's command for mothers to be **"workers at home"** (Titus 2:5) and also the teaching that

---

[10] Gift-giving (flowers, chocolate, jewelry) and card-giving (love notes on Valentines Day) are a part of showing thoughtfulness to a wife. However, men can give gifts in phony ways and with artificial tenderness just because of societal expectations at certain times. A wise wife should realize that these things are not the essence of love. Also, some men who pay insufficient attention to such things still deeply love their wives.

widows of child-bearing years should remarry "bear children" and **"keep house"** (1 Tim. 5:14).

Relative to careers, the Bible does not restrict single women from high positions in society. If a husband supports his wife's working, and she has no maternal responsibilities, that too is fine. If a woman has children, the children, (not career advancement) become the focus of life's energies.

Some mothers believe they can continue to work and place children as the top priority. Others believe they should work full time at home, especially with their pre-school children.

Life presents a wide spectrum. Some are single mothers. Others find they must work to support senior citizen parents. Others face a husband's disability or business failure. Certainly, if a wife and mother absolutely must work to support a family, Christians should be flexible in attitudes. God wants mercy and not harsh criticism (James 2:13). On the other hand, many parents are rationalizing a two-income family during a child's formative years.

Many families simply live beyond their means, piling up debt. Others refuse a lower but acceptable standard of living that would allow more attention upon children. The Bible commands families with children to give first priority to domestic duties. Couples must take this seriously. For some this may involve a need to work to provide basic essentials to survival. Many other couples could actually manage for a mother to stay at home but fail to see its importance. Mothers who feel they must work should choose to work only for the sake of children's genuine economic needs; not mere career advancement. Far more mothers could get by and not work during a child's formative years. Whatever the exact practice, all families are responsible to place children ahead of careers, and mothers need to take seriously the phrase "workers at home" (Titus 2:4) and "keep house" (1 Tim. 5:14). Mothers of young children who work must have a conviction it is absolutely necessary for the sake of their children. [11]

---

[11] Day-care facilities dare not show favoritism. At home, children can be treated as the most special children in the world. In a day-care setting, a child bonds with a worker who will not be a permanent fixture in life. Fifty-cents

Inner Beauty

1 Peter 3:3-5 does not forbid cosmetics (related to the Greek word for adornment), but Peter does prohibit preoccupation with external beauty over inner beauty. Women who give more attention to "the hidden person of the heart" please God with the "gentle and quiet" spirit (see 1 Peter 3:3-5).

Proverbs speaks of the misery caused by irritable, moody, grumbling, and nagging wives. They are like a constant dripping that annoys (Prov. 19:13, 27:15). It is better to live in a desert (Prov. 21:19) or the corner of the roof (Prov. 21:9, 25:24) than with a contentious woman. One husband told me his wife is a black hole. Whatever time, energy, and money he pours into her does not satisfy her.

Those who work on inner beauty bless their husband in addition to pleasing God. The heart of a husband can trust a virtuous wife (Prov. 31:11). She does him good and not evil all the days of her life (Prov. 31:12). While external beauty is nice, it fades over time. Character lasts (Prov. 31:30). Wives with inner beauty bless their husbands and are blessed in return (Prov. 31:28).

Additional Aspects to a Wife's Role

Several important aspects of a wife's role will be reserved for following chapters. The many Bible texts that command parents to instruct children include references to mothers teaching children truth (e.g. Prov. 1:8, 6:20, 31:1). Both Timothy's mother and grandmother taught him the Scriptures at an early age (2 Tim. 1:5, 3:15). Chapter 11 will give more information about training children.

---

per hour someplace else, and the child will get another care-giver. It's safe to bond with Mom. She will always be there to meet every need. In a communal setting there are more communicable child sicknesses. Even in the best of facilities, one cannot guarantee the teaching of a Christian worldview, doctrine, and ethics approved by parents. Marilyn and I started married life quite poor; nevertheless, for the above reasons she was a full time mother.

Also, the Bible commands both husbands and wives to meet each other's sexual needs (1 Cor. 7:3-5). Chapter 9 details much of the Scripture's teaching on sex within the marriage covenant.

Chapter Nine

Procreation (and Sexuality)

Holiness and Restriction

The word "holy" primarily refers to separation. God's own holiness may be classified by a division between majestic holiness and ethical holiness. Majestic holiness means God as infinite Creator is separate (high above) from humans as limited creatures. Ethical holiness means God is separate from sin.

Separation (including restriction) is an essential element in every type of holiness. The Bible is holy. Among other things this means there are restrictions about adding or subtracting to this holy book. Only the Old Testament prophets and New Testament apostles (or those under apostolic supervision like Mark or Luke) could write Scripture. Today no one may add to or subtract from the text. Communion is holy. This means it should be restricted only to those who believe in the Lord Jesus Christ. The Church is holy. Therefore, only those with faith in Christ are spiritually within the Church. By the biblical definition, those who reject Jesus as Savior are restricted from belonging to the body of Christ (the Church) in a spiritual sense.

The Old Testament pictures the relationship between holiness and restriction by the tabernacle and temple. The Ark of the Covenant was placed within the "Holy of Holies." Only the high priest could enter and only on the Day of Atonement (*Yom Kippur*). Restriction is part of holiness.

The primary purpose for God restricting sex to marriage is to ensure its holiness. Only a foolish, immature, and naive person could possibly think that the Bible's restrictions are to destroy "fun" in life. Marriage is holy. Sexuality within marriage is holy. Prohibitions against pre-marital sex (fornication) and extra-marital sex (adultery) serve to keep sexual involvement holy. The marriage bed is comparable to Holy of Holies. All others, except the husband and wife, must stay outside. The "Do Not Enter" regulations are essential to preserve holiness. With separation comes holiness. The Judeo-Christian view of sex has never been that it is shameful or dirty. On the contrary, God's Word imposes restrictions on sex to those within a marriage covenant because sex is supposed to be kept sacred (holy).

Safe Sex

Sexual involvement without God's restriction is less wise or safe than the entire human race driving cars indiscriminately without any traffic laws. It creates many expensive damages, hurts most people, and kills quite a few. In a book on marriage, it is best to stress the holiness of sexuality. God's commandments preserve holiness. However, God also imposed these commandments for our safety. The Bible has so many, they would be hard to miss. "Thou shalt not commit adultery" or some form of it preserves holiness and prevents catastrophe (Ex. 20:14; Deut. 5:18; Matt. 19:18; Mark 10:19; Luke 18:20; Rom. 13:9; Gal. 5:19-21; Eph. 5:3; 1 Thess. 4:3; James 2:11; and Heb. 13:4).

Sociological and medical statistics could be included to warn about sex outside of marriage. In movies and TV shows, an "affair" with few consequences may be portrayed as a harmless distraction or even therapy for life's problems. However, such portrayals are fictional stories with fictional outcomes. In real life, sex outside of marriage leads to broken relationships, ruined reputations, divorce, distrust, terrible venereal diseases, hasty and weak marriages based on guilt, fatherless children, expenses, emotional trauma, loneliness, and on-and-on. The Bible does not use divorce or disease statistics to support its commands on morality, but it does warn those who refuse God's prohibitions are foolish and self-destructive. Various images include fire in one's bosom, an arrow in the liver, a dumb ox, and reduction to a piece of bread (we might say, "he or she is toast!"). Reduction to a piece of bread may refer to poverty arising from blackmail to keep adultery secret or to expensive child-support.

> For on account of a harlot *one is reduced* to a loaf of bread, and an adulteress hunts for the precious life. Can a man take fire in his bosom and his clothes not be burned? Or can a man walk on hot coals and his feet not be scorched? So is the one who goes in to his neighbor's wife; Whoever touches her will not go unpunished [Prov. 6:26-29].

The one who commits adultery with a woman is lacking sense; he who would destroy himself does it. Wounds and disgrace he will find, and his reproach will not be blotted out. For jealousy enrages a man, and he will not spare in the day of vengeance. He will not accept any ransom, nor will he be satisfied though you give many gifts [Prov. 6:32-35].

With her many persuasions she entices him; with her flattering lips she seduces him. Suddenly he follows her as an ox goes to the slaughter, or as one in fetters to the discipline of a fool, until an arrow pierces through his liver; as a bird hastens to the snare, so he does not know that it will cost him his life. [Prov. 7:21-23].

Mental Fidelity

In a philosophy class a "Christian" professor tossed both a Bible and a Playboy magazine on his podium. He proclaimed both are paper and ink. They are morally equivalent. At first I thought he was playing "devil's advocate" and inviting a debate. When I tried to argue, he said he would not allow the Bible to be quoted in a philosophy course. (Ask for a doctrinal statement before giving donations to a college.) Later, I learned this same professor had been caught leaving a strip club in this state's capital city. Evidently, this man was using the classroom to rationalize his own temptations and "mid-life crisis."

The Bible has much to say about mental fidelity. Before the professor told me the Bible could not be used in his "Christian" philosophy course, I was about to say, "In God's Book, not just actions but thoughts can also be sinful. Lust made the all time top ten list. 'You shall not covet your neighbor's wife' " [Ex. 20:17].

The Bible contains many teachings about our minds. On the positive side, Christians are supposed to give God Himself our primary attention. "Thou wilt keep him in perfect peace whose mind is stayed on Thee" (Isa. 26:3 KJV). "Set your mind on the things above, not on the things that are on earth" [Col. 3:2].

Finally, brethren, whatever is true, whatever is honorable, whatever is right, whatever is pure, whatever is lovely, whatever is of good repute, if there is any excellence and if anything worthy of praise, dwell on these things [Phil. 4:8].

Christians are supposed to meditate upon the perfections of the Father, Son and Holy Spirit. We are also supposed to think about truth and good thoughts from the Word of God "day and night" (Josh. 1:8; Psa. 1:2). For our own relational, emotional, and mental well-being, God's commands not only prohibit the sinful act, they prohibit the sinful thought (Ex. 20:17; Deut. 5:21; 2 Sam.11:2; Job 31:1; Psa. 19:14; 139:2, 23-24; Matt. 5:28, 15:19; Rom. 13:14; 2 Cor. 10:5; 2 Tim. 2:22; 1 Pet. 2:11, 4:3; 2 Pet. 2:14; 1 John 2:16).[1]

While it is true that only one sin is sufficient to cause eternal condemnation without faith in Christ (Gal. 3:10; James 2:10), not all sins are equal. Jesus refers to greater and lesser commandments and also greater sins (Matt. 5:19, 22:36-40; John 19:11). Adultery, the action, is indeed a greater sin than lust, the thought. However, this conclusion may not be used to rationalize. Whenever adultery occurs, it starts in the mind (or we could say with a roving eye). A husband or wife who consistently preserves mental fidelity will never commit literal infidelity against a spouse who remains the object of love and passion. Adultery is a more serious sin than lust, but faithfulness to a spouse begins in one's spirit. Prov. 4:23 says, "Watch over your heart with all diligence." Twice God warns in Malachi Chapter Two that treachery in a marriage covenant begins with treachery in the heart (Mal. 2:14-16). The Lord Himself taught that adultery begins in the heart (Matt. 15:19). Those who fight to preserve mental fidelity to a spouse will maintain literal fidelity.

---

[1] Peter said that "fleshly lusts ... wage war against the soul" (1 Pet. 2:11).Not only does slavery to lust show disrespect to one's wife, it may also be a factor in inability to retain knowledge or attain noble intellectual pursuits. One wonders if poor academic test scores are in part due to emotional pain from broken homes and/or minds unable to think deeply because of pornography.

Covenantal Sex

Early in the pages of Scripture we learn that God created male and female and blessed them (Gen. 1:27-28). God designed sexuality and blessed both the original pair and all other married couples with sex. Those who think Christianity is anti-sex have not looked into the topic even to a superficial degree. Prohibitions against sexual involvement outside of marriage only preserve the holiness of sex within marriage and safeguard against self-destructive perversion so that we can be blessed by marital sex.

Our youth group leaders were leading a marriage discussion one evening. They asked those present to rank various issues in order of importance to a strong marriage. The leader wrote "sex" on the board. The group ranked it near the bottom of marital priorities. Later I advised that a university study had concluded that faith and sexual enjoyment are the top two indications that a marriage will last. Abstinence before marriage is holy. Abstinence in marriage is unholy.

In marriage the sexual union is holy. God does not just tolerate or endure sexual union within marriage, he blesses and commands it. Moses wrote, "… they shall become one flesh. And the man and his wife were both naked and were not ashamed" (Gen. 2:24-25). Solomon encouraged a husband to rejoice in his wife, be satisfied with her breasts and "be exhilarated always with her love" (Prov. 5:18-19). Paul compared sexual union to an obligation or debt and forbids married couples from spending too much time apart. Any travel that separates a husband and wife should be brief and only by mutual consent (1 Cor. 7:2-5). Hebrews 13:4 calls the marriage bed undefiled. The word "bed" is a euphemistic translation. The Greek word is literally "coitus." Marital sex is holy.

The Bible clearly blesses males and females becoming one flesh in marriage:

Your two breasts are like two fawns, twins of a gazelle which feed among the lilies. Until the cool of the day when the shadows flee away, I will go my way to the mountain of myrrh and to the hill of frankincense. You are altogether beautiful, my darling, and there is no blemish in you [Song of Sol. 4:5-7].

I have come into my garden, my sister, my bride; I have gathered my myrrh along with my balsam. I have eaten my honeycomb and my honey; I have drunk my wine and my milk. Eat, friends; drink and imbibe deeply, O lovers [Song of Sol. 5:1].

My beloved has gone down to his garden, to the beds of balsam, to pasture his flock in the gardens and gather lilies. I am my beloved's and my beloved is mine, he who pastures his flock among the lilies [Song of Sol. 6:2-3].

The husband must fulfill his duty to his wife, and likewise also the wife to her husband. The wife does not have authority over her own body, but the husband does; and likewise also the husband does not have authority over his own body, but the wife does [1 Cor. 7:3-4].[2]

God designed sex within marriage to bless couples with union and intimacy. In and of itself sexuality alone has value for marriage, but the facts of both Scripture and life reveal God's intent for sexuality also includes the procreation of children. Part of the image of God within humanity is the ability to "create life."

Be Fruitful and Multiply

The command to "be fruitful and multiply" occurs after creation (Gen. 1:28) and again after Noah's flood (Gen. 9:7). The Church is not under the Law of Moses (e.g. Rom. 7:4, 10:4; Gal. 3:24-25) unless a command is repeated in the New Testament. However, the command to "be fruitful and multiply" is pre-law. Also, Paul's statement of 1 Tim. 5:14 and Christ's view of children (quoted below) prove children have been desirable whether the system is Law or Church. Christian couples who are able to have children should have children.

---

[2] There are common differences between men and women in terms of sexual stimulation. Generally, women respond more to touch and emotions, while men respond more to sight. However, the Victorian notion that women have no interest or sexual need does not conform to Scripture (see: Gen. 30:14-16; Ex. 21:10; 1 Cor. 7:3-4).

Throughout the Bible, conception is a matter controlled by God. Those unable to conceive need not experience false guilt. Those able to have children should obey the command to produce a family.[3] The definition of God's blessing in Genesis 1 involves both the creation of sexuality (male and female) and God's design in the ability to reproduce. The ability to be fruitful and multiply is a primary blessing from God for the human race.

Some in modern times view children as a hindrance to career goals, material abundance or freedom from "the good life." The responsibilities in terms of costs, energy, and time in rearing children is viewed as a nuisance if not a curse. The Scripture teaches the view that children are one of the greatest blessings in life. They are one of life's highest rewards and greatest gifts from God. Nothing in a Christian worldview allows the delusion that children are a detriment to life. If God blesses a couple with children, they become one of the reasons to live at all.

Scriptures teach that God either allows, causes, or withholds conception. Children are a reward and gift from God and must not be ignored as if unimportant. Often both truths arise from the same text.[4]

Then the LORD took note of Sarah as He had said, and the LORD did for Sarah as He had promised. So Sarah conceived and bore

---

[3] It is one step beyond the Bible to conclude God would prohibit family planning. While this may be a personal or denominational conviction, biblical evidence falls short of any prohibition for controlling the number or frequency of children. Where the Bible does not give clear teaching, the issue is a matter of Christian freedom. Couples who are able to have children should do so, but the number or frequency is a decision between the couple and God. Whatever a couple decides about family planning is more a personal preference than a matter of right and wrong. The only moral consideration would be judging the salvation or spirituality of others with different personal convictions. To be complete, we must add the thought that abortion is a great evil; not a method of family planning. God is interested and involved in the development of unborn children (see Ex. 21:22-25; Job 10:8-12; Psa. 51:5, 139:13-16; Jer. 1:5).

[4] See also Gen. 4:1, 20:17-18, 25:21, 29:31-35, 30:22-24, 33:5; Judges 13:3-5; Ruth 4:13; Prov. 17:6; Matt. 19:13-15; Luke 18:15-17.

a son to Abraham in his old age, at the appointed time of which God had spoken to him [Gen. 21:1-2].

She made a vow and said, "O LORD of hosts, if You will indeed look on the affliction of Your maidservant and remember me, and not forget Your maidservant, but will give Your maidservant a son, then I will give him to the LORD all the days of his life, and a razor shall never come on his head."....Then they arose early in the morning and worshiped before the LORD, and returned again to their house in Ramah. And Elkanah had relations with Hannah his wife, and the Lord remembered her.... "For this boy I prayed, and the Lord has given me my petition which I asked of Him. So I have also dedicated him to the LORD; as long as he lives he is dedicated to the LORD." And he worshiped the LORD there [1 Sam. 1:11, 19, 27-28].

Behold, children are a gift of the LORD, the fruit of the womb is a reward. Like arrows in the hand of a warrior, so are the children of one's youth. How blessed is the man whose quiver is full of them; they will not be ashamed when they speak with their enemies in the gate [Psa. 127:3-5].

... Truly I say to you, unless you are converted and become like children, you will not enter the kingdom of heaven. Whoever then humbles himself as this child, he is the greatest in the kingdom of heaven. And whoever receives one such child in My name receives Me; but whoever causes one of these little ones who believe in Me to stumble, it would be better for him to have a heavy millstone hung around his neck, and to be drowned in the depth of the sea .... See that you do not despise one of these little ones, for I say to you that their angels in heaven continually see the face of My Father who is in heaven [Matt. 18:3-6, 10].

And they were bringing children to Him so that He might touch them; but the disciples rebuked them. But when Jesus saw this, He was indignant and said to them, "Permit the children to come to Me; do not hinder them; for the kingdom of God belongs to such as these. Truly I say to you, whoever does not receive the kingdom of God like a child will not enter it at all." And He took them in His arms and began blessing them, laying His hands on them [Mark 10:13-16].

Christian versus Pagan Views on Children

The world owes much to the Bible for its view of children. Can those who want to return to paganism actually be serious?

Pagans sacrificed children in fire.[5] Originally, the term "Gehenna" referred to the Valley of Hinnom where apostate Jews burned children in pagan rituals (see Jeremiah 7). The prefix "Ge" arose from the Hebrew word for valley. Good King Josiah stopped these sacrifices and defiled the valley of Hinnom (2 Kings 23:10). Eventually, this location became Jerusalem's garbage dump.

As a trash deposit, "Gai-Hinnom, the Valley of Hinnom," was a place of unending fires burning rubbish and unending maggots feeding on the carcasses of dead animals thrown into the crevice. Since words fail to describe hell, the Lord Jesus used a comparison to the valley of Hinnom, the place of infant sacrifice. The real Gehenna burns endlessly like the garbage dump. There will be eternal rotting and perishing like the garbage dump. (Often the New Testament describes eternal punishment as perishing, i.e. eternal rotting John 3:16; 1 Cor. 1:18.) Among the objects of God's greatest wrath are those who hate children (see also Matt. 18:6). Pagan practices contrast with the Judeo-Christian love for children. Still, even unsaved people normally love their children. [6]

---

[5] *National Geographic* published a book containing pictures of urns with cremated remains of babies burned in sacrifices. Also, an illustrator drew a picture of an ugly Baal idol that served as an incinerator for infant sacrifices. The babies would be placed on the idol's hot metal arms in order to roll into the oven's inferno. The Carthaginians under discussion were immigrants from Phoenicia (i.e. the Canaanites). See Gilbert Charles-Picard, *The World of Hannibal* in *Greece and Rome: Builders of Our World* (Washington, DC: National Geographic Society, 1968) pp. 284-287.

[6] Perhaps even pagan Julius Caesar seemed surprised at the attitude towards children exhibited by the Druid led Gauls. See *Julius Caesar:The Battle for Gaul*, Anne and Peter Wiseman, translators (Boston: David R. Godine Publisher, 1980), p.123. Fathers would not be seen in public with sons too

Normal versus Abnormal Human Psychology

At its worst the unsaved world hates and destroys children. Christianity has long elevated the status of both women and children, especially compared to the time of its origin and to false worldviews. Even though people can sink to horrible treatment of children, the Bible observes that normally even non-Christians love their own children. Abortion on demand and unconcern for children are not just immoral. They are symptoms of sick abnormal psychology.

In lamenting that some in the Roman world had lost normal family love, Paul also believed that "natural affection" (see Rom. 1:31, KJV) for ones own family is normal psychology even for non-Christians. Many unbelievers have normal family affection and love for their own children. Paul also taught that many unsaved parents provide for their children's financial needs (1 Tim. 5:8). Thus, the Bible has elevated the world's view of children. At the same time, however, even the majority of unbelievers have some natural love for their own children. Those who travel widely observe that unsaved parents (especially mothers but often both) usually love their children.[7] Pagans can deeply sin against children, but abuse of children is not an innate component of being an unbeliever. It is abnormal psychology for anyone.

All children are God's blessing. Beliefs and behaviors to the contrary are unscriptural and perverted. God has blessed us with both sexuality and the ability to procreate. He also gave much wisdom on how to raise good children.

---

young for combat. Yet, the Romans themselves were not above abandonment or infanticide of newborn girls. The early Christians would rescue such orphans. See F. F. Bruce, The Spreading Flames (Grand Rapids: Wm. B. Eerdmans, 1979) p. 190.

[7] I have observed Russian, Ugandan and Turkish families who loved their children. In a Russian classroom the middle school children unselfishly offered their own dolls for me to bring to my daughter, Rachel. It was evident to me that their parents loved their children and were doing their best to care for them.

Chapter Ten

Parental Philosophy

The Image of God in Parenting

On a starry August night I gave the message of salvation to a stranger sitting on a bench overlooking Lake George, New York. I quoted John 3:16 and said, "God the Father loves us so much he gave His Son." The man snarled that his own father had given his son up also. He cursed and said he wished his father's grave was in the park so he could urinate on it. I had only experienced exemplary parents and grandparents. This conversation caused a new realization of the connection between parents and the development of theological views about God's nature.

In the course of life, children should begin to develop their views of God from God's image reflected in their parents. It is not without reason that God calls Himself "Father."[1] Obviously, parents who model (in a limited sense, of course) the attributes of God give their children great advantages in life. Such parents make it easier for their children to understand and relate to God.

From a child's perspective, a good father and mother seem omnipresent, omnipotent, and omniscient. They are ever present attending to every need with superior wisdom. To a child, parents seem "ancient of days." They might even be thirty, which is close to eternity from a toddler's perspective. To a child, good parents have a moral system of right and wrong. They are holy and just. Yet, mom and dad give mercy, grace, and unconditional love. Children especially need to know their parents love them with unconditional love, as does the Heavenly Father, (see pages 103-105).

When parents do not reflect the character traits of God, they cause their children to have a distorted view of God the Father. Often

---

[1] See pp. 52-54 for discussion that feminine and/or maternal characteristics are also part of God's image. Thus, while God is Father, His treatment of children also gives a model for mothers.

these children regard God as vindictive and cruel without any grace. Such children can ultimately overcome their disadvantages from bad parental experience through Bible study, fellowship with loyal people in a church family, and mentoring by substitute father/mother figures. These may be relatives (godly grandparents, uncles and aunts) or older role models from a church family.

However, God's plan is that parents model God's traits even before a child can read. Then a child sees that the perfect attributes of God revealed in the Bible have already been made familiar by his or her family experience. At an age of increasing spiritual awareness and ability to read, a child with godly parents more easily relates to and responds to the true God of Scripture. He or she discovers God is like his or her parents, only more perfect. The most important truth for life (including marriage and parenting) is **the admiration and imitation of God**. The best parents can do for children is to reflect God's attributes to them. Specific techniques as to discipline and instruction are vital. However, behavior begins in beliefs. Actions spring from the heart. The Bible teaches children of the righteous have many blessings (Psa. 37:25-26, 112:2; Prov. 11:21, 12:7, 14:26; Jer. 32:39).

> A righteous man who walks in his integrity - How blessed are his sons after him [Prov. 20:7].

Unity on Parenting or a House Divided?

The imitation of God's attributes should be a basic practice in child rearing. How is this possible in a mixed marriage? God forbids a believer to marry an unbeliever in order to save us from troubles, including difficulties in raising children in homes with arguments over views and values. In such cases the believing parent will have to do his or her best to seek those outside the home who can reinforce Christian truths. Raising good children in spiritually mixed homes is possible but not easy.

Even in homes where both parents have placed faith in Christ, it is possible that one or both of the pair has a life that does not reflect God's image to a child. Jesus said, "A wise man builds his house upon the rock" (Matt. 7:24, paraphrase). He defines the rock as His own teaching and authority. The Lord also taught that a "house divided against itself" will topple (Matt. 12:25). Both phrases may be applied to the need for unity of father and mother in the matter of raising children. The best foundation for parents occurs when both have faith in Christ and when both admire and imitate Him. They may not agree on every detail in parenting, but unity on fundamental truths causes foundational strength.[2] Both parents should have a conviction that children are precious, but that children also have sin natures, that God gives parents, not children, authority in the house, and that God's truths give the ultimate wisdom for raising children and the standards by which excellence in children should be measured (not the latest secular magazine article or talk-show).

Children are precious

Chapter 9 lists Bible texts that teach the value of children (see pages 87-88 for many references supporting the infinite worth of children to God). Christian parents believe children are a priority in life.

Behold, children are a gift of the Lord. The fruit of the womb is a reward (Psa. 127:3).

Yet, a contrasting truth about children also reinforces the need to work very hard on parenting. The Bible teaches children are a blessing. It also teaches they are born with a propensity toward sin. If parents neglect God's Word in the matter of raising children, the natural outcome will not be good.

Children and Human Sin Nature

The entire human race with only the exception of the Lord Jesus Christ is born into sin.[3] Children are born relatively innocent

---

[2] During a seminar on parenting, I observed a childless couple get into a public dispute over spanking. He was certain physical discipline is not only approved but commanded in the Bible. She felt it was a sin to spank children at anytime for anything. Either this couple eventually came to truth and unity or had serious trouble raising children.

[3] See 1 Kings 8:46; Psa. 14:2-3, 53:3, 130:3, 143:2; Prov. 20:9; Eccles. 7:20; Isa. 53:6; Rom. 3:9-10, 19, 23; Gal. 3:22; James 3:2; 1 John 1:8, 10. For a

compared to adolescents and adults, but the capacity and tendency to sin begins at conception. David said, "Behold I was brought forth in iniquity, and in sin my mother conceived me"(Psa. 51:5, see also Psa. 58:3).

Both a father and mother should agree that the imitation of God's character gives the background for parenting. Both should agree that no effort is too much because children are precious. If further motivation is needed, parents should fear the outcome if they disobey God's Word about instructions for the family.

Who is in Charge? Children or parents?

Father's Day and Mother's Day sermons can be tricky. It is certainly appropriate to aim a message at parents reminding them of God's commands on child rearing. However, there can be danger of increasing needless guilt among parents who are striving to the limits of human ability to sacrifice for their children. A sermon strictly for neglectful and unspiritual parents usually is not on target for couples that have dedicated themselves to raise children God's way but still make mistakes common to imperfect humans. In order to encourage faithful parents and avoid false guilt, it is wise to direct part of every Father's Day or Mother's Day message to children. There are at least as many Bible commands directed at children as there are commands for parents. While father and mother have many obligations to excellence in child rearing, nowhere does the Bible command, "Honor your father and mother only if they never make any mistakes." Mom and dad will make mistakes, but a teen will make far more mistakes if he or she rebels against good parents. Parents can be doing an excellent job without being supernaturally perfect. Children must honor parents despite human limitations and flaws.

Families where the parents cede control and authority to the children end up teaching dishonor to both parents and ultimately the Heavenly Father. God's Word teaches parents to love children without

discussion of the doctrine of sin see Steven W. Waterhouse, *Not By Bread Alone; An Outlined Guide to Bible Doctrine* (Amarillo, TX: Westcliff Press, 2003), pp. 67-69.

conditions, to instruct, to discipline, to provide. No Bible verse says, "parents obey your children."

Parents fail when they turn all attention and authority in a home over to the children. Part of love is imposing safe limits (Heb. 12:5-11; Rev. 3:19). Part of loving a child is teaching him to honor and obey parents and thereby teaching him to honor and obey the authority of God (presuming the parents are enforcing God's standards).

I observed a church service in which a mother simply would not control her son. He was running between the seats screaming and then hanging over the balcony. The woman sat motionless with her eyes glued on the pastor, evidently thinking no one would notice. One interpretation of this psychology was that she was afraid to stand up to her disruptive son. Maybe she felt that control and domination would turn his love away. Whatever her thinking and motivation, parents do not help their children by fearing to stand up to their bent to sin.

Two biblical characters displeased God and failed as fathers for not restraining their children. Eli raised two sons whom God described as "worthless men." They "did not know the Lord" (1 Sam. 2:12, see also 2:17). God asked Eli "why do you ... honor your sons above me? ..." (1 Sam. 2:29). Because Eli knew of his sons' wickedness, "and he did not rebuke them" (1 Sam. 3:13), the high priesthood was transferred from his family line (1 Sam. 2:35-36; 1 Kings 2:27, 35).

David also made the mistake of not insisting that his sons obey him as father. Of spoiled-rotten Prince Adonijah it is written, "And his father had never crossed him at any time by asking, 'Why have you done so?' " (1 Kings 1:6).

The Bible gives parents authority for the welfare of children. Parents who love their children will not be afraid to cross them or honor God's standards above childish demands. Good fathers and mothers will insist children give them honor and will not be afraid to take charge. Allowing children premature autonomy without loving guidance is the cruel option, and also the option that allows them to turn against parents. Insisting on obedience actually increases the bond of love between parent and child. Parents who love, care enough to insist upon respect for the long-term sake of the child. Children have a way of understanding the parental intent for taking control is for their own good and displays love.

Honor Your Father and Mother

Parents must obey God and strive to measure up to His character traits. Having done so (even imperfectly), the Bible commands children to honor their parents. Jesus Himself set the example in Luke 2:51.

> Honor your father and your mother, that your days may be prolonged in the land which the LORD your God gives you [Ex. 20:12].

> Hear, my son, your father's instruction and do not forsake your mother's teaching; indeed, they are a graceful wreath to your head and ornaments about your neck [Prov. 1:8-9].

> And He went down with them and came to Nazareth, and He continued in subjection to them; and His mother treasured all these things in her heart [Luke 2:51].

> Children, obey your parents in the Lord, for this is right. Honor your father and mother (which is the first commandment with a promise), so that it may be well with you, and that you may live long on the earth [Eph. 6:1-3].[4]

In addition to the many commands to honor father and mother, Scripture gives many warnings about disobedience to parents. We are not under the Law of Moses, but in extreme cases (e.g. serious domestic violence) the Law allowed the death penalty for rebellious adult children (Ex. 21:15; Deut. 21:18-21). Solomon predicted disaster for those who rebel against godly fathers and mothers …. "He who curses his father or mother, his lamp will go out in a time of darkness" (Prov. 20:20, see also Prov. 15:5a).

---

[4] See also Lev.19:3a; Deut. 5:16; Prov. 23:22, 25; Matt. 15:4; Luke 18:20; and Col. 3:20.

96

Perhaps Proverbs 30:17 gives the strongest warning:

The eye that mocks a father and scorns a mother, the ravens of
the valley will pick it out, and the young eagles will eat it [Prov.
30:17].

Paul believed that one of the signs of depravity in the Roman
Empire was widespread disobedience to parents (Rom. 1:30). He also
taught that disobedience to parents would be a sign of the last days (2
Tim. 3:1-2).

Parents have great responsibility to God. So do children and
teens. In teaching and counseling, Christian leaders should stress both.
It is possible for parents to fail. It is also possible for children to
disobey God and rebel against very fine parents. When both parents
and children have a sense of accountability to God's authority, the
outcome will be safety from foolish sins, increased blessings from God,
and love between parents and children.

Nature, Nurture, or Choice

Psychologists study whether children are most influenced by
nature (genetics) or nurture (society and family environments). I
believe both factors influence children. One might have a genetic
tendency to a hot temper or alcoholism, or to a calm disposition with
patience and sobriety. Genetics are a factor but are usually not
dominant over the fundamentals of behavior in life.[5] Likewise, society
and family deeply influence child development. Those born in the 21st
Century will be different from those born in 1500. Those born in the
United States will be different from those born in Kenya. Those raised
in atheist or Buddhist homes will be different from those raised in
Christian homes. Both genetics and social influences help shape a

---

[5] My brother has severe schizophrenia. I still regard him as morally
accountable (especially when improved by medicine) because he exhibits the
traits of moral understanding. He covers up wrongdoing. He blames others.
He has a temper when he is the object of sin. In some cases, medical problems
do blunt or can even remove moral accountability, but for most people and for
most of the time, they do not. However, biological factors do influence
behavior even when they do not predestine it.

child. The many commands to parents, children, and even churches presuppose that family environment is an important factor in the outcome of children. The very reason for including a chapter on parenting is that parents have a huge influence on their children.

However, in order to be balanced, something must be said about change and choice. Those who did not have godly parents can still totally change their lives. They may have disadvantages and/or even emotional pain, but by God's grace, they have hope.

People can also change for the worse. The father of the prodigal son was a good father (Luke 15:11-32). The son alone bore responsibility for his sins as a young adult. In time the son returned to the views and ways of his father. Prov. 22:6 teaches that older children who rebel against good parents tend to return in time. This means parental efforts have value even if there can be times parents wonder whether they have done any good.

At a certain point children become morally accountable to obey God without parents forcing compliance. The entire perspective of the Proverbs is that a father must teach his children. However, having done his best, the father warns he can no longer control his child's choices.

A child might choose foolishness and come to harm. Even after the father has instructed, the child must chose obedience. It is now his responsibility to guard his own heart (compare Prov. 4:20-21 with v. 23). The father instructs. The son should heed the call to obey, but ultimately the son must realize he himself is accountable to God who observes his life (compare Prov. 5:1-2 with vv. 11-13, 21-23). The father pleads with his son not to forget his father's lessons, but the father also warns and limits his own responsibility if the son should choose foolishness (see Prov. 1:20-33).

… fools despise wisdom and instruction [Prov. 1:7b].

Because I called and you refused, I stretched out my hand and no one paid attention; and you neglected all my counsel and did not want my reproof …. because they hated knowledge and did not choose the fear of the LORD. They would not accept my counsel, they spurned all my reproof. So they shall eat of the

fruit of their own way and be satiated with their own devices ....
but he who listens to me shall live securely and will be at ease
from the dread of evil (wisdom personified, but wisdom comes
from God often through parents) [Prov. 1:24-25,29-31,33].

Now then, my sons, listen to me and do not depart from the
words of my mouth .... And you say, "How I have hated
instruction! And my heart spurned reproof! I have not listened
to the voice of my teacher, nor inclined my ear to my
instructors!".... For the ways of a man are before the eyes of the
LORD, and He watches all his paths. His own iniquities will
capture the wicked, and he will be held with the cords of his sin.
He will die for lack of instruction, and in the greatness of his
folly he will go astray [Prov. 5:7, 12-13, 21-23].

Even with the best of parenting, children eventually make their
own choices.[6] In the historical books of the Bible, a godly king could

---

[6] The age of accountability is a topic that usually overlaps with the
criminal/moral liability of young people or the salvation of an infant/child
upon death. Here the idea arises in the context of parenting. When does a
child become accountable for his or her own relationship to God?

Modern cultures vary. The Jewish culture expects accountability at age 13.
Secular society marks age 16 as the age to drive, 18 as the age to vote, and
often 21 as the age to drink. The Bible never gives a precise age of
accountability. Perhaps in God's omniscience it varies with each person.
Several verses give the concept that small children do not yet know right from
wrong (Deut. 1:39; Isa. 7:15-16; Jonah 4:11). Yet, Jeremiah said that King
Jehoichin at age 18 was accountable for having refused to listen to God since
his youth (Jer. 22:21, see also 2 Kings 24:8-9). Many Bible characters were
godly at an early age (Joseph, Daniel, his 3 friends who went into the fiery
furnace, young David who fought Goliath, probably Joseph and Mary, see
Eccles. 12:1). Yet, God did not record Hebrews in the Mosaic census until the
age of 20 (Num. 1:1-3).

The age of personal accountability before God is unknown. Yet, the concept
seems to be true. At an early age children do not know right from wrong.
When Bathsheba lost David's child, the king expected to see the baby again in
the after-life (2 Sam. 12:23). Also, Jesus taught young children have guardian
angels and that the kingdom of heaven belongs to them (Matt. 18:1-6, 10-14,
19:13-15). Infants are not born saved, but should they die, they seem to die

have a spiritually sick son or grandson; but a spiritually sick king might have a son or grandson who led a spiritual revival. Hezekiah, a good king, was followed by his son Manassah, a bad king. Amon, a bad king, was followed by Josiah, a good king. Josiah in turn was followed by three sons and a grandson who were spiritually bad.

Nature influences us, but we are still personally accountable to God. Nurture, (societal or family culture) influences us, but every individual is still personally accountable to God. The Bible makes each generation responsible before God (Deut. 24:16; 2 Kings 14:6; 2 Chron. 25:4; Jer. 31:29-30; Ezek. 18:4,20) and forces individuals to choose for themselves.

See, I have set before you this day life and prosperity, and death and adversity …. I call heaven and earth to witness against you today, that I have set before you life and death, the blessing and the curse. So choose life in order that you may live, you and your descendants [Deut. 30:15, 19].

Elijah came near to all the people and said, "How long will you hesitate between two opinions? If the Lord is God, follow him; but if Baal, follow him." But the people did not answer him a word [1 Kings 18:21].

Joshua's command in Josh. 24:15 presumes responsibility for his own household but also that even the mighty general Joshua had limits to controlling the choice of others. Thus, these words can apply to adult children of godly Christian parents " … choose for yourselves today whom you will serve … but as for me and my house, we will serve the Lord."

Mothers and fathers must imitate the character traits of God. They are responsible to believe both that children are precious and worthy of unconditional love but also that they are sinners and need to

---

saved. See Lightner, Robert. *Heaven For Those Who Can't Believe.* (Schaumburg, IL: Regular Baptist Press), 1977, and Steven Waterhouse, *Not By Bread Alone: An Outlined Guide to Bible Doctrine* (Amarillo, TX: Westcliff Press, 2003), pp. 64-67, (see in particular footnote 4, wherein the author's section on inherited sin from Adam is part of his reasoning for believing God can and does save children under the age of accountability).

be taught respect for God's authority. When parents have disobeyed God, they must confess sin and begin obeying biblical teaching about raising children. When parents have long obeyed these teachings, they should remain free of false guilt if adult children have wandered away from God. Children eventually become personally accountable for their choices to God (Gal. 6:4-5). Personal choice is typically the dominant factor in what a person becomes. Nature (genetics) and nurture (culture and family) do influence us. Thus, parents must raise children in the "nurture and admonition of the Lord" (Eph. 6:4), but children also have an obligation to obey God by honoring this type of parents (even if they are not perfect). When children refuse, the parents may feel pain but need not feel guilt. They may also hope that eventually disobedient children will come to their senses as did the prodigal son (Luke 15:17).

Whatever the future, parents can do no better than following God's wisdom on raising children. Obedience of the parents greatly improves chances for a better outcome. A strong Christian upbringing will at least give children truths to which they can return, and many children will choose to follow their heritage without any periods of rebellion. They will pass from parental example and instruction right to personal choice. They will choose the faith of their parents. They will honor the doctrines and ethics of their parents by realizing they originate in a higher authority. The image of God in parents leads to a clearer idea of the image of God coming from Bible study. Honoring father's and mother's commands grows to honoring God who is the ultimate source of the most important of parental commands.

Chapter Eleven

Parental Practices

Unconditional Love or Trial Acceptance

In a game with a close score a young athlete made a mistake that caused his team to lose in the final seconds. The game itself is completely irrelevant. After the loss, however, the father of an eight-year-old boy ran out on the field and publicly berated the child. I overheard words like, "No son of mine would ever try something so stupid." I was unmarried at the time, yet I instinctively knew the father was worse at parenting than the son ever would be at sports.

In Chapter 10 we argued that the image of God reflected in parents gives children the basis for emotional and spiritual strength. God the Father is the model for parents. There is no need to determine which of God's characteristics is the most important in raising children, but giving unconditional love must be at the top of anyone's priority.

When one trusts in Christ as Savior, he or she becomes a child of God. God wants his children to behave and achieve. As a Father, He rewards and blesses virtuous behavior and efforts that lead to service and achievement. However, God loves His children even if they fail. We might fail by rebellion, or we may have human limitations. Regardless, God loves us without conditions. "See how great a love the Father has bestowed on us that we would be called children of God ..." (1 John 3:1). It is obvious that parents have a moral responsibility to love their children. However, some do not love them in any sense of the word. Many others are confused as to the Scriptural definition of love. It is important that children feel the security of *unconditional love*. Christian love is not based upon performance, ability, or behavior. It is a commitment to do what is best for the object of love whether the person deserves it or not. Parents who mirror this type of love (God's love) instill security in children, teach them to love, and display a model that will generate an attraction to God. It is a major mistake to give the impression that the continuance of love depends upon the child's academic performance, talents, appearance, athletic ability, or *even behavior.* Children need to know love will be there even when there is failure or sin. This is exactly the way God treats His children. He urges righteousness and good works, but we have confidence that He continues to love even when we are unrighteous and fail to achieve. God expects parents to love their children as He loves His children, with *unconditional love.*

The father who embarrassed his son for an athletic blunder was basing love upon achievement and success. Later we will see that the world's standards for measuring success in children (academics, athletics, artistic talent, and appearances) may be off base. God looks into the heart to measure success; beliefs, ethics, attitude (1 Sam. 16:7).[1] But the present point is even deeper. Even when there is a proper standard for measuring true success, parents should never base love on achievements. Yes, the emotional type of love *philos* rises and falls with children's performances in situations that please or displease parents, but *agape* love continues even if a child fails. This is how God loves His children.

Parents giving unconditional love not based upon performance may actually bring about greater achievement in their children. Security in parental love may give children confidence and the freedom to attempt optional endeavors that are difficult. Children unsure of parental love may feel that pursuing a difficult dream is unsafe, a risk to parental love. Children with unconditional love can dream big, precisely because failure would not be a threat to parental acceptance.[2]

---

[1] God's own view is that His ways are simple (Luke 10:41-42) contrasted with the twisted and complex way of sin (Prov. 22:5). His commandments are easy (Matt. 11:28-30; 1 John 5:3) compared to the crushing load of sin. Gaining the acceptance of most in modern society is virtually impossible. Its standards for measuring success are often off base. Frequently, our culture creates a celebrity, and then ultimately destroys that same person just as fast without ever giving any unconditional love or acceptance. There is more than one definition of worldliness. Christians often think of worldliness as various common sins, but a false standard for success and pleasing people above God also is a form of worldliness.

[2] My experience with high school track illustrates. I knew my parents loved me unconditionally. Therefore, I felt secure enough to try athletics though

Children should be taught their motivation for achievement should be to please and honor God (or even please parents) but never from any need to earn love from either God or parents. This type of heart, with an honest and faithful effort, is in itself a success by godly definition, regardless of the objective level of actual skill or performance. The Bible gives the true standard for success stressing character and relationship to God. If societal ways of measuring excellence arise from pride and seeking status independently from God, they do not amount to a true success even if the world judges the performance with high marks.

Parents should approve achievement that arises from a godly heart. However, the love of father and mother must never become something that is earned (or lost!) by performance. It is possible to convey unconditional love to children and teach true standards for measuring success and still tell children that achievement pleases moms and dads. Good parents want performance but will always love limited, imperfect, failing and even sinful children.

Child Support

God requires parents to provide materially for their children's needs. This obligation does not seem to be universally acknowledged in the world as a whole. However, the Bible expects that even non-Christians know enough to be responsible for their children. Among Christians there is perhaps a greater danger of going to the other extreme and giving too much to the children. It is helpful to remember that need and unfulfilled desire can be a basis to teach gratitude and work ethics. Parents must support children, but we do them no favor by spoiling them.

---

without natural ability. Over four years I lost every race against the Michigan high school record holder for the mile run. In the process I set two high school track records, but far more important was the development of a tenacious character that will endure for life. Suppose my parents had based love on a performance basis. Perhaps I would have feared to try, and maybe this would have carried over into fear of trying difficult things in academics or Christian leadership. Unconditional love by parents, not based on achievement, may actually result in achievement.

But if any one does not provide for his own, and especially for those of his household, he has denied the faith, and is worse than an unbeliever [1 Tim. 5:8].

... for children are not responsible to save up for their parents but parents for their children [2 Cor. 12:14b].

Teach the Children Well

The frequency with which the Bible gives teaching responsibility to parents or details parental example is amazing: Gen. 18:19; Ex. 10:2, 12:26ff., 13:8,14; Deut. 4:9, 6:6-9, 11:18-20; Judges 2:10; Prov. 1:8, 2:1-2, 3:1-2, 4:1-4, 10, 5:1-2, 7:1-2, 24, 8:32-33, 12:1, 13:1, 22:6; Luke 2:52; Eph. 6:4; 1 Thess. 2:11; 2 Tim. 1:5, 3:15.

God called Abraham in part so that he would "command his children and his household after him to keep the way of the Lord" (Gen. 18:19). Moses in Exodus and Deuteronomy commands parents to make God known to their children and grandchildren continually. [3]

These words, which I am commanding you today, shall be on your heart. You shall teach them diligently to your sons and shall talk of them when you sit in your house and when you walk by the way and when you lie down and when you rise up [Deut. 6:6-7].

Despite such commands and warnings it took just one generation of failure for another generation to arise that did not know God (Judges 2:10). Disobedience in the matter of parents teaching children can lead to temporal and eternal disaster. The Proverbs give many pleas by a father for a son to heed the father's and mother's

---

[3] Moses' own biological mother became his nurse to raise him on behalf of Pharaoh's daughter. She must have taught Moses well in childhood for as a man Moses chose downtrodden Israel over the power and luxuries of Egypt (Ex. 2:1-10; Heb. 11:24-28). Daniel must also be an example of early training by parents. As a youth, he refused to eat meat sacrificed to idols. This choice was right and beneficial but risked possible insult to his Babylonian captors. Only diligent teaching at an early age explains Daniel's dedication to God (Daniel 1).

instruction (see above list). The most familiar text among them gives hope, "Train up a child in the way he should go, even when he is old he will not depart from it" (Prov. 22:6).

Paul commanded fathers to "bring them (children) up in the discipline and instruction of the Lord" (Eph. 6:4). He also mentioned Timothy's mother and grandmother as praiseworthy models for teaching Timothy in childhood. "And that from childhood you have known the sacred writings which are able to give you the wisdom that leads to salvation through faith which is in Christ Jesus (2 Tim. 3:15, see also: 2 Tim 1:5 which credits Timothy's good background to his mother and grandmother).

Both Samuel (1 Sam. 1:11, 24-28, 2:11, 18, 3:1) and the Lord Jesus (Luke 2:21-24) were dedicated by parents to God in their infancy. Whether in public and formal or private and informal settings, parents should dedicate themselves to raising children to trust Christ as Savior and serve God. The old adage "you can't take it with you" is true of material possessions, but humans have eternal souls. Children who trust in Christ as Savior will be in an eternal relationship with God **and believing parents**. The most basic parental instruction is to teach "wisdom that leads to salvation through faith which is in Christ Jesus"(2 Tim. 3:15). The essential truths in Christianity are the Trinity (One God in three Persons, Father, Son, and Holy Spirit), the Virgin birth and Deity of the Lord Jesus Christ, His death on the cross for our sins, His resurrection and Second Coming, the existence of heaven and hell, the authority of the Bible as God's Word, and the need to place faith in Christ as Savior. In addition to basic doctrines, parents should instill basic morality including, the sanctity of life, marriage, and God's commandments.[4] Given the hostility in our world to the things of Christ, instruction on apologetics also helps (intelligent design in creation, fulfilled Messianic prophecy as evidence the Bible is true, and historical/archaeological proofs for the Bible's trustworthiness).[5]

---

[4] Nine of the Ten Commandments are repeated in the New Testament. We no longer need to worship on Saturday but are still commanded to assemble for worship (Heb. 10:25).

[5] Chapter 13 gives some information defending the trustworthiness of the Bible. Deeper research on apologetics is beyond the scope of this book.

Sometimes secular articles may give insight into child rearing. However, when the philosophy of the world clashes with the Bible, it is wrong and probably dangerous. "See to it that no one takes you captive through philosophy and empty deception, according to the tradition of men ..." (Col. 2:8). Vital truths for teaching children are in the Bible which gives everything needed for life and godliness (2 Pet. 1:3), makes us equipped for every good work, including raising families, (2 Tim. 3:17) and gives sufficiency for wisdom and life (Col. 2:3,10; 2 Cor. 3:5-6; Phil. 4:13). Some aspects to child rearing not in the Bible are matters of common sense or the wisdom of previous generations (naptime, manners, potty training). Not everything advised by secular experts need be rejected as foolish. However, all the points that are vital and true are either already in the Bible or matters of common sense. 1 Cor. 3:11 concerns the local church but applies to a family. This verse asserts there is no other foundation than Christ (see also Matt. 7:24-28).

Ways of Instructing Children: Example

Parents teach by example, by informal instruction through conversation, by formal devotions and lessons, and by involvement in children's ministries. All these methods are important.

Parents constantly instruct their children by example. Unspiritual parents can unknowingly teach their children about complaining, backbiting, slander, lust, cheating, anxiety, unhappiness, etc. Parents who never admit to mistakes might also rear children who always feel they are right. Parents who must have their own way in everything might also rear children with similar expectations. It is ironic that some parents wonder why their older children no longer attend church. If children hear talk of joy in the Christian life and yet listen to their parents incessantly grumble about the miseries of life or the defects in the local church, then it should not be too surprising that they obtain a negative view of Christianity and churches. If these same parents are materialistic, it is even easier to understand why the children reject Christian values. If a home school mother who teaches Sunday School later commits adultery, gets an abortion to cover it up and divorces her husband, all her teaching is worthless. Example makes a deep impression.

Children will tend to adopt parental values and lifestyles. If parents are giving, kind, pure, persistent and disciplined, punctual, honest, dependable, appreciative, courteous, and concerned about others, they tend to instill these traits in their children. It is difficult for a non-motivated parent to teach a child to be persistent in finishing tasks. It is hard for a spendthrift to teach stewardship, for a tardy person to teach punctuality, or for an unethical father to teach morals, or for a cold-hearted mother to teach about Christian love for others. Parents do not need to be perfect, but they should realize that consistency and credibility are among the best teaching tools, and more importantly are required by God. Wise parents will want their children to observe them in prayer (including prayers for the children), Bible study, acts of charity and/or outreach, and service in the church. It is also instructive to have parents admit mistakes and sins when they occur, and for the parents to express affection for each other in front of the children.

God is a Heavenly Father. If children have good parents for a model, they will find it easier to relate to the God of the Bible. If their own parents are unlike God, they will have a harder time understanding God or even desiring a relationship with Him.

A story goes that someone asked which translation of the Bible is the best. The answer was, "my mother's translation." She lived it. Examples of honesty, generosity, service in the local church and fidelity/love in marriage will influence deeply and must accompany verbal teaching. The main purpose for God creating the family seems to be a deeper experience of His character. Parents will only imperfectly reflect God's attributes. They cannot measure up to God's infinite degree of perfection but must at least live in the direction of godliness. Children need to see the admiration and imitation of God in their parents even before reading about God's nature in the Bible.

Ways of Teaching Children: Conversation

Life presents teachable moments. If parents have the presence of mind to realize and use such occasions, they will increase the chance of a child understanding and retaining truth. It is probably true that most effective instruction can be done informally and can occur in the normal course of life's activities. Whenever a Christian teaching applies to a situation a child faces, wise parents will teach the Christian perspective. A young person's life is full of opportunities for the application of Christian beliefs and behavior. There are many moral choices. Times of fear, sickness or need provide occasions to teach faith, prayer, and the attributes of God. Times of prosperity and blessing give occasions to teach gratitude. Confrontations with death can be the ideal situation in which to teach about eternal life. Holidays should be used to celebrate Christian truths. Parents should in general be continually thinking about how the Christian faith applies to their children's experiences.

The Bible envisions that often instruction for children will not occur in a classroom or formal lesson period. Parent-child discussions take place along the road, at home, morning to night. Instruction can take place even in home décor with Christian symbols and Bible verses (see Deut. 6:6-9 and 11:18-20) and in the explanation for holidays such as Christmas and Easter.

Ways of Teaching Children: Formal Studies

Modern times bring animated and visual instruction for children. Children should be exposed to memorable music, poetry, and particularly books of a spiritual tone. Examples of the latter might be a book that goes through the alphabet with a Bible verse for each letter. Another might include the beatitudes or Ten Commandments. Even in a media-filled world small children still love to read with a personal parental presence. Books appropriate to children's age level allow for instruction in the Bible with a graduation to actual Bible reading from an easy-to-understand translation. Other ideas would include a bulletin board with missionary prayer cards; an excellent opportunity to learn geography. A prayer book with pictures of relatives, the local church, the flag, the school, and so forth can be used as an aid to prayer. Beyond the Bible itself, books on creation science (see page 147, footnote 7), Christian biographies, and exposure to traveling students and missionaries can be helpful in instruction. We must remember that Christian instruction also involves limiting exposure to false teaching and evil through television, the Internet, or printed material.

The Bible gives primary responsibility for teaching to parents. However, it requires parents to assemble in a local church (Heb. 10:25) and gives pastors responsibility to equip all for ministry (Eph. 4:11-12). Wise parents will view a local church as reinforcing their own efforts to teach children. If a church no longer teaches the Scriptures, parents should find one that does. Children need relationships with people their own age for a good kind of peer pressure. They also need to have older church family "uncles," and "aunts," and "grandparents" to endorse parental example and instruction. It helps them to see the true scope and size of Christianity and, thus, its importance. Sometimes children grow inattentive to parents, and the same truth taught by others in a church will gain acceptance. Parents should teach about God by all means: personal example, conversations, formal lessons at home, and involvement in a church, including its children's ministries.

Parental Discipline as Love

Someone has said that "discipline without love equals cruelty" but that "love without discipline" is not love at all. Discipline without unconditional love will lead to crushed, bitter, angry children. "Love" without discipline is love misdefined because children will become spoiled and reckless with life. Such may also develop anger for a different reason. Their parents did not care enough to take the responsibility of setting safe and beneficial limits for behavior. Solomon, the author of Hebrews, and the Apostle Paul teach that God's discipline is an aspect of His love for us. Discipline means God cares enough to control us from harming, maybe even destroying ourselves by foolish sin. God is the example of ideal parenting.

My son, do not reject the discipline of the LORD or loathe His reproof, for whom the LORD loves He reproves, even as a father corrects the son in whom he delights [Prov. 3:11-12].

111

You have not yet resisted to the point of shedding blood in your striving against sin; and you have forgotten the exhortation which is addressed to you as sons, "My son, do not regard lightly the discipline of the LORD, nor faint when you are reproved by Him; for those whom the LORD loves He disciplines, and He scourges every son whom he receives." It is for discipline that you endure; God deals with you as with sons; for what son is there whom his father does not discipline? But if you are without discipline, of which all have become partakers, then you are illegitimate children and not sons. Furthermore, we had earthly fathers to discipline us, and we respected them; shall we not much rather be subject to the Father of spirits, and live? For they disciplined us for a short time as seemed best to them, but He disciplines us for our good, so that we may share His holiness. All discipline for the moment seems not to be joyful, but sorrowful; yet to those who have been trained by it, afterwards it yields the peaceful fruit of righteousness [Heb. 12:4-11].

Those whom I love, I reprove and discipline; therefore be zealous and repent [Rev. 3:19].

We should adopt the attitude that discipline is an act of love. It is never loving to condone sin. God loves us. Yet, He does not approve of any wrongdoing, and He will Himself exercise discipline. It is ultimately in our own best interest that He disciplines us. Likewise, we are not doing children any favor or expressing love to them by allowing sin to go uncontrolled and unchallenged. The end results can be so disastrous that a loving parent will gladly endure the unpleasant aspects of discipline in order to spare children from the tragic consequences of sin.

The old adage "an ounce of prevention is worth a pound of cure" is applicable. It will help if discipline is viewed as something done for a child - not something done to a child. The purpose is not to cause pain but to promote safety and righteousness. Does the approach which leads to righteousness or the approach that leads to misery from sin exhibit more parental love? God says, "**Those whom I love, I reprove and discipline** ..." (Rev. 3:19).

The absence of discipline can create insecurity and ultimately disrespect in children. They need guidance, and initially they know it. The limitations imposed by parental discipline cause security and actually give a sense of freedom to develop within "safe" parental boundaries of behavior. One "bright" psychologist thought that fences around playgrounds inhibited the freedom of small children. When they were removed, the children huddled in the middle of the playground because they did not know the limitations of safety and wisdom; and therefore, were insecure and fearful to explore. Without any discipline and direction, children can react initially with fear, then frustration, and then eventually disrespect toward parents. Why should they respect parents who do not seem to know or care enough to guide?

If discipline is an expression of love, it is just as much an expression of faith. Parents discipline not because it emotionally feels good, but rather because they believe in God's wisdom for the home. He tells us what is wise and best. It is an expression of faith to follow His leading.

The order of material in this chapter reflects the conclusion that unconditional love must precede discipline and that caring enough to protect a child from evil is part of the definition of love.

Corporeal Discipline in the Bible: Interpretation and Application

All who have read the Proverbs know that it contains references to corporeal discipline. The derived English proverb is "spare the rod, spoil the child." Here are the actual verses:

He who withholds his rod hates his son, but he who loves him disciplines him diligently [Prov. 13:24].

Discipline your son while there is hope, and do not desire his death [Prov. 19:18].

Foolishness is bound up in the heart of a child; the rod of discipline will remove it far from him [Prov. 22:15].

Do not hold back discipline from the child. Although you strike him with the rod, he will not die [Prov. 23:13].

The rod and reproof give wisdom, but a child who gets his own way brings shame to his mother [Prov. 29:15].

Correct your son, and he will give you comfort; He will also delight your soul [Prov. 29:17].

There are two ways to interpret these teachings from Proverbs. However, the applied result to modern families comes out the same with either view. In Prov. 1:10ff. Solomon warns his son not to associate with murderers and thieves. Later on in the book he frequently warns about the consequences of immorality (e.g. Prov. 2:16, 5:1-6, 6:23-35, 7:6ff, 23:26-28). He also speaks on various other points that seem to concern young adults (e.g. co-signing for a loan, Prov. 6:1ff; work ethics, Prov. 10:1-5). Thus, a case can be made that the statements in Proverbs concern the discipline of a man who is an adolescent or young adult. The rod can be likened to a form of punishment for extremely deviant, even criminal behavior. This is similar to Paul and Silas being beaten with rods and thrown into prison (Acts 16:22). Solomon tells fathers not to worry about sons dying from a beating (Prov. 23:13).

Perhaps Proverbs is not at all concentrating on discipline for small children. It rather concerns the more serious sins of the wayward prodigal. In a strict interpretation Solomon probably refers to very severe punishment for the equivalent of criminal behavior. The nation of Singapore has beaten with canes those convicted on drug charges. Perhaps the words in Proverbs refer to a similar punishment for sins that are virtually crimes.

This interpretation of Proverbs would still recognize that basic applications can be made from Proverbs to parental discipline of small children, i.e. spankings. The Bible gives the principle of corporeal discipline being a God-approved and effective means of discipline.

However, the common view of Proverbs is also very much a viable option. Perhaps even though Solomon warns against sins of older children, he is speaking to a younger child who must be warned against future temptations. The sins may be those committed by teenage children or young adults, but Solomon may be speaking to smaller children to prepare them for adolescence. Also, the rod could obviously have different applications. It could speak of a severe beating that would be administered to young adult criminals but also have a range of meaning broad enough to cover swats to a toddler.

The practical difference is negligible in the two approaches to the precise interpretation of Proverbs. If Solomon is speaking to teenagers and the rod speaks of severe criminal punishment, then the principle of corporeal punishment for younger children would still be established (though, of course, not to the same severity as the adult child engaged in criminal behavior). On the other hand, if Solomon is speaking to a small child and the rod refers to spanking and not beatings; then the principle for corporeal discipline for kids is even more clearly established. Prov. 22:6 can be paraphrased to say, "Train up a child according to the way that is best appropriate for him." Thus, both views of Proverbs establish the basic principle of corporeal discipline. Both views would contend that such discipline should be administered with a reflection upon the age and temperament (natural bent) of the individual child.

In its context Proverbs warns of major sins (joining a gang, visiting prostitutes, stealing, violence). Thus, one must apply the principle of corporeal discipline differently to small children whose sins need correction but hardly are the deep sins actually mentioned in the book. The proper level of corporeal discipline is the least amount needed to change the behavior.[6] Given the actual sins in the context, one may not use Proverbs to justify beating small children with canes or whips to a degree short of death! Pre-schoolers and elementary children as a rule do not commit the types of sins under consideration in the Proverbs. Thus, the Proverbs approve the use of corporeal

---

[6] The purpose of discipline is to train not to harm. Therefore, Christian parents should try to refrain from outbursts of anger and frustration that result in a punishment far out of proportion to the wrong behavior. The proper amount of pain is the amount that causes a forsaking of the behavior. Cruelty will result in resentment, not maturity. Discipline should be fair and in proportion to the degree of wrongdoing.

discipline, but it must be applied wisely (less severely) to small children with lesser sins.

God allows parents discretion on the application of discipline. Scripture gives a general principle but not detailed instructions. Given the commands "do not exasperate your children so that they will not lose heart" (Col. 3:21) and "do not provoke your children to anger" (Eph. 6:4), there is a middle ground between never employing corporeal discipline and using it constantly for every sin or mistake in life.

In our home, we chose danger and the Ten Commandments as general guidelines for the use of corporeal discipline. Dangerous behavior simply must not be repeated. A child may not put hands under the lawn mower, reach up to a pot of boiling water on the stove, consume pills from the medicine cabinet, or run off to the edge while strolling on a pier. With corporeal discipline a given behavior ended after the first infraction.

In addition to danger, we simply would not tolerate lying, stealing, or the attitude of defiance to parents. Long-term parental concession to lying, stealing, and defiance would have allowed habits that destroy children. Such commandments as prohibition of stealing, lying, and dishonor to parents really involve enforcement of God's standards, not just parental preferences.

Children must honor their parents. A child should be able to communicate anything including views that parents have made mistakes. However, they must do so with a tone of respect, not defiance. During the pre-school years, each of our children hit us in a tantrum about being buckled into a car seat. Though this "violence" caused no harm, we reasoned that if such were tolerated, the long-term effect would be a first-rate discipline problem. Therefore, we established a no-tolerance policy of the children hitting their parents. Through the use of corporeal discipline for this offense the attempt was tried once, but never again. Parents are not perfect, but tolerating defiance in children brings harm to them.

Readers will develop their own family policies on corporeal discipline. Balance is in order. The Proverbs clearly teach a general principle of its value, but the situations in the original context are far more serious than splashing water over the edge of a tub or forgetting toys in the backyard before it rains. Long-suffering and mercy are also godly characteristics. Somewhere between never spanking and always spanking is parental wisdom. Danger and the Ten Commandments give prudent guidelines for nipping attitudes and actions that bring grief later in life if not prevented in childhood. Even with corporeal discipline we all raise children with sin natures. In our experience, few applications of spanking were necessary. It virtually stopped the worst behaviors early in life.

While on a trip with a college professor, I observed his parental dealings with his eight-year-old son. Whenever the boy behaved well or gave an intelligent remark, he was praised (positive reinforcement). This excellent habit follows God the Father's example with all of us.[7]

When the boy engaged in questionable behavior, he received warning of future corporeal discipline if there was another occurrence. Since the purpose of child discipline is teaching (not venting anger or pain) instruction before discipline is wise, especially

---

[7] God uses positive reinforcement with His children. Salvation is never earned nor deserved. God's endless love has no conditions. We are forgiven through faith by God's grace. Yet, our Heavenly Father praises and rewards good behavior and diligent service. Heaven itself is not earned, but rewards (crowns, positions of service, and probably even the level of glory in the resurrection body) will come from behavior. Even in this life God gives earthly praises and earthly rewards which reinforce good behavior.

Parents should follow God's example of reinforcement for good behavior. Children should not have to misbehave to obtain their parent's attention. Often verbal praise alone is sufficient to ensure the repetition of good behavior. Sometimes a tangible reward may be appropriate, but the main reward should simply be the happiness of fathers and mothers.

We need also to mention that it can be easy to reinforce negative behavior that might be amusing. If we laugh at a food fight, we might have another food fight. Parents will want to avoid reinforcing bad behaviors by words and extra attention.

117

if the given behavior has never occurred before or rarely occurs.[8] A preventative warning gives instruction and also tests submission or defiance.

The one time the college professor used corporeal discipline he sandwiched it between before-and-after reassurances of unconditional love and forgiveness and also gave instruction both before and after the discipline.[9] His son clearly knew how to correct his misbehavior and that his father accepted him as a person even if he did not accept a given behavior.

Every home and even every situation varies, but a combination of positive reinforcement, warnings with instruction (especially upon the first occurrence), discipline (for danger and Ten Commandment issues), and discipline always followed by repeated instructions and expressions of unconditional love, seems to give prudent policies that others may consider.

Additional Angles to Child-rearing

Both parents should enforce their standards and application of discipline. Commonly, a child will appeal to the parent who most yields to the child's desires. Sometimes it may be father. Sometimes it may be mother. Children should not be allowed a "favorite" parent

---

[8] God as Father has certainly given teaching as to His expectations for His children. Earthly fathers and mothers should make every effort to explain a wrong so that a child remembers and knows what is expected.

[9] God in His role as Father gives assurances of forgiveness (Prov. 28:13; Matt. 6:9, 12; 1 John 1:9). Children should fear wrongdoing but never fear mistreatment or loss of parental love. Parents should direct anger at bad behavior more than the person. The focus should be upon the issue of wrong rather than humiliating the person by name-calling or embarrassing tactics. Verbal cut-downs end up eliciting anger, not respect. Parents should not ridicule or make fun of weakness. It is best to discipline in private and not to discipline unnecessarily before a child's friends. (This does not eliminate discipline for misbehaviors that occur in a public place. Most would advise the child be promptly disciplined in a private spot within the public place or taken home.)

who is lenient and a "mean" parent who gets stuck with all the dirty work of discipline.[10]

Also, it is not wise to compare children with each other: "Why can't you get good grades like your sister?" God's standards are ultimately the measure for excellence, not a sibling's performance. Each can measure self against past behaviors and God's commandments (see 2 Cor. 10:12; Gal. 6:4-5 NIV). In non-moral issues the standard of achievement should be the child's own full potential and progress compared to that child's own past level, not whether a sibling can play the piano better. Measurement of progress should be individual, not competitive. Parental comparison of children may foster a superior feeling in one child and resentment in another. Rivalry to get parental love is unhealthy. The Bible alone gives the measure of excellence. We do not need to put that burden on another child in the family by making him or her the comparison.

The Bible tells us to keep our promises (Deut. 23:21-23; Eccles. 5:4-5; Matt. 5:33 and 37; James 5:12). This means parents should make realistic promises to children and honor them. Regarding discipline, this principle means parents should follow through on any warnings about punishment for misbehavior. If a child is undeniably guilty and parents have threatened discipline, they had better keep their "promise" to act, or they risk losing credibility. If parents frequently back off from discipline, children become skilled at manipulation.

Finally, if corporeal discipline occurs at all, it should take place soon after the infraction in order to increase the learning potential and reduce expectation of "getting away with it." Eccles. 8:11 says, "Because the sentence of an evil deed is not executed quickly, therefore the hearts of the sons of men among them are fully

---

[10] Parents should not discipline their children just to meet the supposed expectations of peers who are also raising children. Keeping up appearances is not a cause for different standards of right and wrong or acceptable and unacceptable behavior. This may be a good time to include the reminder that grandparents have wisdom and honor (Lev. 19:32; Prov. 17:6), but not complete control over how their adult children raise the grandchildren (see Gen. 2:24, where marriage involves independence from father and mother).

given to evil." This statement refers to crimes and punishment by the courts but can apply to families. Any discipline should occur soon after wrongdoing. If it does not, a small child may forget the actual infraction. He or she may not learn as deeply the nature of the infraction and view parents as being mean for no reason. The purpose of discipline is to teach and correct harmful behavior.[11] The Bible teaches corporeal discipline for children but prohibits harshness in its application. Tenderness should exist between father/mother and children. Parents who love their children will discipline them, but children should "fear" parents only in the sense of respect not in the sense of feeling threatened. A father once made a comparison of training children to training guard dogs. He wanted both to fear the master. These are definitely not the conditions Christian parents should create in the home. Sufficient discipline to alter harmful behavior is the proper frequency and amount. The goal is not the most discipline possible. The goal is to raise children who trust, love, and serve God and who value their parents when they are grown. God's Word teaches child discipline but also gives boundaries.

Encouragement

The same truth can be phrased positively or negatively. Either way can be beneficial. Children are baby humans, and all humans need massive doses of encouragement. Verbal and even corporeal discipline is actually one aspect of "encouragement" to do better. Praising children for ethically good behavior or for achievement follows God's own pattern of blessing His children when we do well. 1 Thess. 2:11-12 says, "... we were exhorting and

---

[11] In a world with some extremely depraved parents, it is possible for a parent to abuse authority. If a parent commands something that is obviously a sin, must the child obey? This is another situation when hierarchical ethics plays a role. When a believer is forced into a situation where two biblical commands cannot be followed at the same time, he should temporarily suspend the lesser in order to fulfill the greater. The scriptural injunction to obey parents is in itself a very high principle. Therefore, it should not be suspended lightly. However, "we ought to obey God rather than men" (Acts 5:29). Parental commands that ask children to break major commandments from God ought to be ignored. The Lord placed allegiance to Himself as a greater duty than to parents (see Matt. 10:37 and Luke 14:26).

encouraging and imploring each one of you as a father would his own children, so that you would walk in a manner worthy of ... God ..." (by application see 3 John 4).

God limits discipline that crosses the line of squashing children emotionally. The second part of Eph. 6:4 commands teaching and discipline. The first part commands, "Fathers, do not provoke your children to anger ...." The parallel text commands, "Fathers, do not exasperate your children, so that they will not lose heart" (Col. 3:21). What kinds of child-rearing habits could lead to grown children who are embittered, exasperated, or so discouraged they become indifferent to trying to please parents? These texts do not elaborate, but Bible stories and reflection on Bible truths give some ideas.

In Genesis 27 the father, Isaac, favored Esau. The mother, Rebekah, favored the twin brother, Jacob. This relationship led to trickery in the family. Favoritism of one child over others is one parental failure that could lead to resentment.

Unrealistic parental expectations could also discourage children as they try to meet the impossible, which can also be the unnecessary. **The most important factor in parenting is the admiration and imitation of God.** What standards are the parents trying to instill in their children? It is essential that parents know the virtues of God and the morals of the Bible *and that they acknowledge the biblical standard of excellence and maturity* not so much societal standards. God cares more about our character and beliefs than He does athletic skills, academic achievement, talents, number of college degrees, position, or status. The goal of discipline, therefore, ought to be godliness and Christian maturity. This may indeed involve great achievements, but it is an achievement that is a secondary effort to the main goal of parental discipline, *dedication to God and His Word.* God's Word itself does not require any child to be good at football, to score the top on the SAT, to become a CPA, lawyer, or doctor, to enjoy music or become famous. Parental demands for morality are essential and encouragement to obtain one's highest potential is good. Expectations and demands that go further may cause frustrations to the degree a child no longer cares to please parents (even in the important matters).

Additional aspects to discipline also cause potential for anger or discouragement in children. Inconsistent discipline (verbal or corporeal) can come in several ways. Inconsistent discipline is haphazard and spontaneous (without forethought). It occurs when each parent emphasizes a different standard of behavioral expectations, or when a given behavior is acceptable on one occasion but regarded as a serious wrong upon the next occurrence. Partiality overlaps with inconsistent discipline because it tolerates in one child what is forbidden in another. Any of these types of inconsistent discipline (again verbal or corporeal) would leave a child confused as to parental expectations causing potential anger and "loss of heart."

Another closely related source of frustration for children would be discipline without clear instruction as to the behavior that needs correction or without any expression of unconditional forgiveness and love. Discipline without rational instruction is pointless. Discipline without expression of forgiveness and unconditional love can lead to children giving up on trying to meet parental expectations. Children must know how to avoid disapproval in the future and that parental acceptance can never be lost by any misbehavior.

No doubt Paul has cruelty in mind when forbidding fathers to crush their children's hearts or cause bitterness. Parental authority exists to make choices in the best interest of children. The severity of discipline should be proportionate to the infraction. This means correction, verbal or corporeal, should never cause anything more than temporary pain and only to a sufficient degree to alter behavior. Temporary discomfort can prevent behavior trends that will become dangerous. Permanent scars, physical and/or emotional, are prohibited by the very command not to cause bitterness and discouragement (Eph. 6:4; Col. 3:21).

Finally, children should honor parents even if they are imperfect, but parents need to admit to being human. If we err or sin, it is better to make amends than to give the ridiculous impression of perfection. Children should be able to communicate their feelings as long as they so do with respect. Parents should at least be open to the possibility of having made a mistake. Otherwise, at some point children will be frustrated.[12]

Hope for faithful Mom and Dad

A father and mother cannot improve upon following God's wisdom for raising children. Parenting is a long-range endeavor. Galatians 6:9 is applicable, "Let us not lose heart in doing good, for in due time we will reap if we do not grow weary."

When parents attempt to live out the imitation of God's character traits, teach fundamental truths, discipline in a balanced way to alter damaging behavior, and avoid anything that causes children anger and disillusionment, then a good result can be expected. Either the children will personalize the heritage they received, or they will have Christian roots to which they can return. Personal choice ends up being the greatest factor in what a child becomes, but parental efforts have deep influence. Solomon observed the tendency that the training from a father and mother leaves a permanent impact on their child's life. "Train up a child in the way he should go, even when he is old he will not depart from it" (Prov. 22:6).

---

[12] A pastor gave his children a "free bad behavior" when he corrected them by mistake. By contrast my father always said, "that's for what you did when I wasn't looking." The pastor told me his children would hold on to their "free bad behavior" like a valued treasure. Not wanting to squander such fortune they tried to behave extra-well to keep their "free bad behavior" credit with dad. Still, my father's approach also worked - I later discovered his line was a quote from the Three Stooges and laugh every time I think about it.

Chapter Twelve

Preventing Family Conflicts: Healthy Emotions

The Ideal versus Reality

People seem to know instinctively that the family should be a major source of happiness. Advertisements present images of happy couples on a beach or families laughing together around a meal. Matchmaking services offer the opportunity for happiness that has long eluded the potential client. Music lyrics tell us love is the answer.

At the same time conversation abounds with marriage jokes. The ideal and reality clash. Both aspects are true. Marriage and the family should be a primary source of encouragement and joy. Yet, given human sin nature, relatives can also hurt each other deeply.

This study now moves to potential family conflicts regarding areas of emotions, money, and family communications/decision making. Before any study on dealing with each problem, there will be efforts to prevent the problem or at least build up strength of character to withstand inevitable problems.

Scripture supposes the common sense view that families bring joy. Grandparent/grandchild (Prov. 17:6), husband/wife (Prov. 5:18, Chapter 31; Eccles. 9:9; Isa. 62:5), parent/child (Prov. 23:15-16, 24-25, 29:3) relationships are a source of meaning and joy to life.

Many men need a wife (Gen. 2:18). Many women need a husband (Gen. 3:16). Children obviously need parents. Ideally, each relationship meets needs and gives blessings. Husband and wife are one. Children are also part of father and mother.

A good family is an essential aspect to emotional health, but is not emotional health itself one of the components of building a good family? Which comes first, individual emotional balance and strength creating a strong home; or a strong home bringing emotional health and balance? This question need not be answered. Both are desirable. We need personal spiritual/emotional health to strengthen the home. We need a strong family to support and bring joy to each family member. Ideally, both go together in an upward spiral of strength and blessing.

This topic does raise the point that the family alone divorced from a walk with God will not bring happiness. While marriage is the closest human relationship and meets needs (that even God Himself has chosen not to meet!), marriage and the family were never designed by God to meet all deep needs. If family relationships do not serve to deepen a walk with God, the best of relationships will not produce lasting emotional health and strength. Marriage, children, or extended family relationships alone cannot provide ultimate meaning.

Expectations from Marriage

Solomon's advice in Ecclesiastes was that the best life has to offer is to "enjoy life with the woman whom you love all the days of your fleeting life which He has given you under the sun; for this is your reward in life ..." (Eccles. 9:9). Yes, a good marriage is the best reward from God.

However, it is too much to expect that even the best husband, wife, parent, or child, can become one's "god." Even the dearest and most intimate relative cannot be a Savior or provide all meaning to life. Placing such false expectations upon a spouse, child, or parent is unrealistic and gives our loved one unnecessary stress. A husband or wife cannot be expected to be flawless or fulfill every need. Such expectations are not fair. Over time it inevitably yields disappointment because no human can replace God. Family relationships will not bring the joy God intends unless those relationships are part of a united quest to seek God. God ordained marriage to deepen our experience of His own character traits. Marriage itself is not a god who meets all needs. Limited interest in God brings limited joy and satisfaction with marriage and the family. The best outcome can only take place when a couple (or the entire family) draws close to God. The Bible does teach family relationships are a reward and blessing but as part of a larger experience in life when God Himself is the ultimate source of joy and meaning. The family becomes a source of joy only as it realizes and follows its greater purpose of fellowship with God. Both the purpose for marriage and the family and the process of making a strong family lead back to the **admiration and imitation of the Almighty**.

Joy Comes From Our Attitude towards God

The command "You shall have no other gods before me" (Ex. 20:3) prohibits the expectation that another can fill the role of God in our life, giving all sufficiency for meaning and joy. With such expectations we set up even the best husbands, wives, or children to become a disappointment and failure. If a husband, wife, or child is placed in the role of god and savior, he or she will eventually grow frustrated with such unreasonable demands.[1] Often engaged couples dreaming of marriage place each other in the substitute god role only to discover that marriage, even to a first class husband or wife, is still marriage to a human being.

God alone is the source of joy and meaning. Those who are spiritually strong, and thus emotionally healthy before marriage, make superior spouses (and then parents). When God is our God, then we can view family as a blessing from Him and another major contribution to strength and joy. Joy comes first from God. Then the family gives additional emotional blessings. God's Word presents God alone as God not anything or **anyone** else.

The LORD is my strength and song, and He has become my salvation; this is my God, and I will praise Him; My father's

---

[1] Jeremiah's false expectations concerned his "career," i.e. ministry. He perhaps thought it would lead to a revival or at least be more rewarding. Jeremiah 20:7-9 displays two problems resulting from Jeremiah's expectation that being a prophet would be easier. He gets angry with God (v.7) and is tempted to quit (v. 9). Preaching the Word of God brought him derision and not national revivals.

In marriage, false expectations can also lead to anger and a temptation to quit. Realistically, a family can be the greatest reward in this life but not without hard work. The best spouse or children can not replace God. All are human, and all are sinners.

Jeremiah overcame his problem by three sources of contentment. The same ideals will help everyone. Hope in a perfect God (Jer. 9:23-24), a perfect Word of God (Jer. 15:16), and the call of God on his life (Jer. 20:9, v. 11, also God's presence) gave Jeremiah good emotions even in bad times.

God, and I will extol Him. [Ex. 15:2 (see also: Psa. 118:14; Isa. 12:2)].

Do not be grieved, for the joy of the LORD is your strength [Neh. 8:10b].

The LORD is my strength and my shield; my heart trusts in Him, and I am helped; therefore my heart exults, and with my song I shall thank Him [Psa. 28:7].

And my soul shall rejoice in the LORD; it shall exult in His salvation [Psa. 35:9].

Then I will go to the altar of God, to God my exceeding joy…[Psa. 43:4].

Let my meditation be pleasing to Him; as for me, I shall be glad in the LORD [Psa. 104:34].

Let them also offer sacrifices of thanksgiving, and tell of His works with joyful singing [Psa. 107:22].

Thou wilt keep him in perfect peace, whose mind is stayed on thee: because he trusteth in thee [Isa. 26:3 (KJV)].

I will rejoice greatly in the LORD, My soul will exult in my God; For He has clothed me with garments of salvation, He has wrapped me with a robe of righteousness, as a bridegroom decks himself with a garland, and as a bride adorns herself with her jewels [Isa. 61:10].

Thus says the LORD, "Let not a wise man boast of his wisdom, and let not the mighty man boast of his might, let not a rich man boast of his riches; but let him who boasts boast of this, that he understands and knows Me, that I am the LORD who exercises lovingkindness, justice and righteousness on earth; for I delight in these things," declares the LORD [Jer. 9:23-24].

Yet I will exult in the LORD, I will rejoice in the God of my salvation [Hab. 3:18].

But may it never be that I would boast, except in the cross of our Lord Jesus Christ, through which the world has been crucified to me, and I to the world [Gal. 6:14].

Finally, my brethren, rejoice in the Lord [Phil. 3:1a].

Rejoice in the Lord always; again I will say, rejoice! [Phil. 4:4].[2]

God alone must be our ideal. God alone must be our source of contentment and meaning in life. Our spouse, children, siblings, and others in the family do have responsibilities and do bring blessings, but they cannot be expected to be perfect or fulfill all needs. If God is God in life, then a long list of other relationships and achievements, and even possessions assist in bringing joy. If God is not God in one's heart, the same list of blessings becomes frustrations as they cannot give ultimate joy or meet all needs. Even good aspects of life that are not sin cannot bring joy if we regard them as the ultimate good. Solomon found everything "under the sun" (i.e. leaving God out of the picture) to be meaningless (Ecclesiastes 2). Money, sex within marriage, careers, friends, comedy, music, advanced education, travel, sports, church involvement, etc. are not evil, but they are not "god" either.[3] If subordinated to the true God and exercised under His authority, these aspects of life do increase joy. Nevertheless, if they arise from a life

---

[2] Joy also comes from the Bible, which reveals God's wonderful attributes (Psa. 19:8; 119:14, 162; Jer. 15:16; truth brings joy 1 Cor. 13:6, as does wisdom from the Bible that makes one a wise counselor, Prov. 15:23).

[3] All good things in life come from God (James 1:17). Not everything in this world is bad, but all things that arise from the world alone are bad. Every good aspect to life can be traced to an origin in God. Every intrinsic good is also eternal and, therefore, far more important than temporary material possessions or experiences. God Himself, the Word of God, the Church universal, and the souls of people will endure forever. The eternal and the good give primary meaning to life. God and His Word always have been perfect. The souls of our loved ones and the Church (all believers) will become perfect. Attention in life upon these priorities allows secondary blessings even from other lesser activities and possessions. Neglect of the good and eternal brings a frustrated life and damaged emotions, which in turn drags down families.

that rejects God, or we foolishly try to turn them into our god, then we will end in the same pessimism as Solomon in Ecclesiastes.

A husband or wife can fulfill needs that God intended a husband and wife to meet (it is completely amazing that God created us with any needs beyond Himself). A spouse and those in other relationships can greatly contribute to happiness, but they cannot alone meet all needs or bring all joy. The best a family can do if God is neglected will still fall short of God's intent. Our attitude should be that only God is God. Family members are rewards from God with a purpose of drawing each other closer to God as they together **admire and imitate Him**.

Emotional strength and health comes from our attitude toward God being the source of meaning and joy. It also comes from our own choices and behaviors. To be strong we must avoid sin and act in godly ways. Even if a sin is not directed against a family member, that sin may cause family problems. Even if acts of godliness are directed outside the home, they will help increase the strength in the home.

Joy and Avoiding Sin

In graduate school I observed an experienced counselor helping a couple with marriage counseling. The presenting problem was too much anger in the home. My first thought was giving the couple Bible verses concerning anger.

The counselor asked "Why are you angry?" The wife claimed the husband drank too much. My next thought was Bible verses on drinking. The counselor asked, "Why do you feel a need to drink?"

After probing several more levels came the revelation that the man had been cheating on his income tax for years. This led to guilt and constant anxiety about getting caught. This led to drinking to forget his worries and to disputes between husband and wife. The end was marriage counseling, but the beginning was tax fraud.

Even sins not directed against family members can still harm the family. Emotional well being in life, and thus in a family, is a function of a righteous life in general. The Bible teaches a main ingredient in the recipe for joy is the rejection of sin. "By transgression an evil man is ensnared, but the righteous sings and rejoices" (Prov. 29:6).

People in happy homes try to avoid willful sins. The result is increased singing and rejoicing. The superior course would be never to sin in the first place, but there can be restoration for broken emotions by dealing with guilt.

By faith in the Lord Jesus Christ as Savior we have eternal forgiveness before God in His role as Judge. Then, as the children of God, we obtain cleansing from God as our Father by confession of sins as they occur. The Bible roots inner emotional health to the assurance of God's forgiveness. Blessedness, joy, gladness, and courage arise from confession of sin. (2 Chron. 7:14, 30:18, 26; Psa. 32:1-2, 51:12, 103:8-13; Prov. 28:13, 29:1; Zeph. 3:13-15; Matt. 6:12, 9:2, 26:28; Luke 11:4; 1 Cor. 11:32; 1 John 1:9; give an outline of the benefits from forgiveness through the confession of sins to the Father.)

Individual spiritual strength and health improves family strength and health. Of course, just as health partly comes negatively from the avoidance of sin's poison, spiritual well being arises positively from godly actions.

Joy and Actions We Choose

A word study of "joy" in Scripture yields answers as to how to possess emotional health. From this method, one conclusion is that joy arises from one's attitude toward God as the source of joy. Next, joy increases by avoiding sin or obtaining forgiveness after any sin. Many Bible verses also teach that joy comes from our own actions. Some of these actions are spiritual discipline and habits. Some are matters of Christian ministry for others.

Our emotions improve with spiritual growth within our own hearts. Healthy emotions also increase as we work at worthy and meaningful aspects to Christian service. These contributions to emotional adjustment and well being also improve the emotional atmosphere within the entire family.

Additional Bible study would be valuable in proving the connection between actions (both internal spirituality and external deeds) in bringing joy to life and then into the family. The topics and verses listed below complete our abbreviated study on the causes of joy in the Bible, but the texts in the footnotes would help with deeper research. [4]

God Himself is the source of contentment and joy in life. He is the ideal. Without an attitude focused on Him, we find defects and dissatisfaction in anything and everyone else including relatives. Yet, if God becomes our first source of joy, contentment, and meaning, then a spouse, children, and other relatives can be viewed as blessings despite their flawed humanity. Next, we will increase joy by avoidance of sin or confession of sin. Finally, our spiritual actions both within our soul and in external ministry to others improves individual well-being and also improves family well-being.

The greatest threats to the family are not television or secular education, or politics. The greatest threats are neglecting God and our own spiritual growth. His authority gives wisdom for strong families. **The admiration and imitation of God Himself is the purpose for marriage and the family**. Without attention upon God, any family distant from God will become weak. Treachery to God within an individual results in the greatest danger to homes. With spiritual strength comes emotional strength. "Watch over your heart with all

---

[4] Joy comes from faith (Psa. 13:5; Rom. 15:13; Phil. 1:25), from love for God (Psa. 5:11), from seeking God (Psa. 40:16, 70:4, 105:3), from praise/prayer (Psa. 71:23; Isa. 56:7; John 16:24), from hope in God's truth and promises (Isa. 35:10; Acts 2:26-27; Rom. 5:2; 1 Pet. 4:13; 1 Thess. 4:13). These are spiritual actions within each person though families can share them. Joy also comes from serving God in ministry: evangelism and/or verbal testimony (Psa. 107:22; Isa. 52:7-9; Matt. 18:13; John 4:36; Phil. 1:18), God's work in general (Psa. 126:5-6; Acts 20:24; Gal. 6:4; 2 Tim. 4:7), even suffering for God (Matt. 5:12; Luke 6:23; Acts 5:41; 1 Pet. 1:7-8, 4:13; James 1:2), religious holidays and feasts (Lev. 23:40; Deut. 12:7,12,18, 14:26, 16:11,14 [by application to Christian observances]). By spiritual actions we can influence happiness in life and in turn family happiness.

diligence, for from it flows the springs of life" (Prov. 4:23, see also: Mal. 2:15-16 for the repeated warning, "… take heed to your spirit"). [5]

With emotional strength family strength follows. With a spiritual and emotional strength some family problems never arise. Other inevitable problems will be easier to manage.

Addendum to Spiritual/Emotional Strength

God often teaches us the same truths in different ways. The above material was developed by searching the word *joy* and probing for the sources of joy. We would arrive essentially at the same result by doing biblical word studies on *gladness, strength, hope,* and *peace* (Hebrew, *shalom* often means inner well-being), and we could also follow the words *favor, praise* or *singing* in the Bible to look for ways to increase God's favor and our level of rejoicing. The results from additional angles would still be that emotional health and strength comes from our attitude toward God, our avoidance of sin, and our spiritual actions.

A brief study on biblical priorities in life will reinforce that spiritual strength is foundational to marital and family strength. Misplaced or false priorities in life affect the family for the worse.

Each of us was created to worship God (Rom. 11:36; Rev. 4:11, 5:12-13). One Christmas season I watched people in an auditorium at a noted liberal university stand and sing the "Hallelujah Chorus." Whether these people were believers or not, they looked joyful because they were doing what humans are created to do, i.e. worship.[6]

---

[5] With strong hearts Noah and Elijah remained true to God even when surrounded by prevailing wickedness. The New Testament also tells us to watch ourselves (Matt. 26:41; 1 Cor.10:12; 1 Tim. 4:16a).

[6] Worship involves instruction (praise to God for discovery of great truths about God), admiration, humiliation (need and dependence upon God), contrition (confession of sin), celebration (the gap between a Holy God and sinful self has been bridged by God's grace), a sense of limitation (God is mysterious and awesome), dedication of life, contribution (giving), imitation of God, exaltation (we strive to advance, promote, and honor God), reception (we accept mercy and help in need).

Those who refuse to worship will never be satisfied with anything else because they deny the main purpose of life. Discontent and frustration lead to emotional problems, then to relational problems in the family. Exalting God must be a priority in life to have healthy emotions and a strong family.

In addition to the purpose of honoring God in worship, the process in life must be **the admiration and imitation of God** (Rom. 8:29, 12:1-2; 2 Cor. 3:18; Phil. 1:21, 3:8). Christianity is not totally introspective. We dwell on self enough to confess sin and then give priority in focus upon God. The imitation of God can only happen when one seeks God (Deut. 4:29; Isa. 55:6; Jer. 29:13; Hosea 10:12; Matt. 7:7). We primarily seek God by Bible study. Ideally, seeking God occurs "day and night" (Josh. 1:8-9; Psa. 1:2; Acts 17:11). Those not interested in seeking God as revealed in the Bible cannot obey fully, give God all their hearts, or imitate Him by obedience to the Bible.[7] Without priority on worship, seeking God in Scripture, and growing ever toward the image of God in life, the result will be discontent and emotional problems that directly hurt the family.

Love is the greatest virtue (1 Cor. 13:13).[8] The greatest commandment is to *love God first* (Deut. 6:4-5; Matt. 22:36-40). Those

---

[7] God desires complete allegiance and obedience. How can Christians follow the Lord fully with their whole hearts without complete attention to all the Bible teaches? Here is a fascinating list of verses that give examples or commands to teach all and obey all, following God fully with all ones heart: Num. 22:18, 24:13; Deut. 4:2; Joshua 1:8; 1 Kings 6:12-13, 8:61, 9:4, 11:4,6,38, 15:3,14, 22:14; (see 2 Chron. 18:13); 2 Kings 20:3; 1 Chron. 28:9, 29:19; 2 Chron. 16:9, 17:3-5, 25:2, 31:20-21, 34:2; Psa. 22:9-10 (see 1 Kings 18:12); Psa. 71:5,17, 119:101; Prov. 3:5-6; Isa. 30:21; Jer. 6:16, 23:28, 26:2, 42:2-6; Matt. 28:20; Luke 9:62, 14:27,33; Acts 20:27; 2 Cor. 2:17, 4:2; Gal. 1:10; 1 Thess. 2:4; 2 Tim. 4:2; Rev. 22:18-19.

[8] Humility, which involves a sense of need and dependence upon God, is an overlooked and uniquely Christian virtue. Faith rests on a sense of need and dependence. Love must include selflessness, which is also, humility. By the authority of God's Word, love is the greatest virtue (1 Cor. 13:13), and faith brings salvation and pleases God (Heb. 11:6), but both involve humility. The Lord Jesus Christ taught the greatness of humility, a virtue that greatly improves families (Matt. 18:4, 23:12; Luke 14:11, 18:14; John 13:13-15). Self-

who love end up obeying the rest of the commandments (Rom. 13:10; Gal. 5:14; James 2:8). Because of love, they will not lie, steal, kill, or commit adultery. Without loving God first, all else in life unravels.

Our purpose here is not to give a full treatment of Christian living. Enough has been said to come back to the main point.[9]

A strong and healthy family does not come from spiritually unhealthy hearts. If we refuse to worship and glorify God; if we do not care to seek God in the Scripture and become even more like Him; if we honestly do not love God; then we can not have fulfillment in life. The resulting discontent and emotional weakness will damage a family.

---

hatred would be a false definition of humility. Without Christ we are indeed nothing (John 15:5), but Christ gives completion (Col. 2:10) and sufficiency (2 Cor. 3:5; Phil. 4:13). An independent spirit (pride) leads to failure. Defined properly, humility is not self-loathing but is a sense of dependence upon God and selflessness. Ironically, humility, not pride, brings the power to do great things in life and feel good about self. Real self-worth arises from self in need and dependence upon Christ, not independence from Christ.

[9] Another angle of profitable research would be a study of the Hebrew and Greek words for "happiness". Because these words are usually translated "blessing", they tend to be overlooked. Yet, the approximately 45 occurrences of *asher* in the Old Testament and 55 forms of *makarios* in the New Testament yield truths as to how to be happy. In brief, God is the source of happiness (defined more as satisfaction or contentment rather than thrills or fun). Psa. 1:1-2 and 40:4 teach that those who refuse ungodly counsel but instead delight in God's Word will be blessed (i.e., happy). Only 1 Tim. 1:11 and 6:15 refer to God as "happy." Despite the world's problems listed in 1 Tim. 1:8-10, God is still the "blessed God" (i.e., the "happy" God) in 1 Tim. 1:11. The world may be a mess, but God is still serene and happy with His own perfections. Unless we dwell upon God as the source of happiness, happiness will be elusive. Any biblical concept of the flawless God will tend toward our happiness. Over time we should dwell upon any and all of the following: the unconditional love of Christ upon the Cross, the holy and majestic God upon His throne, Christ at the right hand of God in glory, the power and justice of the Second Coming, the indwelling Holy Spirit, Christ and the believer (the Church) as groom and bride, as vine and branches, as shepherd and sheep. Continual thoughts of God's perfections and blessings tend toward happiness. Without such spiritual thoughts, happiness is not possible.

Strength to prevent or withstand emotional problems in the home comes from God. Spiritual strength brings emotional strength. Emotional strength brings marital strength. Marital strength brings parenting strength. Chapter One argues the very purpose for marriage is to deepen one's experience with God. Thus, a marriage with little concern for God can hardly become successful or fulfilling. Life is about worshipping, seeking, imitating, and loving God. The family was ordained by God to support this purpose and process.

By our attitude toward God, our avoidance of sin, and our acts of inner devotion and external service we build strong and healthy spirits. Then some of the most serious problems will not ever arise. Then the family can endure and even grow stronger by those problems that do come. The next chapter will list common family problems concerning attitudes, feelings, and hard experiences with brief biblical suggestions for overcoming each.

Chapter Thirteen

Preventing Family Conflicts: Unhealthy Emotions

"To dwell above with Saints we love, O that will be glory. To dwell below with Saints we know, that's another story!"

This poem would not rhyme as well if we substituted "relatives" for saints, but it would be true. Problems arise in the strongest of marriages. They will arise in the best of parent/child relationships. The family can bring happiness; but happiness "ever after" is not realistic. The fact that relatives can annoy us the most is a product of our deep love for them. At least we care.

The previous chapter revealed the Bible's recipe for joy and the Bible's priorities for life. Emotional health (spiritual maturity and priorities) helps reduce problems from coming or at least gives greater endurance in overcoming them. We are also better prepared to withstand common problems when we know in advance biblical instruction for handling them. Realistically, it is not possible to list common troubles in order of severity, and of course, problems overlap. One can experience anger and depression and grief all at once. The problems below are in alphabetical order, but a guess at the problem most dangerous to families could well bring the same result. We begin with the topic of anger.

Anger

Anger is a complex emotion.[1] Some people direct anger at God (**the anger of rebellion**). Other times we might become angry with

---

[1] Anger overlaps with hatred, bitterness, and a spirit of revenge. As expressed in this chapter, anger and forgiveness are twin topics. The main text above deals more directly with handling anger. Brief conclusions about the Bible and forgiveness should also be included. The Hebrew word for forgiveness means "to lift up and carry away a burden." The Greek word means "to cancel a debt, release a prisoner, or bestow an undeserved and costly gift." God always requires us to forgive in the sense of refusing revenge, hatred, bitterness (Matt. 5:44; Mark 11:25; Rom. 12:17; 1 Thess. 5:15; 1 Pet. 3:9). In

God because of disappointment or pain in the suffering of life (**the anger of disappointment**). Also, we frequently are angry with other people and can further divide this into **sinful anger** (**the anger of personal self-importance** or impatience and frustration) and **righteous anger** when God's holy laws have been violated (**the anger of God's honor**). The latter might be a situation where one or a group opposes God's work or truth, or it could involve a situation where one is personally the victim of sin.

---

addition, we must always forgive another who sincerely repents (Luke 17:3-4; Matt. 18:21-22).

Yet, a Christian may withhold forgiveness if "forgiveness" were to be defined as "not holding another accountable" for their wrong. We must never hate or seek revenge, but we can choose to withhold forgiveness in the sense of holding another to the burden of moral accountability. Suppose a youth steals and cashes a check from the church offering. The Bible requires forgiveness in the emotional sense of overcoming negative feelings. However, for the youth's own good, he must be held morally accountable to make restitution and ask forgiveness from the church board and the donor.

We must always forgive in the emotional sense, but we might need to withhold forgiveness in the sense of moral accountability until an offender repents (with serious sins insistence on moral accountability is good for the offender). When one is the victim of a wrong, the Bible allows a choice. In most cases he or she should overlook the sin, forgiving in both senses of dropping all emotional resentment and releasing from further moral accountability. Especially in a family setting, most sins should be dropped (Prov. 19:11; 1 Pet. 4:8; Col. 3:13; Eph. 4:32; James 3:2). The opposite extreme is demanding family members to crawl around to obtain forgiveness for "trivial" human failures. "Love covers a multitude of sins" (1 Pet. 4:8).

However, God's Word does allow holding another accountable for a wrong if we in good conscience cannot simply overlook it. Even with many family sins, couples or parents with children may need to privately discuss the matter. Rebuke can be justified if given in a spirit of love, humility, and reconciliation. Whether we overlook a trespass or discuss the problem, the Bible never allows the option of stewing in resentment (Prov. 27:5,6; Matt. 18:15; Luke 17:3; Gal. 6:1; Eph. 4:26-27). If discussion leads to confession and reconciliation, well and good. If not, we may still have to grant release from accountability (forgiveness), even if for the sake of the relationship and inner well-being. With serious sins the Bible allows church discipline and even prosecution by the state for crimes.

Cain was the first murderer in history. Cain's example was actually of anger at God coupled with jealousy towards his brother Abel. Heb. 11:4 says, "by faith Abel offered to God a better sacrifice ... " God required **faith** (not a religion of works in a vain attempt to earn salvation). The closest modern parallel to Cain's anger would be those who rebel in anger because the real God restricts His full acceptance only to those who have **faith in the Lord Jesus Christ**. All other religions, philosophies, and ways of life are unacceptable. Cain illustrated the connection between anger and depression (" ... his countenance fell" Gen. 4:5), and the connection between anger (including anger at God) and family problems.

Sometimes we become angry with God because of suffering in life. We might call this the anger of disappointment rather than the anger of rebellion. The Bible gives examples of respectful "venting" (Job 7:20, 10:7 and 19:6; Psa. 13:1; Jer. 20:7).

If one quickly channels these emotions into a search for understanding, then God tolerates our being upset. Even the Lord Jesus asked, "Why?" (Psa. 22:1; Matt. 27:46). However, Isa. 40:27 shows that being upset with God must be channeled into a quest for deeper understanding of His ways and not be allowed to become anger in the sense of disrespectful rebellion.

Anger directed at God causes depression. So does anger directed at other people. Sometimes people transfer their anger with God to their family. Cain did this to his brother. We must resolve anger with God by confession or by respectfully seeking His purposes. If not, unresolved anger against God will affect family life.

Sinful anger is the anger of personal insult or impatience [2] The offense (or merely perceived grievance) does not involve an attack upon God or a serious violation of His laws. We often rationalize and categorize all anger as being righteous indignation. However, much anger does not really involve a violation of God's holy standards. We become angry over waiting in line or flat tires. We get mad at the

---

[2] Righteous anger is slow (Psa. 103:8; Prov. 14:29; James 1:19). By contrast, sinful anger allows for no long-suffering with another.

human limitations of others or from misunderstanding them. Much anger is sinful and should be confessed as sin both to God and the human victim of our sinful wrath. If not, we risk family turmoil and personal depression. Sinful anger at a close family member by definition is a family problem. However, even anger not directed at anyone in the family may still cause problems for the family (though a prudent person realizes that an angry relative may bring irritating experiences home and such anger is not at all personally directed toward anyone in the household).

In most cases, we will be better off emotionally by forgiving an offense that caused anger even if there is no request for forgiveness. "Love covers a multitude of sins" (1 Pet. 4:8; see also Prov. 19:11). Possessing a forgiving spirit towards family members smoothes over most problems even if the initial anger comes from a legitimate grievance and can be defined as righteous indignation. The same forgiving nature towards non-relatives (co-workers, business contacts, the government, neighbors, church members) will also reduce stress from life brought back into the home.

The Bible never allows hatred. While resistance to an evil act in progress (e.g. a violent assault) is morally acceptable, revenge for past wrongs is not (contrast Prov. 24:11-12 with Rom. 12:17-21). Hatred and seeking revenge are certain paths to family conflicts (especially within the family but even if directed against outsiders). With serious sins, God does allow one who has been grieved to seek repentance and hold another morally accountable.

We never have the option to hate, but we can seek restoration through repentance and perhaps church discipline (Matt. 18:15-17). (God gives the state the authority for justice in criminal sins, Rom. 13:1-4.)

If a sin is too serious to overlook and cover, then we can hold another morally accountable by rebuke and seeking repentance in a private conversation. Sometimes rebuke and blunt discussion may need to take place between a couple or parents and children. If one simply cannot overlook an offense because of its severity, then the issue must be discussed (in a spirit of love and humility seeking restoration). In more severe disputes we can go to the church to ask for counsel or even the government for justice concerning sins that cross into a criminal classification. However, if these fail, we must turn the matter over to God as Jesus did when He was wronged (1 Pet. 2:21-23).

Sinful anger (the anger of personal importance) must be confessed to God and to the object of anger as sin. If not, anger within the home or brought into it from the outside will cause family problems.

Righteous anger is by definition morally right, but it must be handled the Bible's way or it becomes sin.[3] We channel righteous anger into motivation to solve the problem or a quest to seek God's purposes. We should quickly overlook most offenses (especially in the family), or quickly discuss the grievance, first in private, to come to reconciliation.

In the end a forgiving disposition is the solution to angry family conflicts. Within or outside the home, we must confess sinful anger. We must also resolve righteous anger by initially overlooking the offense, or quickly discussing the offense, and ultimately forgiving

---

[3] Some anger is righteous. God's Person or work has been insulted or opposed. When we have been victims of a sin, anger is righteous. God's anger is always righteous (Ex. 32:10a; Mark 3:5). Righteous anger against enemies of faith **should be channeled into motivation** to protect others from their errors. Rebuke might be in order, but it is the type of rebuke that is motivated to help others by reducing sin's destruction. In other words, we oppose people because we love them and do not want to see them harmed because of their false views or sins. Eph. 4:26-27 and James 1:19-20 teach that we must handle righteous indignation carefully and quickly (before sundown!); or it leads to sin, e.g. hatred, bitterness. The Lord's example seems to have given more patience and grace with sinners and stronger rebuke to those leading others into sin.

Righteous anger might involve impersonal opposition to groups, especially leaders of groups, that oppose God. It can also be a personal response when one becomes a victim of another's sin. In most cases, we will be better off emotionally by forgiving an offense even if there is no request for forgiveness. "Love covers a multitude of sins." This is even more true within a family. Even if a loved one has committed an offense bringing legitimate righteous anger, most offenses should just be "swept under" that proverbial rug.

the offense. Whether ultimately resolved or not, all grievances should be turned over to God in the end. The anger should then be put in the past, and we should go on to a happier life and stronger family. Families who imitate the Lord Jesus Christ in the bestowal of forgiveness will defeat problems from anger. Forgiveness overcomes anger. Facts overcome doubt.

Doubt

Most Christians have times when they feel like the man who told the Lord, "I do believe; help my unbelief" (Mark 9:24). Even John the Baptist in prison had points of shaken faith. "Are you the Expected One, or shall we look for someone else?" (Matt. 11:3).

God enjoys our faith just as an earthly father enjoys children who trust his good intentions even when they do not fully understand. "…without faith it is impossible to please Him (God) …" (Heb. 11:6). When my children were small, I used to carry them across the "deep" end (five feet) of the motel pool. They held to me and were safe. At times they had doubts, but they were still safe. They could have trusted completely.

In God's universe, He requires faith and enjoys complete confidence over faith mixed with doubts. Still, Christians with the attitude of "I do believe, help my unbelief" remain safe. They just do not enjoy life as much.

No amount of proof for God's existence, the Bible's accuracy, or Christ's resurrection can make faith unnecessary. However, evidence makes faith the reasonable, most intelligent option. Faith in the Bible and the Lord Jesus Christ is not an irrational lengthy leap into the dark. Faith is a small step in the direction of available facts. Faith in the unseen is not easy. Jesus told doubting Thomas there is a special blessing for those who believe without sight. "Blessed are they who did not see, and yet believed" (John 20:29). Faith is necessary and not easy, but faith in the Lord Jesus Christ is intelligent. He is far easier to believe than competing worldviews, including skepticism. The Christian object of faith is ultimately the Lord Jesus Christ who is both truthful and wise. Everyone chooses whether He is Savior or con artist. He Himself challenged His enemies to convict Him of any sin. Then He challenged His opponents with logic, "If I speak truth, why do you not believe Me?" (John 8:46).

Many objective facts make faith reasonable and make faith in Christ easier than disbelief. The Bible's own system of Messianic prophecies show that Jesus is the promised One and that the Bible is a supernatural book. Before His birth, Christ's life is prophesied in the Old Testament:

- The Messiah would be born in Bethlehem (Micah 5:2).

- His mother would have to claim virgin birth (Isa. 7:14).

- He would be "cut off," i.e. killed, after 69 cycles of 7 years each from the command to restore Jerusalem (Dan. 9:24-27).[4]

- He would come from the line of David, not through Solomon but through Nathan (2 Sam. 7:12-16, Jer. 22:30, Zech. 12:12).

- He would be silent at trial (Isa. 53:7).

- He would be pierced (Isa. 53:5; Zech. 12:10).

- He would sustain wounds on hands and feet (Psa. 22:16).

- He would be considered a criminal but would be buried with the rich (Isa. 53:9, 12).

- Christ would be raised from the dead (Psa. 16:10; Isa. 53:10-11).

This list is deliberately short. If we add indirect Old Testament pictures, there can be as many as 300 Messianic prophecies.[5] No one

---

[4] The Daniel 9 prophecy about the time for the Messiah can be computed to work out to the exact day of the triumphal entry (Palm Sunday). After this the Messiah would be "cut off," and the city destroyed (A.D. 70). A thorough and masterful study may be found in Harold W. Hoehner, *Chronological Aspects of the Life of Christ* (Grand Rapids: Zondervan Publishing House, 1977), pp. 115-139.

can claim Christians went back into the Old Testament after the fact and artificially doctored the Old Testament texts. The Dead Sea Scrolls before the time of Christ contain the same predictions. No one can claim the English translations of the Old Testament have been twisted to create artificial prophecies referring to Jesus. They are in fact accurately translated and find fulfillment in the life of Christ. They were in fact written long before the birth of Jesus. Prophecy identifies the Lord Jesus Christ as the chosen and anointed One. This system of prophecy makes the belief that Jesus comes from God very credible

As to the history of the Bible, there are approximately 100 Bible characters that are also mentioned in ancient literature or archaeological inscriptions. All my professional life I have tried to keep track of the latest discoveries by keeping a list of Bible names and a parallel column of ancient secular sources.

The most impressive historical source is Josephus. Josephus was a Jewish author who lived at the time of the New Testament (c. A.D. 37-100). His writings refer to John the Baptist, Jesus Christ, James the half brother of the Lord Jesus Christ, and most of the political/ religious leaders of the New Testament era (Herod, Pilate, Agrippa I and II, Festus, Felix, etc.) [6] Josephus even wrote that Herod

---

[5] Many Old Testament prophecies refer to the coming Savior in the original context. Others do not. In this second class are many illustrations that do not refer to the Christ in their original setting but give parallels that seem too odd to be mere coincidence. Jeremiah spoke of Rachel as the mother of Israel weeping in her grave for deported children (mostly boys) as they parted for the Babylonian exile from Ramah, the staging area for exile.

Rachel's grave was in Bethlehem (Gen. 35:19). Matthew noted that Herod killed and/or perhaps the families buried the boy infants within the vicinity of Rachel's actual grave marker. Fulfillments like this might be classified as "types" because the Old Testament statements in their original context are not references to the Messiah. Yet, the New Testament often calls them prophecies. By adding these indirect prophecies to more direct predictions, they make impressive evidence that the Bible is of divine origin.

[6] The translation of Josephus into modern English is Maier, Paul. *Josephus: The Essential Writings*. (Grand Rapids: Kregel Publications, 1988). The complete writings of Josephus were translated and published in 1737 by William Whiston who was Isaac Newton's successor in mathematics at

Agrippa I made a speech in Caesarea. The crowd called him a god. He then fell mortally ill on the spot. This account of a public speech confirms Acts 12:20-23. Josephus also mentions that Herod Antipas stole his brother's wife. Such a public scandal made both the New Testament and secular history books.

I have collected 2,000-year-old authentic Bible coins from the eras of the following New Testament leaders: Herod the Great (the Christmas Herod), Archelaus, Herod Antipas (beheaded John), Herod Philip, Pilate, Agrippa I (the stricken speaker), Festus, Felix, Agrippa II, and Aretas (see 2 Cor. 11:32). These coins are physical evidence that the Bible is not a mythological book. Our study will not permit further details, but the remnants of ancient civilization in biblical times do exist. Faith in the Bible is not only the intelligent, but also obvious choice.

The empty tomb of Christ is perhaps the most important historical event. His tomb was definitely empty! How can we be so sure? If Christ's enemies could have produced His body, they would have exhibited the corpse in the Temple or driven it through the streets on a wagon announcing the fraudulent claim of resurrection. The tomb was undeniably empty. How?

None of the natural explanations make sense. If the disciples were having hallucinations (500 having the same hallucination at once is ridiculous, 1 Cor. 15:6), then the body would still have been in the tomb, and it would have been produced by Christianity's opponents. The hallucination thesis will not satisfy.

Some may assert the disciples went to the wrong tomb, got excited and announced the resurrection from the dead. If this happened, the body would still be in the guarded tomb. No one would have believed their story.

Cambridge. At this point it may be mentioned that James is the "half-brother" of Jesus because of Jesus' virgin birth (Matt. 13:55).

At the time, the explanation for the empty tomb was that the disciples stole the body. Yet, no one was ever arrested for the serious crime of grave robbing. Governor Pilate must not have believed the charge and with good reason. Guards in those days never slept (in the Roman army they executed sleeping sentries). Furthermore, sleeping people never make good witnesses. If one is sleeping, it would be hard for one to attest to much of anything. Finally, is it sensible to believe anyone could come at night, with torches, pick axes, and crowbars, roll away a huge stone, unwrap a body from its linens, and never wake anyone? Even at the time, no one with any sense believed alternative explanations for the undeniably empty tomb.

In addition, the psychology and ethics of the disciples make their version believable. After the crucifixion, they became total cowards. They were too cowardly to even have tried grave robbing, and certainly would not have maintained a group cover-up (literally to the death) without someone confessing. The disciples were ethical people grounded in the commandment "Thou shalt not bear false witness." They all died horrible deaths still maintaining Christ's resurrection from the dead. No more honest or motivated witnesses could ever be found for any event. People do die for lies, but they do not die for lies they personally know to be false without having something great to gain. In their case, the disciples would have known the resurrection to be a hoax but have nothing material or social to gain, only suffering, mistreatment and hatred. Christ's tomb was empty on the first Easter morning. Resurrection from the dead is easier to believe than explanations that do not involve a miracle. It takes faith, but the faith is intelligent, not irrational.

The Gospels, especially Matthew, give specific phenomena at the time of the Passion. The sky was dark during the day, the earth shook, the thick veil in the Temple tore from top to bottom, some of the graves in the cemeteries opened, (see Matt. 27:45ff.). In order to believe the main point, the resurrection, people in Jerusalem would have had to find the overall story believable. They obviously did. Christianity took off attracting more and more adherents, beginning in Jerusalem. In the nature of the case, everyone in the city, including Passover worshippers from all over the world, would know whether the sky became black and the city shook. By believing in the resurrected Christ they could expect suffering, but they did believe in great numbers including secret believers within Judaism (John 12:42-43; Acts 6:7).

No one can simply dismiss the Bible or the claims of Christ. Believing the invisible is not easy, but the object of Christian faith is the historical Person, Jesus of Nazareth, who claims to be God's Son and Savior. Faith is still necessary, but faith is intelligent and actually far easier than denial and rejection.[7] God holds the world "without excuse" for not choosing truth (Rom. 1:18-23). Increased study helps with overcoming doubts. Scientific, prophetic, historical or philosophical research makes faith rational. Faith itself brings subjective experience with God, which increases certainty (Rom. 8:16; 1 John 5:10). Those who walk with God in a deep enough way to experience His own character traits have experiential evidences for the existence of God (though such evidence only persuades other believers). Those who take the reasonable step of faith will find additional evidence on the other side of the decision.

Exhaustion/Burn Out

Marriage is hard work. Raising children is hard work. "Burn out" can be a real danger. All homes need balance, priorities, realistic expectations (see Chapter 12), and rest. A family can be improved by simplifying life and saying "**no**" to many options calling for time,

---

[7] Limitations will not allow details on scientific and philosophical topics. Scholars arguing for intelligent design in the universe include Michael Behe, William Dembski, and Phillip E. Johnson. The "Intelligent Design" scholars tend to argue on scientific grounds alone without the Bible. The Institute of Creation Research blends biblical authority with good science (see www.icr.org). Since no two snowflakes are alike and salmon find the stream in which they were born, common sense also confirms the existence of a Creator.

As to philosophy, design shows a designer. Effects prove a cause. The sense of right and wrong proves a Law-giver. All morality is not culturally conditioned. When one is the victim of theft, adultery, a lie, or murder of a loved one, everyone knows right from wrong. Those who argue for empirical evidence as so-called "proof" for atheism fail to observe that the human race everywhere and at all times is spiritually driven and seeks God.

money, and energy. The Church today is not under the Law of Moses, but the Old Testament example of Sabbath provides reason for voluntarily chosen rest. Not only did God require the Jews to rest one day a week, but they had three week-long holidays per year and one entire year of rest out of every seven. Modern Christians are not even close to this degree of rest.

Guilt

Humanism makes a great mistake by responding to guilt with suppression. Guilt in the soul functions as pain to the body. We know something is wrong and needs serious attention fast.

The solution to guilt before God the Judge is faith in the Lord Jesus Christ as Savior (Rom. 8:1, 32-34). Judicially, all sins have been settled by faith in Christ's sacrificial death. Believers are the children of God but still sin. The sins of those who have trusted Christ concern God in His role as Father, not in His role as Judge. Those already forgiven by God the Judge still sin and need forgiveness by God the Father in His Fatherly role. This comes by confession of sin (1 John 1:9). To receive removal of guilt Christians should confess sins to God the Father. True guilt can be resolved by faith in Christ, then confession of sins as a habitual practice in Christian living.

False guilt is also a problem that torments many Christians. False guilt refers to the feeling of guilt even when no biblical sin has been committed. Three main types of false guilt harm emotions.

Unintentional mistakes or being the victim of sin can produce guilt feelings even when no willful sin occurred. We feel guilt if involved in a car accident bringing injury or death to others. Children of divorce or rape victims also experience false guilt. 1 John 3:20 is a good verse to apply to needless false guilt; "In whatever our heart condemns us, God is greater than our heart and knows all things." In addition to accidents or victimization, legalism causes much false guilt, especially among Christians.

It may not be wrong to develop man-made policies that go beyond the Bible's own commandments, but it is wrong to teach such man-made rules as if they are binding with God's authority and that any violation is a sin. If I have been taught that mowing the lawn on Sunday afternoon displeases God, I will feel guilt by doing so. However, this restraint would be a personal preference, not a biblical requirement. Every year someone will argue that it is sinful to celebrate Christmas. Many issues in life are not biblical matters of good and evil. They are personal convictions. They do not involve sin one way or the other until we start judging the salvation or spirituality of others by them.

Guilt arising from legalism is unnecessary false guilt. Bible study will separate clear moral issues from matters of personal preference. Christians can be very good at holding on to false guilt arising from rules that are not even in the real Bible.

A third type of false guilt is holding on to sins that have been confessed to God and, therefore, forgiven. After confession of sin, we should look up to God, not within self. After confession of sin, we should be "forgetting what lies behind and reaching forward to what lies ahead ..." (Phil. 3:13).

Guilt need not make us miserable or weaken relationships in the family. False guilt from accidents, legalism, or not accepting God's forgiveness can be overcome by knowing and believing the Bible. God heals true guilt by faith in His Son, and then confession. He frees us from the emotional paralysis of guilt. "If we confess our sins, He is faithful and just to forgive our sins and to cleanse us from all unrighteousness" (1 John 1:9, see also Psa. 103:12 and Micah 7:19).

Inferiority/A Sense of Worth

Someone has said that American school children rank thirteenth among the nations on academic test scores but are first in self-esteem. A sense of worth and value is indeed vital to emotional health, but there is a big problem with leaving God out of the equation and then stressing self-esteem. Also, secular society itself usually sets the standard that is allowed to judge personal worth.[8]

---

[8] See John 7:24; Rom. 12:1-2; 1 John 2:15 for warnings not to adopt the world's values, including its standard for measuring value and success in life.

Several times under previous topics (such as unconditional love for children and the source of contentment in life), we have already concluded that basing human worth on various achievements is a big mistake. At best, accomplishment can become a secondary reinforcement of the value of one's life, but then only if achieved under God's authority and for God's exaltation.

The underlying basis for infinite human worth has no dependence upon what the world's system defines as "success." One could have many degrees with honors, play professional sports, obtain a huge income, or be famous and powerful, but still fail to measure up to a high quality and productive life as defined by God's Word. A beauty queen or Ph.D. may be a snob. A famous athlete may beat his wife. A powerful TV personality might have a miserable and meaningless life. Identical achievements (high SAT scores, talent, an expensive house and car) may be secondary factors in measuring the worth of life, but they are subordinate to God as the ultimate source and Judge of human worth and human works.

Human life has infinite worth fundamentally because of God's achievements on our behalf not our achievements independent from Him. God has shown the value of every person because all have been created in God's image (Gen. 1:27). God has a plan for each person and is interested in him or her even before birth (Psa. 139:13-16; Jer.1:5). With infinite personal love the Lord Jesus Christ gave His life as a substitute, paying the penalty for the sin of each person (Rom. 5:8; Eph. 2:4; 2 Cor. 5:14-15). This cost for salvation measures the Lord's estimation of each person's value. God has bestowed believers with additional blessings that confirm value. Everyone who trusts in Christ as Savior becomes a child of God (John 1:12; 1 John 3:1). All believers are clothed in Christ's perfect righteousness and spiritually stand before God the Judge with the merits of His Son (Rom. 8:33-34; 2 Cor. 5:21; Jude v.24). Every believer has a spiritual gift that enables him or her to serve God within the Church (1 Cor. 12:7, 18).

These are the primary bases for human worth. Value arises not from what we alone accomplish but from what God has freely given to us and then accomplished through us. One who achieves little by the world's standards as defined by academic, financial, or social power, still has worth to God. God's view of our "self" should be the basis for our own view of self (and not what others think). God's actions on our behalf are the cause of personal worth, not fickle or temporary matters such as physical beauty, popularity, or wealth, which are often not under the complete control of the individual.[9] Human worth is independent of and prior to any accomplishment.

Achievement in a Christian's life can contribute to a sense of worth only by ranking as a secondary measure of value. This assumes that God's truth is the standard by which one measures success and that all achievements are done in a spirit of humility **not** autonomy (i.e. independence from God, a core value in secular humanism). Autonomy from God is the real definition of sinful pride.[10] Paul took a righteous sense of pride in his life's work but only because he recognized such achievements come from humble dependence upon the power of Christ. He had a sense of the value of his life's work, but it came from what God did with him, not what Paul, independent from God, could do.

"I can do all things **through Christ** who strengthens me" (Phil. 4:13, see also 2 Cor. 3:5; 2 Tim. 4:7). One's primary source of feeling worth should arise from God's view of us and His blessings upon us prior to any achievements. An additional secondary sense of worth may then come from what God can do with our lives. The criteria by which God measures success in our accomplishments are spiritual depth and

---

[9] While feminine beauty or masculine strength are blessings (assuming underlying godliness), they are poor foundations for one's sense of worth. Neither beauty nor strength endure (Prov. 31:30; 1 Sam. 16:7; Psa. 147:10). Yet, culture often teaches us to base the core of one's worth upon such temporary features beyond one's control.

Popularity is also beyond the control of the individual. Obedience, faithfulness and pleasing God are in themselves higher and truer standards of success (1 Cor. 3:10-15, 4:2; John 12:42-43) than the degree of popularity or human acclaim. If one has honored God and followed His Word, this alone is success. Human approval of efforts to honor God add to one's blessing but remain secondary. If God has been pleased, this brings the primary sense of achievement and measure of one's efforts.

[10] See pp. 134-135, footnote 8 for additional discussion on the definitions of humility and pride and the need for humility in order to achieve great things for God. Humility should not be defined as self-hatred.

virtues that are accessible to all believers regardless of innate talents or social approval.

Criticism of the self-esteem and self-worth views in secular psychology is not an attack upon the need for feeling worth and esteem. Healthy people do love themselves (Eph. 5:28; Matt. 22:39), but they love God first, and then love others unselfishly. The problem is the stress upon **self**.

God's actions in blessing each human alone give worth. Additional enhancement of human worth comes from achievement but not self-achievement. Each person should have a deep belief in his own worth but first because of what God has done and then because of what God can do through him in the present and future. Basing one's sense of value upon God's view of self brings a true and lasting sense of worth. Living in dependence upon God for the strength and wisdom to achieve much for His glory also provides a feeling of worth, but self-achievement judged by the world's evaluation will end in a feeling of frustration.[11] The world harshly judges its own as failures when strength and ability decline.[12] No one is ever good enough to have the world's approval very long.

---

[11] The world in general is full of fussy, fickle, and capricious people. Culture teaches us to measure our self-worth by factors outside a person's control or by the approval of unpredictable people with unfair and shifting standards. Many cannot be pleased for a minute, let alone over a lifetime. God gives a sense of lasting worth in ways possessed by everyone simply by virtue of being human and then by virtue of being a believer in the Lord Jesus Christ as Savior. Success in life's most vital accomplishments **by God's definition of success** is open to all and within the ability of all.

[12] A man to whom I made a pastoral visit has a Ph.D. from a prestigious university and had served with several Presidents. Now, however, he is largely forgotten by the world in an Alzheimer's unit. He has worth as a creature in God's image and one for whom Christ died. However, if in his remaining lucid moments he fails to accept Christ's payment for sin, he will miss out on the ultimate source of human value from being justified by faith before God the Judge and being God's child. In eternity no level of achievement by the world's standards will matter. "Only one life, twill soon be past; only what's done for Christ will last."

At death everyone dies in "weakness" and "dishonor" (1 Cor. 15:43). Our status totally independent of God is sinful, pitiful, and weak regardless of past accomplishments done for the world or self. Success in a life not under God's authority or for His glory fades quickly. If one lives for God's glory, God promises a life's achievements will be remembered forever.[13]

Self-worth divorced from God's graces (and His working through each life) is an illusion. The truth is that many people figure this out even during their lifetime on earth and grow bitter with age unless they turn to the Lord Jesus Christ. The earlier we believe worth comes from God first and then a life lived for God, the better for our emotions and family relationships. Self-hatred or feeling inferior are not Christian virtues at all.[14] Each one can feel a sense of permanent value if we derive our views of self from God's view of self. Each one can and should sense the worth of life by taking satisfaction in a life of achievement defined by God's standards and lived in dependence of what He can make of us and for His glory.

Laziness/Motivation

Families that work too much can harm themselves. The opposite would be a lazy approach to life, especially by a husband or father. If anything, indolence produces even more family stress. Motivation comes from a few sources. We work for greed, pride,

---

[13] See Dan 12:3; Matt. 13:43; Mark 9:41.

[14] No believer ever need feel worthless. We are all valued by God to the deepest extent. Another problem with basing worth on judgment of the world's standards is the entire system of rivalry. The Bible warns of envy and comparison (2 Cor. 10:12; Gal. 5:26, 6:4-5). Each must first measure self against God's own perfection. Next we evaluate life against our own potential and progress over the past. Other lives may become a bad example to avoid, or model to follow, but we must not measure life by rivalry and comparison to others. Instead, God is the ideal, and each should measure achievement by his own capabilities and by improvement over time. Real accomplishment comes from humble dependence upon God and unselfishness toward others, not independence from God and a survival of the fittest style of "accomplishment."

anxiety … or the glory of God. Greed and pride alone may not provide incentive for a lifetime of hard work, and the same spirit brought home will damage a family. Working from attitudes of panic and insecurity will also bring harm back to a family at the end of the workday.

Only an internal motivation within ones spirit which labors for the glory of God, including love for a family, can bring lasting and healthy motivation. Chapter 14 will cover work ethics and attitudes about money in greater depth.

Loneliness

Marriage and children should reduce loneliness. However, every family unit benefits from extended family and spiritual family relationships. One of the functions of church participation is encouragement (Heb. 10:25). If at all possible, we must promote good relationships with relatives. As for a church family, every community has at least one good church. To say no church is good enough for me says more about "me" than churches. If one church has problems with doctrine, ethics, or personality conflicts, there will be another that is acceptable. Even if difficult to find, good churches are not extinct. (Also, regarding this subject, remember God is the ultimate friend.)

Lust

Pornography addiction, for example, can be a severe marital problem. Also, whenever adultery does occur, it begins in one's mind. This problem was covered in Chapter 9.

Jealousy

" … [L]ove … is not jealous …"(1 Cor. 13:4). Only spiritual immaturity would explain a husband being jealous of a wife's knowledge or success or a wife being jealous of her own husband. Children are perhaps more prone to envy each other, but God forbids comparison and rivalry (2 Cor. 10:12).

There are basically two kinds of jealousy. We can be jealous of one who advances (superficially and temporarily) by evil. Why be jealous in this situation? This so-called success is not success and will eventually end badly (Psa. 37:1-2, 73:1-3, 17).

The other type of jealousy arises when a godly person advances in life. We are supposed to rejoice in this outcome (Rom. 12:15).

Either way, jealousy is a harmful sin that is most unnecessary. The solutions for jealousy are recognition of the true definition of success and trust in the sovereignty of God when He chooses to bless other righteous people. Chapter 14 discusses jealousy in the context of finances.

Materialism

Attitudes toward money can help or hurt a family. Because financial matters can bring severe family conflict, the entire next chapter will cover biblical attitudes toward money. Materialism as biblically defined and followed is the opposite of a godly worldview and ruins many marriages and families.

Pain and Suffering

Complete understanding as to why God permits suffering may not be possible (Deut. 29:29; Prov. 3:5-6; Isa. 55:8-9; 1 Cor. 13:12), but Scriptures do give a theology of suffering. The Old Testament teaches "many are the afflictions of the righteous" (Psa. 34:19). The New Testament teaches believers follow the identical path of the Lord Jesus Christ from suffering to glory.

Any determination of God's purpose for a given hardship is a matter between the individual and God. A counselor giving advice may only point to biblical teaching and encourage the suffering one to wrestle over the issue, seeking understanding from God.

The Bible gives many possibilities:

• Suffering destroys self-sufficiency and keeps us humble (dependent upon God for need, Deut. 8:3; Psa. 56:3; John 6:68; 2 Cor. 12:7, 9).

• In trials we learn to pray (Matt. 26:39; Acts 12:1,5) and study the Bible for strength (Psa. 119:25,28,71).

• Experience with pain makes us sympathetic and gives credibility in ministry to others (2 Cor. 1:3-4).

• Suffering often unites people (Rom. 12:15; 1 Cor. 12:25-26a) and teaches us priorities in life (i.e. spiritual and eternal, not material and transitory matters, 2 Cor. 4:17-18; 1 John 2:16-17).

• Suffering enables testimony to God's power to sustain and allows opportunities for evangelism (John 9:3, 11:4, 12:10-11). One's own pain may drive him to his knees so that he listens to the gospel and trusts Christ (Luke 15:16-18).

• By suffering we see the value of all human life including the weakest (Matt. 25:40 by application). Sometimes it is in pain that we count our blessings and learn to appreciate (Psa.103:1-4).

• Suffering can be a test of loyalty to God as was the case in the book of Job (Job 1:8-12, 13:15a, 23:10; 1 Pet. 1:7-9). A given trouble can be chastisement to cause a forsaking of sin (John 5:14b; Heb. 12:6a, 7,11). Punishment from God is by no means the only reason He permits suffering, but if a person has lived in disobedience; chastisement is one of the possibilities.

• Suffering causes us to understand God's strength and wisdom by contrast to our own weakness (Isa. 40:27-31).

• Finally, trials in life produce strength of character just as exercise produces physical strength (James 1:2-3).

Other important reasons why God allows suffering extend beyond the above list developed from specific biblical teachings. Perhaps God permitted evil to enter the universe so that He could once and for all destroy evil rather than evil remaining an eternal hypothetical possibility. The Bible does teach that this life is part of a mysterious process of experiencing and becoming more like God. The main thesis of this book is that **God created marriage and the family**

so that we would have a deeper imitation of His character. Suffering also deepens experience with God's virtues in a committed believer's life. We follow Christ's pattern from suffering to glory (Luke 24:26; Rom. 8:18; 1 Pet. 2:20-21, 4:13, 5:1, 10; Heb. 2:10).

By permitting evil and suffering, God wants us to learn mercy (pity for the suffering); grace (kindness for the undeserving); forgiveness (God's permission for the existence of sin was required for such); long-suffering (enduring people's failures); unconditional love (tested by sin); and loyalty to a covenant relationship (also tested by sin). Without suffering in the universe, we would not experience God's greatest virtues (the same is true for family relationships).

Bereavement has to be among the greatest pain. Death is not the end of existence. Theologically, death may be defined as separation. The soul departs the body and separates from family and friends. Even Jesus felt sorrow over his friend, Lazarus (John 11:35). Grief over losing a dear one drives us to the promises and hope recorded in Scripture. The most important aspect to faith is the object of faith. Christians place faith in Christ. He is the One who gives hope over death. The Lord Jesus Christ is both wise and worthy of confidence in His teaching about resurrection, heaven, and eternal life. In reference to the heavenly city, the Lord said " ... if it were not so, I would have told you" (John 14:2). A modern paraphrase might be: "You can trust me about this heavenly city. I would not mislead you about such a serious matter."[15]

Perfectionism, Efforts to Make Everyone Happy

Excellence is a virtue but perfectionism, whether imposed by self or society, produces depression and creates problems at home.

---

[15] A selected list of sub-topics and verses include: eternal glory after a believer's suffering (Rom. 8:18; Psa. 23:5-6; 2 Cor. 4:7-10, 17-18; Rev. 14:13); victory over death (Psa. 23:4; Heb. 2:14-15; 1 Cor. 15:55-57); resurrection for believers in Christ (Job 19:26; Matt.22:29-32; John 5:25-29, 11:25-26; 1 Cor. 15:51-58; Phil. 3:20-21; 1 Thess. 4:13-18; 1 John 3:2; Rev. 20:6); heaven and reunion with believers who have died (John 14:1-6; 1 Thess. 4:13-18; Rev. 21:2-4, 22:1-5).

Moses was literally suicidal because he could not fix or control the people he was leading (Num. 11:11-15).

God wants us to strive for excellence, but He does not expect we can do everything, solve every problem, or make people do as they should. "There is a God, but I am not He" gives a common-sense realization. God does not expect the impossible from us. We need to accept human limitations and God's grace for our inabilities and flaws (Psa. 39:4, 103:14). Married people and parents must obey Psalm 127:1-2, which teaches the vanity of working to frustration and collapse either from worry or being a perfectionist. We work toward excellence, but we must concede humanity.

> Not that I have already obtained it or have already become perfect, but I press on so that I may lay hold of that for which also I was laid hold of by Christ Jesus [Phil. 3:12].

A related problem is that of trying to make everyone happy. Just as with perfectionism the direction is good but the degree can be unrealistic. As much as possible we should want to be helpful and live in peace with all (Rom. 12:18; 1 Pet. 2:20, 3:17). Certainly, Christians want a good reputation and should live in ways that would not needlessly displease or antagonize others (1 Tim. 3:7; 1 Pet. 2:12). At the heart of Christianity is a selfless spirit (Phil. 2:3-4).

Yet, the Bible itself places limitations as to pleasing people. If the choice lies between pleasing God or pleasing an employer, customer, or neighbor, God expects to be honored first (John 12:42-43).

More pertinent to marriage is that there is a legitimate aspect to a husband pleasing a wife and a wife pleasing her husband ahead of other people. 1 Cor. 7:33-34 comes in a context of persecution and danger. Paul suggests at such times, being single can be better for ministry. The apostle was free to travel and take risks because he had no family obligations. Yet, married people do have to put a spouse's needs and interests first.

> [B]ut one who is married is concerned about the things of the world, how he may please his wife ... but one who is married is

concerned about the things of the world, how she may please her husband [1 Cor. 7:33, 34b].

Applying this Scripture to the subject at hand, God expects married people to care for their families above trying to make everyone else happy. Not only must one please God above man, one must have more concern for relationships at home than other relationships. In many cases there will be no tension. However, it is possible to work so hard to please unreasonable people that the pain they cause is brought back home. Demands for attention, efforts, and time commitments from those outside a family can put a strain on the family. God wants us to do what we can to help, but within balance and within the limitations of not bringing turmoil, frustration, and distraction back to the home. At a point, married people may need to go on with life and set limits for how much they try to please others. A spouse has a greater right to time and consideration than others.

Sometimes customers, employees, relatives, or fellow church members demand both body and soul with impossible demands that make balance in life and priority attention to the family difficult. Unless a matter is a clear biblical command, one may need to say "no" to "one more" optional commitment in order to preserve strength and time for the home. If others criticize, we should remember the Bible sets limits to how much criticism and judgment must be tolerated for non-ethical issues. Fussy people do not have a right to destroy a family by impossible demands for strength and time, or judgment by legalistic standards. Paul told his associates there were limits to putting up with others (1 Cor. 4:3; 1 Tim. 4:12; Titus 2:15). God is easier to please than a world full of imposing people who drain time and strength from priority relationships (Psa. 109: 28, 30-31; Matt. 11:28, 30; Luke 10:40-42; 1 John 5:3). Pleasing a godly spouse comes next. Others may expect and claim limited attention but not to the degree where pleasing them damages either one's own relationship with God or with his or her own family. God and the family matter far more than unfair demands or criticism. Family life improves if we give up trying to be perfect or to please everyone.

Worry

Worry can lead to frustration, then anger. Fears also contribute to depression. In the long term, anxiety will lead to enough irritation and exasperation in life that disputes arise within a family. In reality unbelievers should be worried. In their worldview, the universe has no hope. They should be terrified. Believers can and should manage their fears because faith in a God who superintends life should make life's troubles bearable (1 Cor. 10:13).

Alarm based upon external and present danger is a healthy kind of fear. We should brake the car when someone swerves in front of us. We should head for shelter when the tornado siren goes off. Worry in the sense of concern for responsibility or needs can be godly (2 Cor. 11:28; Phil. 2:20). However, the Bible forbids anxiety that does not stem from any present danger (worry about what could possibly happen in the future) and even anxiety over real and present troubles to the point of lack of faith or loss of peace and joy. The fruit of the Holy Spirit says nothing of a life tied in knots over worry (Gal. 5:22-23).

By giving more attention to the Person of God and presence of God than any problem, the Bible promises us a peaceful mind (Isa. 26:3; John 14:1,27; 2 Tim. 1:7). Worry beyond a reasonable concern to remedy a given problem is defined as a sin in the Bible because worry is the opposite of faith (Matt. 6:34; Phil. 4:6; 1 John 4:18). God offers us joy (see Chapter 12, also John 16:24; 1 John 1:4).

We can reduce fear by trusting God's promises.[16] Next, we do what we can about a problem but must turn unsolvable problems over to God (Psa. 55:22; 1 Pet. 5:7). Instead of worry, God tells us to pray (Phil. 4:6-7). Those who live one day at a time obey Christ's wisdom in the Sermon on the Mount, "so do not worry about tomorrow ..." Matt. 6:34). Practicing the presence of God reduces worry (Matt. 28:20;

---

[16] Bible promises that help us in times of worry include: reminders of God's love, care, and protection (Psa. 23, 27:1, 34:4,6-8, 55:22, 118:6, and Psa. 121; Isa. 40:11; Matt. 6:25-34, 11:28-30; John 10:1-18; Rom. 8:28, 31-32, 37-39; 2 Tim. 2:1; Heb. 13:5-6; 1 Pet. 5:7); reminders of God's power (Josh. 1:9; Job 5:17-21; Psa. 31:24, 46:1, 10-11, Psalm 91; Isa. 40:28-31, 41:10 and 13; Nahum 1:7); reminders of God's guidance (Psa. 32:8; Prov. 3:5-6); reminders to count our blessings (Psa. 103:1-18; Eph. 5:20; 1 Thess. 5:18; James 1:2-4); reminders to increase faith, not fear, when we face difficulties (Psa. 37:5, 42:5, 56:3-4; Prov. 3:5-6; John 14:27).

Phil. 4:6-7; Heb. 13:5-6) as does counting blessings and substituting negative thoughts of worry for positive thoughts of good (Lam. 3:22-23; Psa. 103:1-8; Phil. 4:8-9). Sometimes doing good works takes the mind away from worry (Psa. 37:3; Matt. 6:33) as does fellowship from supportive friends in a church family (Heb. 10:25). Contentment in life, especially with the attributes of a perfect God and His perfect Word, reduces worry over a world full of defects and worry about money (Phil. 4:11; 1 Tim. 6:6; Heb. 13:5).

Above all else, deeper faith in God reduces worry. He watches over us in all our problems. They will either be removed, or God will give the strength to endure. With either outcome, God leads and preserves every believer (Psalms 23 and 121).[17]

Depression

Depression has been included last in this chapter because it overlaps with so many of the preceding problems. Christian thinking and secular thinking often debate past each other in the therapies for depression. Some Christians conclude that depression is never a medical problem. No one should ever need a prescription. By direct contrast, the secular world often views all depression as medical ignoring the spiritual, emotional, and relational factors that can also cause depression. The best advice is to probe all non-medical causes for depression before taking medicine. Yet, sometimes medicine is needed.

---

[17] The following suggestions are helpful in reducing worry. Refuse to worry about the past or future (Matt. 6:34; Phil. 3:13). Concentrate on present and real problems. Accept what cannot be changed. Don't worry about worry. Focus on the solutions to a problem not the enormity of it. Also, God is stronger than any trouble. Imagine the worst. Then consider how God would reverse this difficulty (either in this life or eternally). Listen to Christian music for encouragement (1 Sam. 16:23). Attend church for encouragement (Heb. 10:25). Get recreation, exercise, and rest (including rest from worry and problem solving, Psa. 127:1-2). Do what you can. Leave the rest with God (Psa. 55:22). Talk with a trusted friend about the source of worry. Do not put off responsibilities that can be accomplished now. This only increases pressure and makes worry more likely. Make a list of possible solutions with pros and cons to each. Perhaps set a time limit on concerns and efforts to solve long-term problems.

Those who need medical help should not feel false guilt and should realize those who need medicine still need God.

The Bible gives at least nineteen potential causes for depression. These may be further classified into four main categories. Depression can arise from sinful factors (personal sin), non-sinful factors (such as being the innocent victim of a grievous sin), holding false ideas, or having medical problems. Since God Himself and God's work in one's life is the source for joy, it is not surprising that most of the factors causing depression can be traced back to taking attention off God to self or things. For our purposes, it will be necessary to cover the complex topic with brevity, following only the outline of a previous study. [18]

Sinful Factors in Depression

Guilt causes depression. David was depressed when he covered up his adultery (Psa. 32:3-5,10; 38:1-10,18, 51:7,12). We solve our guilt by faith in Christ as Savior and then ongoing confession of sin to God.

Greed brings depression. King Ahab was depressed because Naboth would not sell him a certain piece of land (see 1 Kings 21:4-6; Eccles. 5:10,12). We must refuse the many advertisements telling us to buy more in order to obtain happiness. That process leads to depression.

Anger can cause depression. Cain was angry with God, then he took it out on his brother Abel. Cain "became angry and his countenance fell" (Gen. 4:5). We must confess sinful anger and forgive others who have wronged us, or we risk depression. Hatred is closely related to anger. Several Bible stories also tie hatred with serious depression (Haman was anti-Semitic, Esther 5:11-13; Jonah hated gentiles, Jonah 4:1-4, 8-9). We benefit emotionally by forgiving and loving even our enemies (Matt. 5:44; Rom. 12:19-20; Prov. 20:22, 24:29).

---

[18] See Steven Waterhouse, *Life's Tough Questions* (Amarillo: Westcliff Press, 2005), pp.19-61.

Saul was one of the Bible's most depressed characters. Among his problems was jealousy of David's success (1 Sam. 18:6-12, 15, see also pp. 154-155 and 169-170). A lazy, indolent life can lead to depression (Eccles. 3:13, 22, 5:18-19) as can the absurd but common notion that sex alone and outside of God's authority can become the basis for meaning in life (2 Sam. 13:1-4, 14-15).

Worry can cause depression if problems do not drive us to increased faith in God. Both Saul (1 Sam. 18:12, 29) and Elijah (1 Kings 19:2-4) illustrate that fears can bring depression to the point of suicidal despair.

Finally, perfectionist attitudes can bring depression as in Moses' life (Num. 11:11-15). This problem may or may not be classified as sin. However, if we know that we must realize human limitation but persist with perfectionist expectations to the point of thinking life is hopeless (as did Moses), then being a perfectionist is fairly classified among sinful causes of depression.

Guilt, greed, sinful anger, hatred, jealousy, laziness, looking to sex alone as "god", worry, perfectionism, rejection of Christ, and dabbling in the occult all cause depression. They may all be classified as sins and have in common attention upon self above God.[19]

Sometimes even otherwise non-sinful causes of depression eventually involve a lack of attention upon God. This is especially true if we do not bring the problem to God and thereby persist in depression.

Non-Sinful Factors in Depression

---

[19] Two additional factors that cause depression are rejection of the Anointed One and involvement in the occult. By definition, a believer has accepted Christ as Savior. Judas rejected the Lord, and then became depressed enough to kill himself (Matt. 27:5). This is the fulfillment of the Old Testament type, Ahithophel, who betrayed his close friend King David and later became depressed to the point of suicide (2 Sam. 17:23; Psa. 41:9; John 13:18). No one can deny Christ as Savior and escape depression at some point. Also, occult involvement in Bible days did sometimes lead to serious depression (Mark 5:5, 9:20, 22a). Satan brings the antithesis of joy.

The children of Israel experienced depression by Pharaoh's mistreatment (Ex. 6:9). A case can be made that the Lord Jesus Christ endured depression in the Garden of Gethsemane facing "victimization" by taking the punishment for the sins of the world (Matt. 26:38). Of course, He handled His need by entrusting Himself to His Father (1 Pet. 2:23) and by forgiving (Luke 23:34). Thus, in His non-sinful depression, He increased attention upon God. Often we do not follow His example.

False guilt (see pp. 148-149) can cause depression. We must avoid false guilt from accidents, legalistic standards, or failure to accept God's forgiveness.

Dashed dreams can cause depression. This was probably one of the several factors in Elijah's case. Perhaps he expected a national revival in Israel after defeating the prophets of Baal on Mt. Carmel. When revival did not happen, he became depressed to the point of wanting to die. The statement "I am no better than my fathers ... " reveals Elijah's depression because no past generation of spiritual fathers (i.e., spiritual leaders) had been successful in changing Israel either. Later he says, "I have been very zealous ... the sons of Israel have forsaken Your covenant ... I alone am left" (1 Kings 19:10).

Even today noble dreams go unrealized. However, faithfulness and pleasing God is within everyone's grasp. Taking pleasure that God has been honored helps when the specific project was not "successful." David never fulfilled his dream to build the temple, but God commended David's heart (2 Chron. 6:7-9). Again, attention upon God reduces depression. The same is true for a non-sinful depression stemming from rejection, even betrayal, and unfair criticism by people (see David in 2 Sam. 16:5-14). To overcome depression from rejection we have to go to God for unconditional love and security as did the ultimate "reject", the Lord Jesus Christ (Isaiah 53).

Loneliness causes depression. Elijah felt alone even when he was not (1 Kings 19:10). Sometimes loneliness can be caused by sinful rejection and withdrawal by others. Therefore, loneliness has been listed among the non-sinful factors that can bring depression. However, if we refuse to obey the command to assemble in a local church family, we can bring loneliness on ourselves. Also, in addition to human companionship, God is our ultimate friend (Heb. 13:5-6).

Non-sinful causes of depression (mistreatment, being the victim of sin, false guilt, dashed dreams, rejection and/or unfair criticism, loneliness) typically involve problems arising from other people. If these drive us to God as the source of healing for emotional wounds, we overcome depression. On the other hand, if we refuse to look to God in our needs caused by others, we may remain in depression and bear some responsibility for mishandling what otherwise are non-sinful causes for depression. A third major category that brings depression involves false ideas, especially a totally false world-view.

False Ideas

There is a direct connection between good theology and good psychology. Likewise, there is also a direct connection between false theology and bad psychology. Paul was worried about the Thessalonians being "shaken from composure" or "disturbed" because of false doctrine (2 Thess. 2:2). The heresy that there is no resurrection or life after death causes misery (1 Cor. 15:19). Denial of such things as creation or life after death produces worldviews that are inherently causes of depression. The only reason false views might be classified as a non-sinful cause of depression is that many are led astray by false teaching. Still, all are ultimately without excuse (Rom. 1:20) and required to seek truth (Acts 17:27). Persistence in a false doctrine, especially a totally non-Christian worldview, will at some point bring depression.

Sometimes personal sin causes depression. Sometimes being sinned against causes depression. False ideas cause depression. Finally, primary medical factors can cause depression, or depression that originates from another cause may eventually bring medical problems. Then we need both medical and spiritual help.

Medical Aspects to Depression

Exhaustion was a primary factor in Elijah's depression. Rather than delving into immediate counsel, the angel of the Lord told Elijah to eat and then let him rest. "Arise, eat, because the journey is too great for you" (1 Kings 19:7). Elijah's example gives biblical support that biological weakness can be a cause for depression. Psalm 102 gives the prayer of a sick person. Verse four describes sickness that causes a "smitten" heart "withering" on the inside and loss of appetite.

Some overemphasize biological factors, but it is also a mistake to ignore them. If one rules out the many non-medical causes of depression listed above, then the next step would be to try healthy practices including rest. If the spiritual/emotional causes for depression can be ruled out, and one tries a healthy lifestyle without alleviation of depression, then medicine may well be needed.

Conclusion

God's Word gives wisdom for all our problems. By looking to God as the source of joy and following His priorities for life we can eliminate some problems that could adversely affect the family.

When inevitable problems do arise, God has given instruction so we can either remove the problem or have a strong family in spite of the problem. Marital and family problems are nearly always underlying spiritual problems. This is not the same as concluding all problems originate in personal sin. Some do. Others do not. Regardless, each problem demands a response to the authority of God's Word. **If a couple has a commitment to the authority of the Bible and views life as a process of the admiration and imitation of God, no problem need ruin a family.**

Chapter Fourteen

Preventing Family Conflicts: Finances

Attitude or Amount?

Financial choices and habits reveal much about a person. The use of wealth reflects interests and philosophical values. Jesus said, "… where your treasure is, there your heart will be also" (Luke 12:34, see also Matt. 6:21).

Harmony in a home regarding money has more to do with attitude than amount. A couple fought over a $2.50 expenditure. They were deeply in debt so that a small amount caused great friction. Another couple had much money. They not only had money in the bank, they were heavy investors in their own bank. Nevertheless, they also fought over a $2.50 expenditure because the purchase of a pack of colored pencils for the children had not been planned in the budget and would lower the amount saved that month.

One assumption might be that lack of money produces broken homes. It certainly can. However, in modern times divorce rates have increased while the standard of living has also increased. In previous generations poor families with many children were virtually unbreakable. Proper attitudes toward God, life, and money created family strength despite financial difficulties. Attitude, not amount, determines family unity regarding money.

Contentment as a Financial Goal

From a Christian perspective, the issue is not whether money can make us happy but whether we can find contentment whatever our level of wealth. The world typically believes that the secret to contentment lies in a greater amount of money. God's Word teaches the secret to contentment regarding finances comes from attitudes and obedience in pleasing God. The world thinks, "I will find happiness and peace in life if and when I accumulate enough to feel secure and support my desired standard of living." The Bible teaches God alone gives security and satisfaction. The purpose of money is to exalt God. I can be content regardless of income level.

> Not that I speak from want, for I have learned to be content in whatever circumstances I am. I know how to get along with humble means, and I also know how to live in prosperity; in any and every circumstance I have learned the secret of being filled and going hungry, both of having abundance and suffering need. I can do all things through Him who strengthens me [Phil. 4:11-13].

> But godliness actually is a means of great gain when accompanied by contentment. For we have brought nothing into the world, so we cannot take anything out of it either. If we have food and covering, with these we shall be content [1 Tim. 6:6-8].

A biblical perspective on wealth allows for contentment in life, including family life. Amounts are secondary. Based upon God's authority, we must all agree that Christians in third world countries can be just as content and possess equally strong families as those in affluent areas. A few important truths about wealth are essential to bringing contentment.

God as Owner

God owns all. To Abraham God was "possessor of heaven and earth" (Gen. 14:19, 22). God told Moses that He owns the land (Lev. 25:23, see also: Deut. 10:14; Job 41:11; Psa. 24:1, 82:8). He told David He owns "the cattle on a thousand hills" (see Psa. 50:10-12). Haggai 2:8 asserts, " the silver is mine, and the gold is mine, declares the LORD of hosts."

God's claim upon all possessions puts us in the role of administrators of the money God has entrusted to us. God does not measure financial success by the amount accumulated at the end of life but by the degree of faithfulness in managing His possessions.

Initially, it may seem difficult to see any joy or contentment in the principle that we own nothing. The world does not see any connection between God and contentment in finances. Yet, given that

God owns everything, then we may feel secure in His ability to provide. A belief in God's ownership helps reduce burdens and worries about unpreventable loss in wealth or damage to possessions. We have an obligation to ethics in work habits and financial choices, but Christian living is not constant stress and obsession over money. In the final analysis, God can preserve, enlarge, or dispose of what belongs to Him. Those who live as if God owns everything have more responsibilities but less stress. They also have an attainable way of contentment and an accurate definition of success.

God as Distributor

God owns everything. Next, God distributes wealth as He pleases.

In the day of prosperity be happy, but in the day of adversity consider - God has made the one as well as the other so that man will not discover anything that will be after him [Eccl. 7:14].

The LORD makes the poor and rich, he brings low, He also exalts [1 Sam. 2:7].

For not from the east, nor from the west, nor from the desert comes exaltation; But God is the Judge; He puts down one and exalts another [Psa. 75:6-7].

For who regards you as superior? What do you have that you did not receive? And if you did receive it, why do you boast as if you had not received it? [1 Cor. 4:7 (see also Ex. 12:36; Deut. 8:18; 1 Chron. 29:12)].

One must know far more about a person's life than financial statements in order to measure a life. Godly people can be poor (Christ, the Apostles, Lazarus). Godly people can be rich (Abraham, Job, Solomon). Wicked people can be poor (poverty as judgment in Lev. 26:15ff.; Deut. 28:15ff.; Prov. 6:10-11, 28:22; Hosea 8:7; Haggai 1:6; 2 Thess. 3:10). Wicked people can be rich (Ahab and Jezebel, the rich fools in Jesus' parables Luke 12:13-21, 16:19-31).

A bank account alone does not give enough information to determine the quality or importance of a life. Perhaps the last category in the preceding paragraph is the most difficult to understand, the wicked rich. Some gain wealth as a result of God's blessing. Others temporarily prosper in wickedness. Sometimes evil people grow rich not just despite wickedness but directly from it. Drug dealers, abortion clinic investors, and pornographers often have more money than missionaries.

Belief in the Bible's teaching that God distributes wealth helps with financial contentment in life. Perhaps God causes a certain income level. It may be that He temporarily allows it, as in cases of those who prosper by evil. Belief that God is sovereign in the distribution of wealth allows for contentment despite the short term inequities we may see in life.

One of the secrets in being content with little or much is the realization that God knows which degree of wealth will make us most efficient in His service. If we are working faithfully at a task that is God's calling, we can leave the amount of income up to God. Recognition that God distributes wealth helps reduce snobbery toward others with fewer possessions and jealousy (or partiality) towards others with more. If God does make a righteous person rich, then his or her abilities and work were a part but not the entire factor in wealth. God's blessings were an even greater factor. Therefore, an attitude of smug superiority is never valid.

On the other hand, if a virtuous and hard-working Christian never becomes rich, he or she still has no basis for jealousy, resentment, or feelings of inferiority. God evaluates attitudes and faithfulness in handling money regardless of amount. He may judge the poorer Christian's life as having as much or more value. As administrators of God's wealth, our primary goal is to be faithful, not necessarily rich (1 Cor. 4:2). [1]

---

[1] Proverbs 30:8-9 presents an interesting middle-class mentality. Extreme wealth or extreme poverty both bring their own temptations. " ... give me neither poverty nor riches; feed me with the food that is my portion."

God as Provider

Those who obey God need not worry about financial uncertainties. God promises to supply all needs. These promises, however, are addressed to the righteous. God does allow the rebellious (Luke 15:11ff.) and the lazy to suffer need (2 Thess. 3:10). Conditions mentioned in texts that promise to meet need include: "righteousness" and "seeking first the Kingdom of God." Paul's promise in Phil. 4:19 that " ... my God shall supply all your needs" ... comes in a context of sacrificial giving. To the Philippians who had given to Paul's ministry God promised to supply their needs.

> Behold, the eye of the LORD is on those who fear Him, on those who hope for His lovingkindness, to deliver their soul from death and to keep them alive in famine [Psa. 33:18-19].

> I have been young and now I am old, yet I have not seen the righteous forsaken or his descendants begging bread. All day long he is gracious and lends, and his descendants are a blessing [Psa. 37:25-26].

> But seek first His kingdom and His righteousness, and all these things will be added to you [Matt. 6:33].

> For all these things the nations of the world eagerly seek; but your Father knows that you need these things. But seek His kingdom, and these things will be added to you [Luke 12:30-31].

> And my God will supply all your needs according to His riches in glory in Christ Jesus [Phil. 4:19].

God owns and distributes all wealth. God provides for His obedient children. An individual or family's view of wealth is that we are fund managers of the assets God entrusts to us. Our concern should be with the amount of faithfulness in managing God's wealth, not amount of money.

> He who is faithful in a very little thing is faithful also in much; and he who is unrighteous in a very little thing is unrighteous also in much [Luke 16:10 (see also: Matt. 25:21, 23)].

In this case, moreover, it is required of stewards that one be found trustworthy [1 Cor. 4:2].

Part of a Christian's attitude towards money includes basic truths about God. God is the owner, distributor, and provider. Relative to attitudes directly towards money itself, the Bible warns us not to make money the master of life (Matt. 6:24), the measure of life (Luke 12:15), or the motivation to live (1 Tim. 6:9-10). Those who transfer trust for security in life from God to money itself or live to worship money are called fools (Luke 12:20, 1 Tim. 6:9). Yet, if we view possessions as a blessing from God, and not a "god," then God intends us to enjoy possessions.

...God, who richly supplies us with all things to enjoy [1 Tim. 6:17].

Since contentment arises less from amount of assets than amount of faithfulness, we must study the Bible to determine God's instructions about managing His wealth. The knowledge and practice of God's truths about money enables the financial aspects of life to improve a family, not weaken it.

The Bible's Teachings about Debt

The conclusion that all debt is sin goes beyond the Bible. However, unlike modern practices, the Bible would classify all debt as extremely undesirable. Debt is a form of slavery. "The rich rules over the poor, and the borrower becomes the lender's slave" (Prov. 22:7; see also 2 Kings 4:1; Matt. 5:25-26, 18:21ff.).

Debt may not always be sin, but it is always negative. While debt for emergency expenses may be unavoidable, other types of debt are foolish and can be sinful.

Knowingly incurring debt that will never be repaid becomes an ethical matter. "The wicked borrows and does not pay back ..." (Psa. 37:21). If we continue to borrow even when we know in advance we cannot or have no intention to repay, this type of debt is sin.[2] Some

---

[2] Psalm 37:21 can be applied to the government.

kinds of debt do not arise from any material need but from several related sinful attitudes. We may go deeply in debt purchasing goods that we think will give us status. Such debt is ultimately based in pride not material need. Of course, there need be no sin in acquiring products beyond the basics if one has the means to do so with cash and at the same time maintain a balanced obedience to all of God's commands about money. Assuming these factors, including a rejection of snobbery, Christians who have jewelry or Italian suits need not have sinned. [3] The subject under consideration is debt. If one cannot afford beyond the basics, then he or she should be content with the basics and not try to obtain any elusive "status" financed by needless debt.

Another form of debt arises from what may be called "debt therapy." Advertisers encourage debt for unmet emotional needs. Contentment in life arises from a perfect God, a perfect Word of God, and the intrinsically valuable souls of family and friends. Purchases will not bring inner peace. On the contrary, purchases by debt in efforts to bring inner peace increase personal and family stress.

In addition to debt with no intention to repay or debt to obtain status or for emotional therapy, the final type of debt is based on pure greed and is often a delusion of feeling powerful. When we spend money, we feel important and in control. Greed is a sin problem whether we pay with cash or credit, but debt for the thrill of feeling power brings weakness to a family. Debt, not for emergency basic need, but rooted in selfishness and the illusion of power, does involve moral issues.

Not all debt is sin, but all debt is negative. When one never intends to repay, when debt arises from pride to obtain status, or misguided attempts to meet psychological needs, or selfish greed with a false sense of power, these types of debt do involve spiritual/ethical

---

[3] Christians must obey all the Bible teaches about greed, debt, and giving. We should try to live below, not above, our incomes. Still, many have enough affluence to obey and also to have nice possessions. Class envy and jealousy are not virtues. Believing God causes or allows the distribution of wealth helps with temptation to envy.

issues and can, if unchecked, lead to serious problems for a marriage and family.

Less Objectionable Types of Debt

Since the Bible tells us to lend to people in need, debt arising from genuine need must not be sinful (though obviously undesirable).

> Now in case a countryman of yours becomes poor and his means with regard to you falter, then you are to sustain him, like a stranger or a sojourner, that he may live with you [Lev. 25:35].

> If there is a poor man with you, one of your brothers, in any of your towns in your land which the LORD your God is giving you, you shall not harden your heart, nor close your hand from your poor brother; but you shall freely open your hand to him, and shall generously lend him sufficient for his need in whatever he lacks [Deut. 15:7-8 (see also Ex. 22:25-27; Deut. 15:1-2, 6, 23:19-20a, 24:10-13, 17; Neh. 10:31; Ezek. 18:5,7-9; Matt. 5:42; Luke 6:34-35)].

Some types of situations, such as a medical emergency or natural disaster, are need by anyone's definition. Debt incurred in order to produce an income (such as education) is less objectionable than debt for rapidly depreciating luxury goods (a boat). Debt for a product necessary to life, which at the same time holds high resale value, is also less objectionable than debt for a rapidly depreciating luxury good with minimal resale value. Sometimes the same product can be either in the need or luxury category. Transportation makes a good example for consideration.

Basic transportation is essential to produce an income. Virtually every employment ad for even "entry level" tasks requires transportation. Yet, transportation financed by debt can also be classified in the far beyond minimal need category. It is common for people to finance cars or trucks that exceed basic transportation requirements and enter the "debt to obtain status," "feel-good debt therapy," or "debt for greed and false thrill of power" classification.

Those with means to obey all of God's commands and still pay cash for luxury cars need not feel false guilt for being so blessed. Those with less should always ask "What do I need?" not "What gives me status, or good feelings, or a sense of control and self-importance?" Many times a need for transportation to produce an income can be met debt free with a less expensive or used car.

With some couples, debt for any reliable car may be a necessity. If so, they need feel no panic or false guilt. A balanced philosophy towards debt will avoid sinful and foolish debt but allow for emergency or necessary debt to live.[4] Viewing all debt as negative and concentrating on needs will go a long way toward reducing marital feuds over money.

When We Have Debts

The Bible assumes we will avoid all unnecessary debt and view all debt as negative. Those with debt have an obligation to repay. While unforeseen setbacks such as injury, disease, or a job loss might cause inability to repay, or bankruptcy, Christians without such disasters have an obligation to repay creditors. When the means to repay are available, we must get free from debt as opposed to using disposable income for other optional purchases (or even going deeper into debt). Proverbs Chapter 3 concerns charity, but its principle may be applied to repayment of debt.

> Do not withhold good from those to whom it is due, when it is in your power to do it. Do not say to your neighbor, "Go and come back, and tomorrow I will give it," when you have it with you [Prov. 3:27-28].

Paul's teaching in Romans 13:8 is that believers are to "owe nothing to anyone except to love one another ... " At the very least, this means

---

[4] Those who have experienced injury, disease, or disasters need not feel any guilt for the resulting unavoidable debt.

Christians in debt have a duty to discharge that debt as soon as possible. [5]

Here is a brief list of practical suggestions to become debt-free:

♦ Make a list of all your assets (cash, bonds, insurance, coins, real estate, personal property) and evaluate whether you should sell assets to reduce debt.

♦ Make a policy to pay cash. Either destroy credit cards or use them only for the convenience of making a purchase (with funds already in an account to pay off the debt before interest is charged). When in debt, accumulate no new debt.

♦ Make a list of debts. Try to pay off those with the highest interest rates more rapidly.

♦ When one creditor is paid off, apply that money to another debt rather than feeling free to dispose of that money on some new purchase.

♦ Seek additional income to apply to the debt (odd jobs, a temporary second job, garage sales), but do not waste this income on more foolish buying habits.

♦ If debts are unmanageable, take a repayment schedule to creditors and explain what proportion of the debt can be paid and estimate how long before the obligation is met.

♦ Be content with what you have *as the Bible commands.*

By compliance with the Bible's philosophy towards possessions and its views on debt, a family can reduce conflict and increase strength. When financial conditions permit saving, a family

---

[5] In its context the Romans 13 text commands us to pay taxes. No family needs the stress of being in trouble with the government. God's Word tells us to pay all taxes owed (Matt. 17:24-27, 22:17-22; Luke 20:25; Rom. 13:5-7). The Proverbs also warn about co-signing for another's debt (Prov. 6:1-5, 17:18, 22:26-27).

will also face less stress by building a reserve in order to meet inevitable future needs.

The Bible on Saving

The phrase "lay not up for yourselves treasures upon earth" (Matt. 6:19 KJV) definitely forbids hoarding wealth. Endless saving in order to insulate self from all potential need is both contrary to the Bible and ultimately impossible. We cannot possibly save enough to shelter from all imaginable catastrophes. The attempt to do so insults God by not trusting in His care or putting Him first in life. Many Scriptures forbid hoarding to the point of turning money into an idol, the sole standard for greatness, or the source of ultimate security.[6]

An overemphasis upon saving is wrong, but it is also a mistake to conclude God is in favor of squandering (or even giving away) absolutely everything. Sometimes Jesus asked an individual to give up all (or be willing to give up all), but this may not be transferred to a universal command for everyone. The rich young ruler in Matt. 19:16-22 may be taken as an example of riches being a barrier to faith and thereby to salvation. Jesus told him to give up all his possessions and "… come follow Me" (v. 21). Any possession that prohibits faith in Christ as Savior should indeed be discarded, but this truth does not prohibit Christian families from saving money.

Joseph is the ultimate biblical example of saving during years of abundance so that a surplus exists for years of greater need. Genesis 41 tells the story of Joseph being called from prison to interpret the Egyptian Pharaoh's strange dream. God told Joseph that the dream predicted seven years of abundant crops followed by seven years of

---

[6] See Deut. 8:10-14, 17-18; Psa. 49:6-9, 10-11; Prov. 11:25, 23:5, 30:8-9; Haggai 1:4-7; Mal. 3:10; Matt. 6:19-21, 24; Luke 12:15-21; 1 Tim. 3:3, 6:7-10,17; 1 Pet. 5:2; James 5:1-3. Solomon concluded, "He who loves money will never be satisfied with money … when good things increase, those who consume them increase. So what is the advantage to their owners …. "(Eccles. 5:10-11). Someone wise has observed, "Money will buy a bed but not sleep, books but not brains, food but not an appetite, a house but not a home, medicine but not health, luxuries but not culture, amusement but not happiness, a crucifix but not a Savior."

famine. Joseph was promoted from prison to prime minister by advising saving during abundance to withstand future difficulty.

> Let the food become as a reserve for the land for the seven years of famine which will occur in the land of Egypt, so that the land will not perish during the famine …. Now Joseph was thirty years old when he stood before Pharaoh, king of Egypt. And Joseph went out from the presence of Pharaoh and went through all the land of Egypt. During the seven years of plenty the land brought forth abundantly. So he gathered all the food of these seven years which occurred in the land of Egypt and placed the food in the cities; he placed in every city the food from its own surrounding fields [Gen. 41:36, 46-48].

The Proverbs give us wisdom about saving by telling us to observe ants. They store in the summer to provide a reserve for a time of future need (Prov. 6:6-8, 30:24-25). Another proverb reads, "There is precious treasure and oil in the dwellings of the wise, but a foolish man swallows it up" (Prov. 21:20; by application see also 22:3 NIV).

In related parables the Lord revealed he was not against all saving, whether bank accounts or investing (Matt. 25:14-29; Luke 19:12-24). Paul taught that parents are to save up for their children (2 Cor. 12:14). More verses warn against miserly hoarding than encourage saving, but balanced saving is a biblical and prudent aspect to Christian living.

Proverbs 24:27 gives a farm analogy that may be applied to other lifestyles. "Prepare your work outside and make it ready for yourself in the field; afterwards, then, build your house." This truth may be applied to those who are not on a farm. Solomon advised working to develop income producing skills and/or building up a business before plunging into life's greatest expenses. By extension, it is wise for young people to develop careers that will generate an income before they buy things like a house or maybe even prior to marriage itself.

The Bible is not averse to making an income. Saving can be done to an unwise extreme, but saving during good times so that there is a cushion for bad times follows the Bible's own example and advice.

Some Bible verses caution against get-rich-quick-schemes, but also endorse diligent plans to build up saving gradually.

Dishonest money dwindles away, but he who gathers money little by little makes it grow [Prov. 13:11 NIV (see also Prov. 21:5, 28:20)].

Families should enter into debt reluctantly. In time of excess, the first thought should be toward a saving plan to reduce pressure when the next time of greater need arises. Not only would biblical principles encourage efforts to maintain self-reliance into old age if possible (by application Acts 20:34; 2 Cor. 11:9; 1 Thess. 2:9), they commend building up enough to give an inheritance to following generations.

A good man leaves an inheritance to his children's children ... [Prov. 13:22a (see also Gen. 24:36, 25:5)]. [7]

Excellence in Work

Every married person must attempt to balance work and Christian service responsibilities with the family. Just as the Bible encourages saving but forbids hoarding, there are also many commandments to work hard but other teachings which caution against overworking out of anxiety over income.

Humans were created to work. We derive a sense of purpose by serving God with work and imitating His image as "Creator." Even before sin entered the world, God instituted work as a part of the

---

[7] As a general rule the righteous try to leave an inheritance for the next generation. We cannot take anything with us (Job 1:21; Eccles. 5:15; 1 Tim. 6:7), but we can send some ahead to the "treasury" in heaven (Mal. 3:10; Matt. 6:19-21) and can often choose how the rest is dispersed after death. Often a family can trust the next generation with inherited money but not always (Prov. 20:21; Eccles. 2:18). Some children would only use the money for evil, not God's honor. It is not a biblical requirement that an inheritance be left to all adult children or even divided equally. Parents are responsible to provide for minor children. This should include life insurance and making a will that entrusts children to willing and godly adoptive parents.

original Creation (Gen. 2:15). Distasteful aspects to work are a result of the curse. However, in our love-hate relationship with work, there are aspects to employment that are rewarding (Gen. 1:28, 9:1, 7).

Since our purpose is only to consider how work fits in with family life, we will only quote a few proof-texts (with more references listed for the reader's additional study).

The Bible commands excellence in work habits.

Whatever your hand finds to do, do it with all your might ... [Eccl. 9:10].

[A]nd to make it your ambition to lead a quiet life and attend to your own business and work with your hands, just as we commanded you, so that you will behave properly toward outsiders and not be in any need [1 Thess. 4:11-12; (see also Ex. 20:9, 34:21; Prov. 6:6-11; Rom. 12:11; Eph. 4:28; 2 Thess. 3:10)].

The Bible gives historical examples of hard work.

And she said, "Please let me glean and gather after the reapers among the sheaves." Thus she came and has remained from the morning until now; she has been sitting in the house for a little while…. So she gleaned in the field until evening. Then she beat out what she had gleaned, and it was about an ephah of barley [Ruth 2:7,17].

You yourselves know that these hands ministered to my own needs and to the men who were with me. In everything I showed you that by working hard in this manner you must help the weak and remember the words of the Lord Jesus, that He Himself said, "It is more blessed to give than to receive" [Acts 20:34-35; (see also Jacob, Gen. 31:38-42; Nehemiah, Neh. 4:6, 21; and Paul, 1 Cor. 4:12; 1 Thess. 2:9)].

The Bible promises good results from diligent labor. Any given day may not be profitable, but over a life the trend is that hard work pays.

Do you see a man skilled in his work? He will stand before kings; he will not stand before obscure men [Prov. 22:29].

The sleep of the working man is pleasant, whether he eats little or much; but the full stomach of the rich man does not allow him to sleep [Eccles 5:12; (see also Prov. 10:4, 12:11, 24, 14:23, 25:13, 28:19a)].

The Bible forbids and ridicules laziness.

The way of the lazy is as a hedge of thorns, but the path of the upright is a highway [Prov. 15:19].

The sluggard buries his hand in the dish, but will not even bring it back to his mouth [Prov. 19:24].

A little sleep, a little slumber, a little folding of the hands to rest, then your poverty will come as a robber and your want like an armed man [Prov. 24:33-34].

The sluggard says, "There is a lion in the road! A lion is in the open square!" As the door turns on its hinges, so does the sluggard on his bed [Prov. 26:13-14].

Through indolence the rafters sag, and through slackness the house leaks [Eccl. 10:18; (see also Prov. 10:5,26; 12:11,24; 13:4; 14:23; 18:9; 19:15; 20:4,13; 21:25-26; 22:13; 23:21; 28:19)].

The Bible on Working Too Much

Just as God's Word encourages saving but condemns hoarding, the Bible requires hard work but limits workaholic attitudes and habits. Work honors God in many ways.

Social contacts through business generate frequent ministry opportunities for evangelism or counseling. All honest professions honor God and should be viewed as working in a ministry to the Lord.[8]

> Whatever you do in word or deed, do all in the name of the Lord
> Jesus, giving thanks through Him to God the Father .... whatever
> you do, do your work heartily, as for the Lord rather than for
> men, knowing that from the Lord you will receive the reward of
> the inheritance. It is the Lord Christ whom you serve [Col. 3:17,
> 23-24 (see also Eph. 6:5-8; 1 Tim. 6:1-2; Titus 2:9-10; 1 Pet.
> 2:18-19)].

Our vocations are not substitutes for "God" providing the
reason to live any more than the income generated by working. Profit
motives should be to "honor the Lord from your wealth" (Prov. 3:9a)
by obeying biblical commands about finances, including giving (see
next section).

Work is a means to bless the family (1 Tim. 5:8), to become
self-reliant when there are no physical limitations upon labor (Acts
20:34; 2 Cor. 11:9; 1 Thess. 2:9, 4:11-12), to help the weak (Acts
20:35; Eph. 4:28), to worship God by financial sacrifice and offering
(as opposed to Old Testament animal sacrifices, Phil. 4:18-19) and to
obtain "fruit" (ministry results) by giving (Phil. 4:17; Rom. 15:28).
Work is not the goal in life but a secondary means to the greater
purpose in life of worship and service to God.

Taken to an extreme, overworking can hinder our relationship
with God, and our service to God. Instead of bringing blessings to the
family, work looked upon as the reason to live harms marriage and the
family. Perhaps human nature tends to laziness. Therefore, the Bible
contains more commands to work, but some important texts warn of

---

[8] Scripture contains a complete business philosophy beyond the scope of this
book: honesty in measuring products (Deut. 25:13-15; Prov. 11:1, 16:11,
20:10,23; Hosea 12:7; Amos 8:4-7; Micah 6:10-11), strict ethics in agreements
(Prov. 10:2, 15:27, 16:8, 19:1, 20:17, 21:6; Isa. 33:15-16; Jer. 17:9-11; Micah
2:1-2, 6:10-12), prohibitions against embezzlement (Titus 2:9-10) or laziness
(see pp. 179-181), or slandering co-workers (Prov. 30:10) or discontentment
over salary to the point of violence (Luke 3:14). Employers must pay fair
wages (Lev. 19:13; Deut. 24:15, 25:4; Neh. 5:1-12; Isa. 5:8-9; Jer. 22:13;
Amos 5:11; Mal. 3:5; Matt. 23:14; Mark 12:40; Luke 10:7, 20:47; Eph. 6:9;
Col. 4:1; 1 Tim. 5:18, 6:10; James 5:1-4).

needless excess. In addition, the Old Testament Sabbath supports the need for balance in work habits. Work is virtue but not to the degree of crowding God out of life or harming marital or parental relationships.

Six days you shall labor and do all your work, but the seventh day is a sabbath of the LORD your God; in it you shall not do any work, you or your son or your daughter, your male or your female servant or your cattle or your sojourner who stays with you [Ex. 20:9-10]. [9]

Do not weary yourself to gain wealth, cease from your consideration of it. When you set your eyes on it, it is gone. For wealth certainly makes itself wings like an eagle that flies toward the heavens [Prov. 23:4-5].

Unless the LORD builds the house, they labor in vain who build it; unless the LORD guards the city, the watchman keeps awake in vain. It is vain for you to rise up early, to retire late, to eat the bread of painful labors; For He gives to His beloved even in his sleep [Psalm 127:1-2].

The sleep of the working man is pleasant, whether he eats little or much … [Eccl. 5:12a].

And He said to them, "Come away by yourselves to a secluded place and rest a while." (For there were many people coming and going, and they did not even have time to eat) [Mark 6:31].

Life itself will require most families to work hard. Yet, there is a crossing point at which additional work hinders, rather than helps a family. Balance between work, family and church improves life. Wise Christians give attention to and make progress in all areas rather than

---

[9] The Sabbath is the only one of the Ten Commandments not carried over into the New Testament. Yet, as a personal choice for life we will be better if we choose to balance work with strong convictions about time for worship and rest. Eric Liddell would not have sinned to run Olympic trials on a Sunday, but he had an honorable personal conviction. Under the Law of Moses, the people not only rested one day in seven but observed lengthy holiday periods every year.

focusing on one to the neglect (or even ruin) of others. These three main areas of life are intended to reinforce each other.

To give balance in finances we must include one additional topic: giving. The Bible teaches about debt (spending), saving, and giving. A full treatment is not needed for a book on marriage, but ignoring charity would be a mistake. With correct attitudes, giving becomes a spiritual matter, improving our relationship with God and bringing increased purpose and satisfaction to life, including family life.

Giving As a Blessing

God does not need our help. He is not bankrupt. His Kingdom and plans are not on the verge of ruin (Psa. 50:10-12; 1 Cor. 13:3; 2 Cor. 8:12, 9:7). If a bad attitude exists, it is best not to give at all ("not grudgingly or under compulsion" 2 Cor. 9:7).

Purposes in giving include: acknowledging God, not money, as Master (Matt. 6:24), blessing by support for noble projects and precious people (Acts 20:35; Phil. 4:17), coming to realize God as owner, provider, and authority over wealth and our continual debt to Him (1 Chron. 29:14). Giving develops character by increasing faith in God to provide replacement of our gifts, by deepening humility both in terms of dependence upon God and an unselfish nature, and by learning obedience (1 Tim. 6:17-19). When we share, we are improved and God is honored above money. [10]

God wants to create a certain spirit within those who give. Certainly, donors should not seek pride or vain publicity. The Bible teaches that sharing includes (or should include): an attitude of worship and dedication to God (Luke 12:21; 2 Cor. 8:3-5), modesty and humility (Matt. 6:1-4), genuine love (1 Cor. 13:3; Heb. 13:1-2; 1 John 3:17), a sense of unity and fellowship with other Christians who are also giving to a ministry project (1 Cor. 12:25; Phil. 1:5; Rom. 15:26), submission to God as a first priority over materialism (Prov. 3:9-10;

---

[10] Commands to give include: Matt. 5:42, 6:19-21, 10:8c; Luke 3:10-11, 12:33-34; Gal. 2:10; 1 Tim. 6:17-19; Heb. 13:16.

Matt. 6:33), increased faith in God to provide after sacrificial giving (compare 2 Cor. 8:3; with Phil. 4:10-19), a willing attitude without a grudge (1 Chron. 29:9; 2 Cor. 8:12, 9:7), an attitude expecting God to bless in His own manner and time (Acts 20:35; Luke 6:38; 2 Cor. 9:6).[11]

God's way of evaluating our sharing is less about the amount of money than the amount of dedication and sacrifice. He cares more about what we give up in order to give than in the amount given. The story of the widow giving her small mite illustrates that God grades on a "curve" in the ministry of giving (Luke 21:1-4).

A married couple struggling with finances must not think giving is unimportant if amounts cannot be large. In God's economy,

---

[11] We must be cautious about concluding that the Bible gives inevitable results for sharing. Likewise, we must be cautious about concluding inevitable results for a refusal to share. There are biblical examples of righteous people who were not blessed with wealth (e.g. Luke 16:19ff.; 2 Cor. 8:2; Heb. 11:37ff.). There are also biblical examples of wicked people who were blessed with wealth (Luke 12:16ff., 16:19ff.). It is not correct to assume that those who share are always automatically blessed with riches, nor is it correct to conclude that God automatically takes wealth away from stingy people. The Bible does not promise that generous believers will always be blessed with wealth; neither does it warn that miserly people will always end up in poverty.

However, there are passages that teach givers will often prosper. Likewise, there are passages which teach those who are greedy often end up with less or at the least end up in misery. Christians should not think that sharing is an automatic way to financial rewards. There is no absolute promise or guarantee of monetary prosperity for generosity. However, it seems as though prosperity (either financial or spiritual) is a common, usual, and frequent blessing for faithfulness in sharing. On the other hand, misery and stinginess go together. It is common for the greedy to find themselves diminished in wealth. (It is relevant to repeat here that the promise to supply all need is delivered to the righteous. Thus, for the righteous there is always the blessing of being under His protective care.)

Here are some verses which show the general principle that sharing often leads to blessings, and refusal to share often leads to diminished blessings: Psa. 41:1-3; Prov. 3:9-10, 11:24-25, 22:9, 28:27; Eccles. 11:1-2; Haggai 1:2-11; Mal. 3:8-10; Luke 6:38; 2 Cor. 9:6.

He figuratively can multiply our donated "loaves and fishes." With biblical attitudes, God can cause ministry impact far out of proportion to our ability to give. A family should by all means give something according to its ability. God's standard for giving is proportional to income (1 Cor. 16:2, "as he may prosper," see also Acts 11:29; 2 Cor. 8:12-13). [12]

By sharing, a family obtains God's blessing, improves its own character, teaches the children God's own outlook and values in life, and feels purpose in contribution to important causes. Giving deepens a walk with God and helps our efforts in life rise far above the trivial pursuits of materialism. [13] Sharing is part of truly living (consider 1 Tim. 6:19!).

Budgeting As Smart

---

[12] 1 Cor. 16:2 gives God's method for giving. Giving should be individual and include all Christians, "... Each one of you ..." It should be regular as to frequency, "on the first day of the week ..." We should plan in advance so that giving is a thoughtful, not haphazard part of our budget, "... put aside and save." Finally, giving should be proportional to income, "... as he may prosper ..." When Christians obey this method, it will prevent frantic fund drives. That is exactly Paul's point. When is the last time you heard a sermon on "so that no collections be made when I come" (1 Cor. 16:2)?

[13] The Bible condemns and prohibits giving to false teachers (Ezek. 34:1-2; Mark 11:15-17, 12:38-40; Luke 16:14; 1 Tim. 6:3-5; 2 Pet. 2:2-3, 14-15; especially 2 John 7-11, Jude 11). We should also try not to support laziness (2 Thess. 3:10). Recipients or projects worthy of giving include: needy relatives, especially senior parents (Matt. 15:4-6; 1 Tim. 5:4, 8); hospitality to believers (Rom. 12:13; Heb. 13:1-2; 1 Pet. 4:9); needy widows and orphans (1 Tim. 5:4, 9-10; James 1:27); poor Christians (Lev. 25:35; Acts 2:44-45, 4:32-35, 6:1-3, 11:29; Rom. 12:13, 15:26-27; 1 Cor. 16:1; 2 Cor. 8:13-14; Gal. 6:10; Eph. 4:28; James 2:15-16; 1 John 3:16-17); the poor in general (Ps. 41:1-3; Prov. 14:21,31,19:17, 21:13, 22:9, 28:27; Matt. 5:42; Luke 6:34, 10:33-37, 14:12-14; Acts 11:29); Christian workers (Matt. 10:10; Luke 8:3, 10:7; 1 Cor. 9:14; Gal. 6:6; Phil. 4:10,14-17; 1 Tim. 5:17-18; 3 Jn.5-8) and by application Christian buildings (Ex. 35:29, 36:5-7; 1 Chron. 29:6-9).

There does not seem to be direct references to family budgeting in the Bible, but many verses call for counsel and planning (Prov. 11:14, 12: 15, 15:22, 19:20). Jesus assumed any sensible person would sit down and plan for an expensive building project (Luke 14:28-30).

Creating and using wealth are major scriptural topics. Finances reveal much about a person. Disregard to God's principles on debt, saving, hoarding, sharing, work, and overwork, will bring trouble to a home. Sometimes continued disobedience destroys a home. All of God's commandments are for our benefit, including those on money. Compliance brings increased financial and relational security.

It may be impossible to choose whether greater stress upon modern homes arises from finances or poor communication. The next chapter considers help from the Bible with communication and decision-making.

Chapter Fifteen

Preventing Family Conflicts: Communication

The book of Joshua closes with an event showing the importance of communication. Israel settled into the Promised Land with two and one-half tribes on the east bank of the Jordan River. Those east of the Jordan built an altar purely as a memorial to unity with the rest of Israel. However, their brethren west of the Jordan took this for apostasy and "gathered themselves at Shiloh to go up against them in war" (Josh. 22:12). Fortunately, before starting to fight the sides met for a discussion. All preparations for battle ceased with the explanation the altar was not intended for actual sacrifice but only as a memorial for future generations of the oneness of all twelve tribes. Those on the east bank intended to gather for worship only at the Tabernacle built by God's command to Moses (Josh. 22:21-29). Here is an example of a potential fight based upon lack of communication and a complete misunderstanding. A positive moral to the story would be that communication prevents needless conflict.

The actual word "communication" occurs very few times in the English Bible. In Bible times the same truths were taught by the numerous references to the "tongue," "lips," or "mouth." When classified, these references give a veritable "theology of communication." We will apply these teachings to marriage and the family, but they would also give wisdom for communication in politics, education, business, or church life.

The Power of Speech

Communication is vital to healthy relationships because the tongue is an instrument of blessing or cursing, building-up or tearing down. God's Word gives both outcomes to speech. "Death and life are in the power of the tongue ..." (Prov. 18:21). Proverbs calls words "dainty morsels" because "they go down into the innermost parts of the body" (Prov. 26:22). Morsels first make us think of goodies. Words to a husband, wife, or child can be a treat. Another Bible comparison would be "fruit" Prov. 18:21. Yet, words can also give us the emotional equivalent to "food poisoning."

The old rhyme, "sticks and stones may break my bones, but words will never hurt me" has some value in teaching children not to take every mean word to heart, but it is not true to say "words will never hurt me." James says, "But no one can tame the tongue, it is a restless evil and full of deadly poison" (James 3:8). Job's so-called comforters hurt him deeply by their speech, "How long will you torment me and crush me with words?" (Job 19:2).

We might paraphrase Proverbs 18:21 to teach *marital life and death are in the power of the tongue.* The importance of the **admiration and imitation of the Lord Jesus Christ** to marriage overlaps with the topic of communication. "What would Jesus say?"

Communication and Gender Roles

Chapters 7 and 8 support traditional roles for husband and wife but also stress that decisions should be made only after a couple communicates about the matter. While final authority in a Christian home should rest with the husband, the Bible tells husbands to "live with your wives in an understanding way" and to "show her honor" (1 Pet. 3:7). In God's view of leadership, the leader always serves the best interests of those under authority. The Bible's commands for communication should not be considered authoritative in other areas of life only to be cast aside within a marriage.

If we will obey God and communicate, most of the time both husband and wife will either agree or at least come to a consensus about a decision. If a deeper disagreement arises, they might wait. In situations of a deadline, the Bible gives a husband the authority to decide. When he has exhibited a past of honoring, understanding, and loving his wife, then she should be able to yield without resentment, safely trusting his intentions even if disagreeing with his judgment.

Reasons for Poor Communication

Lack of communication is always a poor sign in a marriage. However, diagnosing the precise cause matters greatly. Just as a cough may only be an irritating tickle, or it may be lung cancer, communication problems arise from different sources and may or may not be serious. Accurate diagnosis matters because a solution must fit the real problem. We do not want to consider drastic surgery for a tickle or vice versa.

Sometimes people are insecure or preoccupied. Others have been hurt in the past, or they simply have trouble verbalizing thoughts. If lack of communication stems from insecurity, a gentle and supportive approach is in order. A spouse needs encouragement for insecurity or troubles in communicating his or her ideas.

Oftentimes people clam up from anger or the conclusion that talking things out will just lead to rejection or will not make any difference. This is obviously a more serious reason for lack of communication. Here, there may be need for love mixed with confession, forgiveness, or even rebuke.

The starting point for resolving communication problems depends upon its cause. Rebuke and calls for an apology, for example, would only cause more insecurity when timidity is the real problem. It helps to keep in mind the cause for silence determines suggestions for improving communication. Also, how a person has been treated in the past or his own personality bent influences the degree of present communication skills or comfort with revealing themselves. Our present response to our spouse can encourage or squelch communication. Try to understand the cause of silence before making a plan for improvement. There is a vast difference between a spouse withdrawing into a snit or a shy and timid soul hesitant to bring topics up out of sensitivity of saying the wrong thing.

Listening: A Basis for Communication

The first rule in communication is to become a careful listener. People in our hectic, mobile and stressful world simply do not pay close attention to others. Listening is a great act of love.

Listening involves love because it takes time. Few in our busy world can afford time. Yet, of all people, those in our family deserve complete attention more than anyone else. They deserve first priority in one's schedule for their needs. James 1:19 commands, " ... everyone must be **quick to hear** ... " If obedience to this command begins in the family, it will prevent trouble and strengthen the home.

Prov. 18:13 says, "He who gives an answer before he **hears**, it is folly and shame to him."

Listening carefully displays love and respect. Wise people do not answer (communicate) until they first listen.

Couples on the verge of divorce quit listening to each other. When we dislike another we interpret their intents and words with the most unfavorable twist. When a couple argues in private, the conversation reported to others becomes a case of "he said" and "she said." Often third parties cannot even tell what really transpired. In marriage counseling sometimes a "time out" is helpful, followed by inviting Mr. X to speak, then inviting Mrs. X to slowly repeat what Mr. X has just said. Then Mrs. X might be invited to speak, and Mr. X is invited to repeat what Mrs. X said. This exercise forces a couple to listen to each other carefully without subjective interpretation or exaggeration.

Misunderstanding can arise from never talking, but also from talking without really listening. Listening demonstrates honor and respect. Couples who listen have a basis for sane and profitable communication. God's Word tells us to be "quick to hear." Next the Bible commands us to think before we reply and to begin with gentle words.

Thinking Precedes Talking

Sensitive topics require reasoned responses. In a dispute, the first words in our sinful hearts might best be restrained. With diplomats or negotiators the first words may well be restrained in order to prevent war. In a family setting thoughtless words may even win the argument and put our spouse (or child or parents) on the defensive. Even though careless and spontaneous words may win an argument, they can easily lose in terms of the relationship or solving the problem. What profit is there in "winning" an argument when it damages the relationship?

After the phrase "quick to hear" in James 1:19 comes "**slow to speak**" and "**slow to anger**". The person who gives thought before a reply can spare everyone much grief.

When there are many words, transgression is unavoidable, but he who restrains his lips is wise [Prov. 10:19].

The heart of the righteous ponders how to answer, but the mouth of the wicked pours out evil things [Prov. 15:28].

The heart of the wise instructs his mouth and adds persuasiveness to his lips [Prov. 16:23].

He who guards his mouth and his tongue, guards his soul from troubles [Prov. 21:23].

A fool always loses his temper, but a wise man holds it back [Prov. 29:11].

Do you see a man who is hasty in his words? There is more hope for a fool than for him [Prov. 29:20].

Diction and Tone

How we talk can be as important as what we are trying to say. Choice of words, attitude, volume, rate, pitch, and gestures are all a part of communication. The same message can be delivered in ways that gain acceptance or in ways that cause fights. Suppose I would like for my wife to bake a blueberry pie. I could remark at supper, "It has been so long since you've made anything good; you've probably forgotten how to make blueberry pie." The same message can be delivered in an acceptable style and get results. "You make such good pies. If I bring home the ingredients after work, can I get a pie?" This pie illustration is silly, but far less silly than the way many married couples communicate about far more serious topics. Indeed, there can be a time for blunt and firm family conversations. Yet, all talks should start with gentleness.

A gentle answer turns away wrath, but a harsh word stirs up anger [Prov. 15:1].

A man has joy in an apt answer, and how delightful is a timely word! [Prov. 15:23].

The wise in heart will be called understanding, and sweetness of speech increases persuasiveness [Prov. 16:21].

Pleasant words are a honeycomb, sweet to the soul and healing to the bones [Prov. 16:24].

Like apples of gold in settings of silver is a word spoken in right circumstances [Prov. 25:11].

Goals for Communication

Every Christian must in principle yield to the Bible's authority on speech. If anything we should be even more ready to obey these commands within our family than at church or when talking to strangers. The goals for Christian communication should be to understand another more deeply, to meet another's needs, to edify (a Bible word meaning to build up not tear down), to restore. The goal of a conversation should never be to embarrass, to inflict emotional wounds, or to win an argument at all costs.

In church disputes the underlying problem that needs to be solved can be forgotten. The goal in the conversation no longer remains to understand, to solve, and to meet needs. In resentment the goal becomes to win the argument even if the relationship is ruined or the problem remains unsolved. If anything, it is more disheartening when such attitudes occur within a Christian home. The following verses remind us that the goals of conversations should remain deeper understanding, love, edification, and the well being of our family members. Attitudes commanded in these texts prevent a win-at-any-cost approach where a secondary argument is won at the expense of wrecking the underlying relationship.

Brethren, even if anyone is caught in any trespass, you who are spiritual, restore such a one in a spirit of gentleness; each one looking to yourself, so that you too will not be tempted [Gal. 6:1].

[W]ith all humility and gentleness, with patience, showing tolerance for one another in love [Eph. 4:2].

Let no unwholesome word proceed from your mouth, but only such a word as is good for edification according to the need of the moment, so that it will give grace to those who hear [Eph. 4:29].

[M]ake my joy complete by being of the same mind, maintaining the same love, united in spirit, intent on one purpose. Do nothing from selfishness or empty conceit, but with humility of mind regard one another as more important than yourselves; do not merely look out for your own personal interests, but also for the interests of others [Phil. 2:2-4].

Let your speech always be with grace, as though seasoned with salt, so that you will know how you should respond to each person [Col. 4:6].

Notice the attitudes and actions in the preceding verses: humility, gentleness, patience, forbearance, love, unity, prohibitions of selfishness and conceit, interest in others, grace, edification. Such wisdom in communication prevents or solves family conflict.

The willingness to forgive also allows communication to continue or be restarted, "He who covereth a transgression seeketh love" [(Prov. 17:9a (KJV)]. Those who **admire and imitate Christ** will "forbear" and "forgive" (see Eph. 4:32; Col. 3:13). Covering a multitude of sins (see 1 Pet. 4:8) enables communication. The flip side of the willingness to forgive is openness to our own mistakes or sins. It is difficult to communicate with anyone who cannot imagine the possibility of ever making an error. Yet, experience and Scripture warn that it is human nature to be blind to ones own faults. "The way of a fool is right in his own eyes" (Prov. 12:15; see also 16:2, 20:6, and 21:2; Rom. 12:3; Gal. 6:1, "looking to yourself," and James 5:16a). By imitating the Lord Jesus in the matter of forgiveness and by refusing the attitude of a perfectionist oblivious to faults in self, we increase healthy communication and strengthen the family.

Bible Warnings about Destructive Speech

The Greek word for gossip is the same as the word for "devil." The devil is a slanderer or gossip. The original word is *diabalos. Dia* means "through" as in diameter. *Balos* refers to throwing like a ball. Originally, a spear would be literally cast through a person. Over time *diabolos* meant to pierce another with a verbal spear.

In a family situation, gossip refers to broadcasting to others the defects we find in our husband, wife, child, parent, or sibling. There may be a need to bring up problems to a trusted counselor or pastor who can keep a confidence while offering support and advice. However, indiscriminate complaints or whining about a family member can destroy trust and stop future communication. Serious family problems are not improved by leaking matters for "prayer requests" or belittling a spouse in a small group setting. When this occurs, a family member will soon learn it is not safe to communicate with one who will betray secrets often without much of a motive to obtain help but rather with a motive to embarrass. Prov. 17:9b can be applied to the home. "But he who repeats a matter separates intimate friends" (see also Prov. 16:27, 26:20-21).

Solomon applied the problems of complaining and nagging to the home. He compared a fussy wife to the annoyance of a constant dripping (Prov. 19:13, 27:15). He also taught it is better to live in the desert or in a corner of what we would call an attic than with an argumentative, whining, never-satisfied wife (Prov. 21:9, 19).

Silence is not golden one hundred percent of the time. If truth is suppressed about a major irritation or sin, there is the possibility of hidden resentment eventually exploding. Serious issues will not go away by themselves if we stew in silence. Some family problems must be resolved by open and honest communication. Eph. 4:15 gives the balance to "speak the truth in love." When we must talk about a problem, we should seek objective truth in love. Even rebuke with the goal of constructive criticism may be used if done in love. "Open rebuke" when the goal is to improve our loved-one and strengthen the marriage (or family) is better "than love that is concealed" (Prov. 27:5 see also: 9:8 and 27:6). For the sake of our spouse or family member difficult issues must sometimes be confronted in love.

Another category of "rebuke" is in reality just fussing over trivial matters. Sometimes a husband or wife constantly complains and fusses over minor imperfections, nags for the impossible, or verbally manipulates a spouse to achieve selfish ends. **That** is the type of vexation and contention to which Solomon objects. Except for serious sins where our beloved hurts self or the family, we should either overlook the fault entirely or bring the matter up rarely. With "mid-level" problems we might need to break silence on occasion to express a desire for a resolution but drop the matter most of the time, accepting our loved one for what he or she is. Very few things matter to the point of being a constant irritation to a family member.

He who covereth a transgression seeketh love ... [Prov. 17:9a (KJV)].

A man's discretion makes him slow to anger, and it is his glory to overlook a transgression [Prov. 19:11].

And Jesus answered and said unto her, Martha, Martha, thou art careful and troubled about many things: But one thing is needful: and Mary hath chosen that good part, which shall not be taken away from her [Luke 10:41-42 KJV].

Be kind to one another, tender-hearted, forgiving each other, just as God in Christ also has forgiven you [Eph. 4:32].

[B]earing with one another, and forgiving each other, whoever has a complaint against anyone; just as the Lord forgave you, so also should you. Beyond all these things put on love, which is the perfect bond of unity [Col. 3:13-14].

Above all, keep fervent in your love for one another, because love covers a multitude of sins [1 Pet. 4:8].

Suggestions for a Marital Discussion or Family Conference

Routine communication can take place constantly and in any setting. Marilyn and I have gone out at least once a week for decades. For years we have gone for coffee in the morning. Talk without any planned agenda helps keep intimacy.

If communication involves a potential conflict, the following list of suggestions may be of assistance:

- Ask God for wisdom and control of emotions (James 1:5; Gal. 5:22-23; 2 Tim. 1:7).

- Decide what is best for the family regardless of who originated the idea or gets the praise.

- Remember, verbal remarks directed against you may well be provoked by exasperation unrelated to you (a flat tire, a lost item, a headache).

- Attack the problem not the personalities involved. Give the benefit of doubt to trust your spouse's intentions.

- Try to be flexible, willing to compromise, objective as to the real level of importance of the subject or objective as to ones own flaws (see Matt. 7:3-5; Rom. 12:3).

- If possible, prepare the setting for any disagreement (privacy, in a peaceful place with few interruptions, at a time of rest, not cranky exhaustion).

- Never forget to listen. There may be a need to repeat the opposite point of view back to the verbal antagonist to ensure complete understanding.

- Back up criticism with specific facts but be gentle and offer suggestions for improvement.

- Reject absolute language ("you **always** act this way, or you are **never** fair"). Do not malign relatives or appearances. Attacking in-laws or cruel comments about looks can cause long-term strain. Also, avoid exaggerations, loud volume, and cutting humor.

- Do not resort to threats or gossip to "win" the argument.

- Try to state your viewpoint in a specific and positive manner, not a vague and negative manner.

- Stay on the subject. Avoid tangents.

- Be willing to ask for forgiveness. Be willing to grant forgiveness.

- Deal with the present problem without rehashing old unrelated spats.

- Since the topic has already been opened, the silent treatment is not longer an option. Work towards solutions and try not to just end the conversation by walking off in silence.

- "To keep your marriage brimming in the loving cup, when you're wrong, admit it, when you're right, shut up." [1]

- Make the goal of every conversation to express love, deepen understanding, meet needs and solve problems, not just to win the debate at all costs, and especially not to inflict emotional pain. [2]

While some situations call for communication over matters of disagreement, a couple's sharing should be dominated by routine and more enjoyable talk. Another major type of communication is decision-making. How does a married couple or family determine the will of God?

Decision-Making and the Will of God

---

[1] Ogden Nash quoted by H. Norman Wright, *Communication: Key to Your Marriage* (Ventura, CA: Regal Books, 1974) pp. 154-55. Several of the ideas listed here derive from this fine book.

[2] It is not wise to make time or work commitments involving a spouse without prior communication. Also, without communication it may not be accurate to assume a spouse's opinion and feelings by speaking on his or her behalf.

How do we know what God wants us to do in life?[3] The subject of God's will should be of interest to both singles thinking about potential marriage and couples making decisions about their family. Before delving into suggestions for knowing God's will, it is necessary to give some definitions and a distinction.

God's General Will/God's Specific Will

The phrase "God's general will" may be used to refer to God's will for all Christians in all places at all times. God wants all Christians to be holy. God wants all Christians to pray, study the Scripture, evangelize, give, assemble for worship and so forth. God's general will is identical for believers in America, Europe, Africa, or Asia. It is identical for those who live in the present as it was for believers who lived in previous centuries. Of course, God's general will comes directly from the Bible and never changes. Those who miss it are without excuse; "So then do not be foolish, but understand what the will of the Lord is" (Eph. 5:17).

The phrase "God's specific will" may be used to refer to God's will for an individual, family, church or Christian organization. The Bible itself gives precedent for individual guidance and destiny.

Not only did God call Abraham to move to the Promised Land, or Moses to lead the Exodus, or Paul to spread the early church; God called ordinary individuals. In Luke 9:60 Jesus called a common man to " … go and proclaim everywhere the Kingdom of God." Simply by reference to different categories of people and ministries, the Bible presupposes individual leading by God. Individuals have different spiritual gifts. This assumes an individualized leading process by God to determine one's own gift. Some are led to become elders and deacons. Others are not. Some are single. Others are married. Some

---

[3] During a restless night as a young student, I walked to the Lincoln Memorial in Washington D.C. To my surprise I ran into another Christian also wondering about life and destiny. We had both been staring at the contemplative face of Abraham Lincoln as we wondered how to know God's plan for life. Some aspects of this topic are mysterious, but pursuit of God's will is vital. The earlier one seeks God's will, the better the results will be. "Remember your Creator in the days of your youth … " (Eccles. 12:1).

serve God in travels (Matt. 28:19). Others stay in one location (Mark 5:19).

Unlike the general will of God, the specific will of God varies from person to person and changes over time. Even with a person or family, God's will may change over time as one changes vocations or moves to another place.

The distinction between God's general will and God's specific will is common sense, but they overlap in two important respects. First, God's specific will never contradicts His general will. No one may rationalize a subjective impulse to disobey the Bible and call it God's will. God does not lead a college student to cheat on exams, or a businessman to embezzle, or anyone to lie to the IRS. Regardless of any internal feelings, it is not God's voice urging a man or woman to commit adultery.

Individual subjective leading from God never violates the revealed objective leading from God written in the Bible, "Your word is a lamp to my feet and a light to my path" (Psa. 119:105, see also: Psa. 73:24).

A second vital truth linking God's general will to God's specific will is that the only way to know God's specific leading comes only by obeying His general leading. Those who refuse to obey the clear commands of the Bible are likely to be confused as to any individual direction. Why would God be obligated to give a specific turn in life to those moving as fast as they can in an evil direction? [4] Those who run away from God on matters of basic Christian living can not expect to understand the finer points of God's individual plan for their life. Even if God were to give such advice, the individual does not have a spiritual aptitude open to discernment.

---

[4] Dietrich Bonhoeffer used a train illustration. When the respected Lutheran seminary professor was asked to join the Nazi party, he was told he might be able to serve God as a Nazi. He replied that if a train ran fast in the wrong direction, it would do very little good to run to the back of the train. Those who disobey God in general can hardly be expected to find His specific will on the details.

The main secret to finding God's specific will is a habit of obedience to His general will, revealed in the Bible. One of the few Bible texts on knowing God's specific will clearly links individualized direction to a life of overall compliance with God's revealed will.

The Basis for God's Specific Guidance

Romans 12:2 is one of the few places in the Bible with a reference to knowing God's specific will ("that you may prove what the will of God is ..."). Since the following context teaches about individual spiritual gifts, the topic in Rom. 12:2 must be God's specific individualized direction.

Therefore, Romans 12:1-2 gives a formula for finding "proof" (cf. the KJV translation) or "evidence" for knowing God's specific will. It does not provide answers to all mysteries, but Paul gives a start to the process. The way to ultimate discovery of God's specific will begins with compliance to His general will. Those who refuse servanthood to God in a general way are likely never to discover their specific gifts for service.

Before getting to the material about individual leading, Romans 12:1 and 2 gives three conditions for a believer prior to any knowledge of God's specific will. First, one must **present self to God as a sacrifice**. Second, one must **refuse conformity to the world's lifestyle** and goals. Third, one must **be renewed in mind**.

Presenting self as a sacrifice draws on the Old Testament picture of an animal sacrifice. It calls for obedience, worship, and sacrificial dedication and work for God.

Next **not being "conformed to the world"** means rejection of the world system, ideas, values and pursuits whenever they conflict with God's Word.

Finally, **mind renewal** takes place by the knowledge and practice of Scripture. Those who study and follow the Bible become very much unlike the world. Those who study the Scripture and submit to it undergo **mind renewal toward the image of Christ** (2 Cor. 3:18).

When a couple or family refuses to present life to God, becomes worldly, and has no interest in mind renewal (i.e. the **admiration and imitation of Christ**), they may miss much of the way God would have otherwise lead them in specific areas. By contrast, when a couple or family has obeyed "present self a holy sacrifice," "do not be conformed to this world" and "be transformed by the renewing of your mind," then they can trust God's promise to give specific leading.

Rom. 12:1-2 does not give all secrets as to God's leading. Much still remains mysterious. The text does give the comforting truth that those on the right road will by some means in God's time be given the right steps. One is reminded of Abraham's servant who said, "I being in the way, the Lord led me ..." (Gen. 24:27 KJV).

A couple or family must be traveling the path of the **admiration and imitation of Christ** in order to pay attention to God's specific will. Decision making arising from a life of habitual disobedience is likely to mistake proud, covetous, or fleshy impulse for the call of God. In rebellion, we rationalize our desires as God's. To avoid peril every married couple should wisely submit to God and remain dedicated prior to major decisions. One conclusion is certain: Any discovery of God's specific will begins by compliance with God's general will.

More Clues to God's Specific Will

Romans 12:1-2 gives the starting point towards discovery of God's specific will (present self to God, be not conformed to the world, be transformed in the mind). Other texts also provide steps towards knowing God's will.

James 1:5 tells us to pray if we lack wisdom because God "gives to all generously and without reproach." Here the Bible does not say how prayer will bring wisdom to a bewildering decision, but promises that it does.

Prov. 15:22 suggests we get advice from "many counselors." Research on a decision helps one explore options, weigh risks, and uncover ideas that would otherwise be overlooked. Maybe the Bible actually does address the decision under consideration. A counselor with greater Bible knowledge may give the exact chapter and verse. Even on non-moral issues, Jesus remarked it is just common sense to "count the cost" before starting a project. Difficulty alone may not rule out something as being God's will, but consideration of difficulty will help even if we are not bound to follow every bit of counsel. 1 Cor. 7:17ff. allows for changes but counsels a general stability in life with a conservative approach to frequent and drastic moves. Also, 1 Tim. 3:1-7 teaches elders should be stable and not given to rash judgment. Thus, problems may well bring about a decision to make a change, but God does not want drastic changes for no other reason than to escape problems.[1] Getting counsel from others need not mean we slavishly follow them, but the process still helps with better understanding of a decision.

Often Christians will make a decision and say they had "peace" about it. Assuming the decision does not contradict the Bible, there can be validity in this. God's will may have difficulties and unpleasant struggles; but still doing God's will brings joy. Psa. 40:8 uses the word "delight" in reference to God's will, "I delight to do Your will, O my God ... ". Romans 12 calls God's will "good, acceptable, and perfect." A spiritual person will not find God's will odious but will have a "measure of faith" within his heart that this way is right. ("Measure of faith" in Rom. 12:3 refers to an internal measure of confidence regarding knowing one's spiritual gifts.)

The text used to support peace being an indicator of God's will actually refers to a different kind of peace than peace within one's mind. Colossians 3:15 says, "Let the peace of Christ rule in your hearts." Here the Greek pronoun "your" is not singular but plural. Peace among the church (not peace within) gives guidance as to God's will. All things being morally and doctrinally true, decisions in the church should try to keep peace in the church family.

A literal family should follow the same principle. Life can present serious ethical challenges. Some things are a matter of core principles. Other decisions can get blown all out of proportion. If one

---

[1] A change in location will not remedy a flaw in character.

way destroys peace in the relationship, but the other preserves or even deepens it, only a fool chooses the first option just to agitate or take control. Unless there is a serious doctrinal or moral issue, keeping the peace should be kept in view in the decision-making process.

Assume a marriage has been based upon obedience to God's general will contained in the Bible. Furthermore, the family has prayed, obtained counsel and considered the impact of a choice upon the peace and unity in the family. At some point the topic of God's specific will enters subjective areas such as feelings, burdens, promptings or impressions. The primary way God directs is by the Bible. We can even assert the main leading of the Holy Spirit is Scripture since the Holy Spirit wrote the Scripture. Thus, no one may claim the Holy Spirit leads contrary to the Bible. Also, no one who is disobedient to the Bible may safely interpret any impulse as from the Holy Spirit (except conviction of sin). Yet, for those who strive to obey God's revealed will, we must make room for subjective and internal leading in the decision process.

God's Leading Within

Some room can be given in anyone's theological system for God's subjective guidance.[6] Disobedient Christians cannot trust their

---

[6] This raises the topic of God's leading by audible voices. This may occasionally happen, especially in emergencies. Nevertheless, there are biblical restrictions. Particularly, any "message" that claims divine authority over others should be rejected. God gave the apostles and prophets revelation binding in authority upon the entire Church. To be a part of Scripture a book must have been written either by an apostle or under apostolic supervision. In our own time God may give a **strictly personal message** that may be audible in nature, but no one today can claim to speak for God with authority over others (beyond simply teaching truths already in the Bible). An apostle had to have seen the risen Lord (Acts 1:21-22; 1 Cor. 9:1, 15:8). No one today has revelation from God with binding authority on others.

Even with strictly personal messages, those in the Bible to whom God spoke audibly were humbled by the experience. Paul did not mention it for 14 years (2 Cor. 12:2ff.) The more one boasts about hearing an audible voice from God, the less others should be inclined to give such experience credence. For more study on this topic see Steven W. Waterhouse, *Not By Bread Alone: An Outlined Study Guide to Bible Doctrine*, 2nd edition (Amarillo, TX: Westcliff Press, 2003), pp. 260-61.

feelings to indicate God's desires or leading. Yet, several Bible passages support that God does give internal promptings and burdens to those in a pattern of compliance to God's general will given in the Bible.

Psalm 37:4-5 may be interpreted that God places desires within the hearts of those who commit life to Him and delight in Him. "Delight yourself in the Lord, and He will give you the desires of your heart" (v. 4). Paul believed Christ lived within and lived through him (Gal. 2:20). Perhaps Phil. 2:13 is even more clear; "... for it is God who is at work in you, both to will and to work for His good pleasure."

Those who have a track record of obeying God's will as commanded in the Bible may then safely consider what we might call impulses, promptings, burdens or convictions as indication of God's will. Augustine has been quoted, "love God and do as you please." Some qualifications may be in order, but he was close. Love God first by obeying all His revealed will, after that "what you (subjectively) please" will probably become what He also pleases.

Regarding the decisions of life, a married couple should **practice the admiration and imitation of Christ as the foundation to building godly judgment for choices in life.** With this foundation and after prayer, counsel, and consideration of peace in the family one may consider a strong and lasting feeling that one ought to do something as an indication of God's will.

If one never senses any "measure of faith" (i.e. confidence, see Rom. 12:3) about a decision, it might be best to wait. Waiting on God is also a biblical option (Psa. 27:14). Circumstances might force a change, and change may be in God's will, but there is no virtue in reckless change or just quitting a difficult but noble task. We are supposed to follow God, but without clear leading, we are also supposed to put our hand to the plow and not look back (Luke 9:62). Paul told Timothy to "fulfill your ministry" (2 Tim. 4:5). Without strong convictions one can wait to see whether they ever come. With a spiritual life followed by enduring promptings to make a change, one should trust God to work within, and trust the Bible, which teaches that He does work in the hearts of the committed.

No regret if …

More important than any secondary decision is the prior choice to obey God's revealed will completely. Yet, sometimes even those with complete dedication to God make decisions that may from hindsight seem to have been mistaken because of the problems they cause.

Many Bible verses tell us we will not totally understand God's will in this life. If we acknowledge God's authority in all things and then trust Him in the unknown areas of life, the Bible promises He will direct our paths (Prov. 3:5-6). This means that obedience to the Bible and then to any perceived inner leading will still be a mysterious process. To use the hymn title, we must trust and obey, but we simply will not understand God's entire plan for this life.

In many respects full understanding is not necessary, nor is false guilt for decisions made in submission and good faith that later turned out to include troubles. If we submit to the *general* will of God, the *specific* will of God will take care of itself even without full understanding. Flexibility that grants God the right to veto our choice or allows unexpected events is also a part of Christian living (Prov. 27:1; James 4:13-16). As a good Father, God knows our needs better than we do. God has a wonderful plan for each Christian couple and each family. We trust and obey. Sometimes we understand. Sometimes we do not understand, but we can always trust God to superintend godly families for good and His own purposes and praise.

> The secret things belong to the LORD our God, but the things revealed belong to us and to our sons forever, that we may observe all the words of this law [Deut 29:29].

> For He performs what is appointed for me, and many such decrees are with Him [Job 23:14].

> Does He not see my ways and number all my steps? [Job 31:4].

> Delight yourself in the LORD; and He will give you the desires of your heart [Psa. 37:4].

Trust in the LORD with all your heart and do not lean on your own understanding. In all your ways acknowledge Him, and He will make your paths straight [Prov. 3:5-6].

Watch the path of your feet and all your ways will be established [Prov. 4:26].

The mind of a man plans his way, but the LORD directs his steps [Prov. 16:9].

Many plans are in a man's heart, but the counsel of the LORD will stand [Prov. 19:21].

A man's steps are ordained by the LORD, how then can man understand his way? [Prov. 20:24].

I know, O LORD, that a man's way is not in himself, nor is it in a man who walks to direct his steps [Jer. 10:23].

"For My thoughts are not your thoughts, nor are your ways My ways," declares the LORD [Isa. 55:8].

"For I know the plans that I have for you," declares the LORD, "plans for welfare and not for calamity to give you a future and a hope. Then you will call upon Me and come and pray to Me, and I will listen to you. You will seek Me and find Me when you search for Me with all your heart" [Jer. 29:11-13].

And we know that God causes all things to work together for good to those who love God, to those who are called according to His purpose [Rom. 8:28].

[b]ears all things, believes all things, hopes all things, endures all things [1 Cor. 13:7].

Therefore, my beloved brethren, be steadfast, immovable, always abounding in the work of the Lord, knowing that your toil is not in vain in the Lord [1 Cor. 15:58].

Holy Matrimony: Basic Conclusions

Marriage is the deepest human relationship. A husband or wife can even fulfill needs that God Himself has chosen not to meet. The relationship of a parent to a child adds yet another intimate union, even another form of oneness, to life's experience.

God joins husband and wife together in a holy and spiritual union ("what, therefore, God has joined together ..." Matt. 19:6). A couple's beliefs about the origin of marriage shapes that marriage in direction and outcome. Marriage is not just a legal and economic union or a cultural tradition; nor did God intend family relationships to be ends in themselves. Even the best husband, wife, parent, or child cannot replace God as a substitute source of ultimate meaning or happiness.

God created marriage and the family as a means of deepening human experience with Himself. God's purposes for marriage include: companionship, safe and holy sexual union (restriction of sex to marriage reflects and preserves holiness), procreation, emotional and financial security, and spiritual growth (1 Pet. 3:7).

God created countless angels without marriage or reproduction. By amazing contrast, God created one man and one woman. He developed the rest of humanity by marriage and the family. Through the family, humans learn God's character traits in deeper ways, especially His loyal-love in a covenant relationship.

Marriage begins in a covenant before God (Mal. 2:14). His pattern for marriage is one man and one woman for life (Matt. 19:4-6). By making such a covenant, God intends that husband and wife imitate His own loyal-love to covenant relationships (Ex. 34:6-7).

The **admiration and imitation of God** is at the heart of God's purpose for marriage and the family. The Old Testament picture of God is as husband to Israel (Isa. 54:5). In this role, God's character and actions becomes the model for marriage. The New Testament expands upon this theme.

God's will for a Christian husband is the **admiration and imitation of Christ** in His relationship to the church (Eph. 5:25ff.). Christ's sacrificial love and servant-leadership give the ideal for husbands.

God's will for a Christian wife is the **admiration and imitation of Christ** in His relationship within the Trinity. As God the Son, Christ is co-equal to the Father in Person and worth, but He chose to submit in the position and work of the Godhead. He becomes the model for a wife submitting and being a helper to her husband though she retains equal worth to him. (1 Cor. 11:3 gives Christ's submission to the Father as a wife's role model.)

Good parenting also leads back to the **admiration and imitation of God** as the ideal Heavenly Father. The best parents reflect God's character traits, teach God's truths, and discipline as God disciplines His own children (2 Tim. 3:15; Heb. 12:5ff; Rev. 3:19). Good parenting involves the admiration and imitation of God so that a child forms a healthy view of God from parental treatment even before he or she can read in the Bible about the Father in heaven.

As the ultimate family expert, God's wisdom in the Bible sustains families with difficult emotional, financial, or communication problems. The Bible's counsel prevents some problems from occurring or enables a family to withstand them. Also, the Bible gives help with family decision-making and clearly teaches God has a blessed plan for every family even if that plan is not fully understood at all times.

It is not possible to have God's greatest blessing without having interest in God Himself. Only those who have experienced Christ's unconditional love by faith in His work on the cross have sufficient experience with true love and forgiveness to become an excellent husband or wife.

The strength or weakness of a marriage depends upon whether both husband and wife feel accountability to the authority of God's Word. Success or failure in the family is ultimately a spiritual matter. Does a **husband admire and imitate Christ** in His relationship to the Church by giving sacrificial love and servant-leadership? Does a **wife admire and imitate Christ** in His relationship to the Father? Will she be an equal in worth who chooses to be a helper in God's work? Do **father and mother admire and imitate God's virtues** (in a flawed but earnest effort) so that through them a child can make an easy transition to knowledge of the Father in heaven? Both God's purposes for marriage (and family) and His process for a strong marriage (and family) merge in the **admiration and imitation of God.**

TOPICAL INDEX

Abortion   87fn 3
Abraham   106
Accountability   29
Accountability for adult children   97ff.
Achievement in children   104
Adultery   23, 25, 31ff., 42, 82-83
Agape (love)   63, 75
Age of accountability   99 fn6
Anger   137ff.
Apologetics   142-147
Augustine   71fn 5, 206

Beauty   78
Bible authority   7, 108
Bible reliability   142-147
Blessings for children of the righteous   92
Bonhoeffer, Dietrich   201fn 4
Budget   186

Cain   139
Celibacy   5
Celibacy after divorce   24, 30ff., 43
Child abuse   90, 114ff., 122
Child evangelism   107
Child support   105ff.
Children, biblical value   87ff.
Choices or parental influences   100
Christ and women   54
Church attendance   110, 154
Cohabitation   19, 45
Communication   66, 189
Companionship   3, 70
Comparisons of siblings   119
Conception   87ff.
Contentment   167
Corporeal discipline   113ff.
Covenant   9, 19, 40, 209

Dating   3
David, example as father   95
Death and the marriage covenant   14
Debt   172
Decisions   66, 190, 199ff.
Dedication of children   107
Depression   161ff.

Desertion for religious grounds   33fn 8
Discipline as love   111
Disobedience in children   96-97
Divorce   23, 26
Doctrines, basic   107
Domestic violence   28
Doubts   142-147

Eli, example as a father   95
Elijah   164-165
Encouragement   120
Equality of genders   51, 71
Esau, mixed marriage   36
Evidences for faith   142-147

False expectations   126, 129-130
False guilt   148ff.
Favoritism towards children   121
Feminine traits in God's image   52ff.
Feminism   58fn 13
Forgiveness   29, 137, 137fn 1, 140, 148

Gender interdependence   53
Gentlemen   54, 58fn 13, 76
Giving   184
God as our role model   8, 61, 64, 69, 91, 121,134,
    (continued)   209-211
God the Father   52, 91ff.
God's will   200ff., 207-208
Government and marriage   17, 24, 43
Grandparents   119fn 10, 125
Grief   157
Guilt   148ff.
Guilt , false   148

Happiness   135fn 9
Heart, purity   84
Helper, wife as   70
Heterosexuality   11
Hierarchical ethics   73fn 8, 120fn 11
Hoarding money   177fn 6
Holiness of marriage   1, 27, 32, 40, 48, 81
Homemakers   76
Homosexuality   11ff.
Hope for marital problems   27
Hosea   32
Human value   150
Humility   134fn 8

Husband's role	61ff.
Image of God, in parents	91ff.
Image of God, male and female	52
Imitation of God	6, 61, 69, 91, 121, 134,
(continued)	209-211
Infant death and salvation	99fn 6
Inferiority	149ff.
Infertility	87
Interracial marriage	47
Isaac and Rebekah	2, 18, 36fn 2
Jealousy	154, 169-170, 173fn 3
Joseph	177
Joy from family	125
Joy from God	127ff., 132fn 4
Laziness	181
Leadership, in husbands	66-67ff.
Limits to criticism	159
Licenses for marriage	17, 24
Listening	191
Love (*agape)*	63, 75
Love for God	134
Love (*philos)*	62, 75
Love, unconditional	61, 103ff.
Luke on women	56fn 10
Lust	83-84
Marriage between races	47
Marriage between unbelievers	48
Masculinity	75-76
Mental fidelity	83
Messianic prophecy	143
Mixed marriage (believer to unbeliever)	35ff., 45, 92
Monogamy	11
Moses	25, 47, 106, 158
Motivation	153
Mr. or Mrs. "Right"	2
"Nagging" texts	75, 78, 196
Nash, Ogden	199
Natural affection	61, 90
Nature or nurture?	97ff.
Obedience, children	96ff.
Obedience to God	134fn 7
Origin of marriage	1
Overworking	181-183

Pagan views of children | 89
Parental authority | 94ff.
Parental consent | 41, 46
Parental example | 108
Parental instinct (love) | 90
Pattern for marriage | 11, 20
Paul on women | 57
Perfectionism | 157, 163
Performance and reward | 117fn 7
Performance and unconditional love | 103ff.
Permanence of marriage | 14, 27, 40
Philos (love) | 62, 75
Pleasing everyone | 158
Polygamy | 11
Pornography | 83
Positive reinforcement | 117
Pregnant bride | 44
Priorities | 133ff.
Procreation | 4, 86ff.
Prodigal son | 98, 101

Rabbinic quotes on women | 55
Reconciliation | 29
Reflection of husband's love by wife | 75
Remarriage, after divorce involving adultery | 31-33, 43
Remarriage, after divorce without adultery | 24, 29-30, 42-43
Remarriage after spouse's death | 15
Remarriage, permanence | 25fn 4
Reproduction, commands for | 86
Rest | 147-148, 182-183
Resurrection of Christ | 145-147

Safe-sex | 82
Samson | 36
Savings | 177
Security, safety | 6, 28, 104, 113
Seeking God | 134
Self-worth | 149ff.
Separation, marital | 28
Sex | 4, 81ff., 86fn 2
Sin, impact on family | 130
Sin nature in children | 93
Solomon, polygamy or mixed marriages | 12, 36ff.
Speech | 189
Standards for children | 95, 103-104, 119, 121
Submission | 65-66, 72ff.
Success defined | 149ff., 168 ff.
Suffering | 155ff.

Index

Teachable moments	110
Teaching children	106ff.
Tough love	29
Violence	28
Vows	20, 40
Wealth and God's sovereignty	168ff.
Wedding customs	21
Widows	15
Wife's role	69ff.
Women in society	57
Work and the family	179
Working mothers	76
Worry	160
Worship	133, 133fn 6

SELECTED SCRIPTURE REFERENCES

OLD TESTAMENT REFERENCES

GENESIS

1:27	52
1:27-28	85-86ff., 150
2:18	3, 71, 125
2:23	70
2:24	11, 46, 85
3:16	72, 74fn 9, 125
4:5	139
5:1-2	52
9:7	4, 86
18:19	106
24	2, 18, 203
41:46-48	178

EXODUS

20:12	96
20:17	83
22:16	44
34:6-7	9, 53, 209

NUMBERS

12	47

DEUTERONOMY

6:4-5	134
6:6-7	106
24:1-4	25
24:16	100

JOSHUA

24:15	100

JUDGES

2:10	106

RUTH

3:1	5, 28

1 SAMUEL

1:11, 27-28	88, 107
2:7	169
2:12, 17, 29	95
16:7	104, 151fn 9

1 KINGS

1:6	95
11:1-4	37
18:21	100

JOB

19:2	190

PSALMS

37:4-5	206
37:21	172
50:10-12	168
51:5	94
55:22	160
75:6-7	169
102	166
127:1-2	183
127:3-5	88, 93
139:13-16	87fn 3, 150

PROVERBS:

1:8-9	96
2:17	3, 19
3:5-6	207-208
3:11-12	111
3:27-28	175
4:23	84, 132-133
5:18-19	85
6:6-8	178
6:26-29	82
6:32-35	83
7:21-23	83
12:15	195
13:11	179
13:22	179
13:24	113
15:1, 23	193
15:17	37
15:22	203

16:21	194
17:9	195, 196
18:13	192
18:21	189
18:22	54, 67
19:11	138fn 1, 140
19:13	37
19:14	2, 67
19:18	113
20:20	96
21:9	37
21:20	178
22:6	98, 107, 115, 123
22:7	172
22:15	113
22:29	181
23:4-5	183
23:13	114
24:11-12	140
24:27	178
24:33-34	181
27:5	196
29:15	114
29:17	114
30:8-9	170
30:17	97
31	54, 67, 76, 78

ECCLESIASTES

2	129
5:10-11	177
5:12	181, 183
7:14	169
9:10	180
12:1	200

SONG OF SOLOMON

4:5-7	85
5:1	86
6:2-3	86

ISAIAH

50:1	32
54:5	8, 209
55:8	208

JEREMIAH

3:8	32
7	89
9:23-24	128
29:11-13	208

EZEKIEL

18:4, 20	100

HOSEA

2:2	32

AMOS

3:3	36

HAGGAI

2:8	168

MALACHI

2:14-16	3, 10, 19, 26, 84, 133, 209

NEW TESTAMENT REFERENCES

MATTHEW

5:32	23, 32
6:19	177
6:21	167
6:33	171
7:3-5	198
7:24ff.	38, 92
12:25	38, 92-93
18:3-6, 10	88
18:15-17	138fn 1, 140
19:3-6	1, 11, 14, 17, 23, 32, 209
19:16-22	177
20:28	66
22:30	15
22:36-40	134

MARK

6:31	183

10:2-12	11, 14, 23
10:13-16	88-89

LUKE

2:21-24	107
2:51	96
10:41-42	197
12:34	167
15:11-32	98
16:10	171
16:18	23

JOHN

2:1-11	21
4	19, 54

ACTS

20:34	179

ROMANS

1:31	61, 90
7:2	15
12:1-2	202
12:3	198, 204, 206
13:1-4	18
13:8	175

1 CORINTHIANS

4:2	170, 172
4:3	159
4:7	169
7:3-4	86
7:10-11	24, 29, 42ff.
7:12-14	26, 41
7:15	33, 33fn 8
7:33-34	158-159
7:39	15, 39
9:5	39
11:3	69, 210
11:9	70

2 CORINTHIANS

3:18	202

6:14	38
10:12	119
12:14	106, 178

GALATIANS

3:28	57
6:1	194
6:14	129

EPHESIANS

4:2	194
4:32	138, 138fn 1, 195, 197
5:22	57, 72-73
5:24	72
5:25	61, 75, 210
5:28	63, 66, 75, 152
5:29	53
5:33	72
6:1-3	96
6:4	107, 116, 121ff.

PHILLIPPIANS

2:13	206
4:4	129
4:6-7	160
4:11-13	168
4:13	151
4:19	171

COLOSSIANS

2:8	108
3:11	47
3:13	138fn 1, 195, 197
3:15	204
3:17, 23-24	182
3:19	63, 67, 75
3:21	116, 121ff.

1 THESSALONIANS

2:7	53
2:11-12	120
4:11-12	180

1 TIMOTHY

4:12	159
5:8	68, 90, 106
5:14	15, 77
6:6-8	168

2 TIMOTHY

1:5	107
3:15	107

TITUS

2:4-5	72, 75
2:15	159

HEBREWS

12:4-11	112
13:4	85

JAMES

1:5	203
1:19	191-92
3:8	190

1 PETER

3:1	40-41, 72
3:3-5	78
3:5	72
3:7	5, 65, 75, 190, 209
4:8	138fn 1, 140, 197
5:7	160

1 JOHN

3:20	148

REVELATION

3:19	112
19:7	21
21:2	21
21:9	21